UNDERDOGS

Underdogs

SOCIAL DEVIANCE AND QUEER THEORY

Heather Love

The University of Chicago Press

CHICAGO AND LONDON

The University of Chicago Press, Chicago 60637
The University of Chicago Press, Ltd., London
© 2021 by The University of Chicago
Published 2021
Printed in the United States of America

30 29 28 27 26 25 24 23 22 21   1 2 3 4 5

ISBN-13: 978-0-226-66869-7 (cloth)
ISBN-13: 978-0-226-76110-7 (paper)
ISBN-13: 978-0-226-76124-4 (e-book)
DOI: https://doi.org/10.7208/chicago/9780226761244.001.0001

Library of Congress Cataloging-in-Publication Data

Names: Love, Heather, author.
Title: Underdogs : social deviance and queer theory / Heather Love.
Other titles: Social deviance and queer theory
Description: Chicago ; London : The University of Chicago Press,
2021. | Includes bibliographical references and index.
Identifiers: LCCN 2020030291 | ISBN 9780226668697 (cloth) |
ISBN 9780226761107 (paperback) | ISBN 9780226761244 (ebook)
Subjects: LCSH: Queer theory—History. | Deviant behavior—
Research—United States—History—20th century. |
Sociology—United States—History—20th century.
Classification: LCC HQ76.25 .L683 2021 | DDC 306.7601—dc23
LC record available at https://lccn.loc.gov/2020030291

⊚ This paper meets the requirements of ANSI/NISO Z39.48-1992
(Permanence of Paper).

My sociological reference group was clearly of the naturalist-ethnographic-underdog school.

Laud Humphreys, *Tearoom Trade*

Contents

Preface

This book offers a genealogy of queer theory, tracing its roots in American social science from the period after World War II. It is a story that has been told before by social scientists, for whom the connection is evident. This has not been the case for queer scholars in the humanities, who see few links between queer inquiry and empirical research on marginal sex practices and communities in the era before Stonewall. Having been trained in the philosophical version of queer theory that emerged in the late 1980s and early 1990s, I was slow to acknowledge the connection. Queer theory seemed to change everything, not only challenging gender and sexual norms but also the nature of scholarship itself, allying it with activism and popular protest. From this vantage, with gender relations laid out for view and apparently up for grabs, it was hard to see the interest of community studies of "queers and peers" or of the careful mapping of vice districts in urban centers. *Underdogs* records the results of my reeducation, which has not turned me away from queer thought so much as it has made me see the necessity of integrating it with earlier approaches in the history of sexuality. Queer thought, even at its most critical and utopian, owes a great deal to studies of social deviance conducted in the postwar period. This claim is true, as I will argue, not just in the general sense of creating the conditions in which queer thought might flourish. It is also true more directly: deviance studies contributed ideas and frameworks that appeared as if newly minted in 1990.

My inability to appreciate such connections before is not merely an individual failing. Rather, it is part of the ruling mythology of the field of queer studies, which has understood itself as existing outside of traditional academic lines of influence. According to this view, the roots of queer theory should be located in activist ferment and traditions of radicalism coming out of the AIDS crisis, the women's health movement, in debates in feminism, and in movements for gay and trans liberation that emerged in the late 1960s. These were indeed crucial sources for the field, feeding its confrontational politics, its most sweeping challenges to heteronormativity, and its flouting of academic decorum. But queer theory was never merely an outsider to the academic world, even as it refused to play by its rules. It was also an inheritor of many traditions within the academy. While some of these influences were eagerly embraced—Marxism, poststructuralism, feminism, psychoanalysis, Foucauldian analysis of power and language—others, such as deviance studies, social interactionism, and microsociology, were incorporated without fanfare. It is my strong conviction that queer scholars should acknowledge these legacies at last.

This is not a heroic origin story, or even one that is very comfortable to tell. The critique of queer theory as mired in class, racial, and national privilege is in some measure bolstered by delving into the field's roots in American social science. The aim of this narrative is not to justify the field or to exonerate it, however. For many readers, it will have the opposite effect, amplifying yet further a well-established critique of the field. Although I acknowledge the justness of many of these arguments, it is not in the service of a critique of queer theory that *Underdogs* marshals its evidence. I remain invested in the field both intellectually and politically, and do not see its links to older forms of scholarship as necessarily damning. Rather, my aim is to inquire more deeply into aspects of queer thought that have proven contentious: its stance against identity and legislative politics; its universalism and its comparative reach; its focus on individual experience, small-scale interactions, and the politics of gesture and self-presentation; its focus on the impact of homophobia, rather than more positive aspects of queer culture; and its reliance on strategies of exposure to shake the hold of gender and sexual norms. These aspects of queer thought, so marked by their emergence at the end of the twentieth century, have in each case important precedents in midcentury sociology. Determining what aspects of queer thought continue to be salient and effective in the twenty-first century depends on a reckoning with this past.

Queer scholars' unwillingness to recognize the influence of midcentury social scientists is not surprising. Because of the changes in US social life from the 1960s onward, research *about* sexual and gender minorities by experts in the human sciences would seem to have little in common with research *by* those who identified themselves as such. This shift led to a major movement against sexual and gender normativity. In this sense, the birth of queer theory was a clear political advance, a declaration of independence from apologetic studies of homosexuality. But looking more closely at this history proves that the transition from studies of sexuality to queer theory was less a clean break than a complex process of debt and disavowal.

To the extent that this earlier scholarship has been acknowledged, it has been as a deeply limited and incomplete precursor. Doing this work, I realized how much I had underestimated a previous era of scholarship, crediting secondhand accounts of works rather than reading them for myself. Instead of seeing midcentury empirical scholarship as a less enlightened version of our own, I began to see in it a robust and meaningful alternative to the queer account of politics. What had appeared as a straightforward narrative of political progress turned out to be a profound difference in the understanding of what counted as political. While queer scholars and activists worked to challenge the categories by which we define ourselves, empirical researchers in the postwar period sought to establish categories in order to make space for behavior considered illegitimate.

I came to understand this difference regarding political strategy as deeply influenced by disciplinary history. Queer theory's commitment to disruption is an orientation that it shares with the interpretive humanities. This was especially true in the last few decades of the twentieth century, when scholars of literature and philosophy rigorously questioned the grounds of knowledge and experience. The commitment to stabilization might be understood to characterize the social sciences in general; although there are key differences among them, social scientists share a commitment to making the sublimely unknowable social world intelligible and meaningful. This task took on particular urgency at midcentury. In light of changing morals and standards of behavior, researchers turned tools of quantification, taxonomy, and description on social groups that were barely understood as part of the social world. These were people whose activities so contravened norms of decency, honesty, and mental fitness that they could only be understood as sick or evil individuals: homosexuals, but also con men, professional gamblers, drug addicts, juvenile delinquents, prostitutes, and so on. The motive for claiming that these groups' activities were socially patterned, meaningful, and predictable may have been professional: to claim more territory for sociology. But the political effects were profound; claiming that these outsiders had a share in ordinary life brought them into the realm of the recognizably human.[1]

Reframing political conflict as disciplinary or methodological conflict entails a direct challenge to queer thought. As queer theory coalesced in the academy, it understood itself as opposed to professionalism and institutions, even as it took hold in elite enclaves of academia. But many of its key tenets were more suited to fighting in the street than to standing at a lectern. Of course, now that queer studies is widely acknowledged as an integral part of academic life, it is hard to remember it as the scrappy upstart that it was. But this anti-institutional, antidisciplinary aspect of the field is still central to its self-understanding, which can make calling attention to its place in the history of the disciplines sound like an affront.

But the emergence of queer theory and activism around 1990 is both a signal political event and a fascinating moment of intellectual history. The field combined the activist energy of the 1980s with an ascendant American poststructuralism. In that context, it seemed both urgent and possible to counter presumptive heterosexuality through an excavation of the epistemological structure of the closet; to refuse the straitjacket of biological sex through the foregrounding of linguistic performativity; and to counter the ever-tightening association of homosexuality and death by a refusal of the terms on which "the homosexual" had become an object of knowledge. This revolution of ideas had powerful effects, influencing everything from the shape of popular protest to the course of research on HIV/AIDS. But it also fit well into the context of the university and into the academic humanities, where the opposition it encountered because of its real political challenges was offset by its intellectual resonance and theoretical fluency.

Underdogs looks back on this moment, now thirty years ago. We are living through a period of greater uncertainty, both about the effects of rhetorical analysis on public discourse and about the future of the university. The changes wrought by the queer movement serve to remind us of the critical force of thought itself, and of how activism can be brought to bear on academic life. But holding on to what is most valuable in queer critique means letting go of what is not. The dream of addressing all forms of marginality through the term queer, under strain from the beginning in the context of the US, has failed to reckon with political and economic difference beyond its borders. The long-standing tensions around gender inequality that attended the attempt to transition from *lesbian and gay* to *queer* have never been fully resolved. As the LGBT community has been more widely included in civic organizations and has staked a vigorous claim on marriage and family, the bright line between normativity and antinormativity is harder to maintain. And in a moment when institutions are so visibly under threat, and the survival of state-funded education appears tenuous, queer theory's critique of academic institutions and its antistatist politics feel out of step with current reality.

Yet despite these tensions, *queer* continues to flourish, and not simply as a global brand. I remain deeply committed to the vision of queer that has enabled generations of scholars and students to think and act differently. The fusions of theory and activism, creative praxis, and the remaking of academic life that queer theory inaugurated have profoundly impacted me and have affected the lives of countless others. My sense is that to continue to do this work, queer studies stands in need of a renewed look at its founding assumptions, methods, and place in the university. *Underdogs* seeks to make that look backward possible by staging an encounter with a history that may not look like our own.

Introduction

BEGINNING WITH *STIGMA*

> What's the point of accentuating the negative, of beginning with stigma, and for that matter a form of stigma—"Shame on you"—so unsanitizably redolent of that long Babylonian exile known as queer childhood? But note that this is just what the word queer itself does, too: the main reason why the self-application of "queer" by activists has proven so volatile is that there's no *way* that any amount of affirmative reclamation is going to succeed in detaching the word from its associations with shame and with the terrifying powerlessness of gender-dissonant or otherwise stigmatized childhood. If queer is a politically potent term, which it is, that's because, far from being capable of being detached from the childhood scene of shame, it cleaves to that scene as a near-inexhaustible source of transformational energy. There's a strong sense, I think, in which the subtitle of any truly queer (perhaps as opposed to gay?) politics will be the same as the one Erving Goffman gave to his book *Stigma: Notes on the Management of Spoiled Identity*. But more than its management: its experimental, creative, performative force.
>
> Eve Kosofsky Sedgwick, "Queer Performativity"[1]

In her essay "Queer Performativity: Henry James's *The Art of the Novel*" (1993), Eve Kosofsky Sedgwick proposes to replace the ordinary language philosopher J. L. Austin's example of a statement that does rather than describes ("I do") with the phrase "Shame on you." By shifting from the marriage ceremony to a scene of childhood shame, Sedgwick questions the normativity of Austin's examples of felicitous or effective speech acts, which are taken from a repertoire of socially approved scripts and occasions. What would it mean, she asks, to understand performativity in the context of unauthorized or debased social experience—for instance, in the context of "gender-dissonant or otherwise stigmatized childhood"? But Sedgwick, too, knows how to choose her moments: as the lead article in the inaugural issue of the journal *GLQ: A Journal of Lesbian and Gay Studies*, "Queer Performativity" is an especially significant intervention into queer studies at the moment of its ascendance.[2] Sedgwick takes the opportunity to respond not only to Austin but also to Judith Butler, whose essay "Critically Queer" follows hers in the special issue, and who was, at this time, the author of the most influential discussion of performativity in queer studies: *Gender Trouble* (1990). Although Sedgwick's explicit target is not *Gender Trouble* but its readers (those making use of a version of performativity as "they think they are understanding it from Judith Butler's ...work" [15]), her ambition to claim this concept for a different version of queer studies is clear. Sedgwick declares that, for her, "the deepest interest of any notion of performativity ... is not finally in the challenge it makes to essentialism" (14), thus citing, negatively, Butler's central argument. Homing in on what was understood, even by Butler, as a weakness in the book, Sedgwick points to the limits of parody as a framework for reading queer culture: "I'd also—if parenthetically—want to suggest that shame/performativity may get us a lot further with the cluster of phenomena generally called 'camp' than the notion of parody will" (14).[3]

Gender Trouble ends by articulating the utopian possibility that the proliferation of genders will "expose [the] fundamental unnaturalness" of gender, and so weaken the violent hold of the sex-gender system.[4] Sedgwick pursued a similar approach in her 1990 book *Epistemology of the Closet*, using the tools of critical genealogy to denaturalize sexual orientation and thus to "render less destructively presumable 'homosexuality as we know it today.'"[5] But "Queer Performativity" marks the beginning of a transition in Sedgwick's work, away from the strategy of denaturalization (or what she later called "faith in exposure"[6]) to an emphasis on affect and embodiment. This shift—from epistemology to phenomenology; from cognition to affect; from psychoanalysis to object relations; from strong to weak theory—was crucial to Sedgwick's intellectual trajectory and to the broader field of queer studies.[7] Like other transitions, this one required sacrifices: here, it is the framework of philosophical poststructuralism, so formative for both Butler and Sedgwick, that is sacrificed, as Sedgwick redefines performativity as a bodily, affective, and social phenomenon. After a preliminary engagement with Austin, Sedgwick turns to the affect theory of the postwar psychologist Silvan Tomkins and to the rhetoric of shame in Henry James's prefaces to the *New York Edition* of his novels. Sedgwick argues that experiences of shame make identity but in a way that is ripe for "misconstrual and misrecognition" (14). Describing circuits of interaction and interrupted interest, Sedgwick redefines performativity as a social scene, and a form of attunement; rather than relying on dissidence and exposure as the basis for social change, she imagines a queer collective of "those whose sense of identity is for some reason tuned most durably to the note of shame" (14).

Sedgwick's attempt to reorient the field—away from its poststructuralist antecedents and toward that bio-psycho-social hybrid now known as "affect studies"—was remarkably successful. My dissertation ("Failure as a Way of Life") and first book (*Feeling Backward*) were deeply influenced by the "affective turn," and especially by Sedgwick's assertion of the political value of negative feelings. I was moved by the moral seriousness of this account of queer life, which had the power to dignify experiences that might otherwise be deemed simply abject. At the same time, I struggled to reconcile Sedgwick's pronouncements about queer feeling with more pedestrian accounts of gay, lesbian, and transgender identity. Would the focus on feeling, particularly childhood feelings, displace rather than supplement attention to sexual practices and communities?[8] "Some of the infants, children, and adults in whom shame remains the most available mediator of identity," Sedgwick writes, "are the ones called (in a related word) shy. ('Remember the fifties?' Lily Tomlin asks. 'No one was gay in the fifties; they were just shy.')" (13). Riffing on Tomlin's joke about the closet, and the recoding of homosexuality as shyness in the McCarthy era, Sedgwick goes on to suggest that shyness—but not homosexuality—might *define* queerness: "Everyone knows that there are some lesbians and gay men who could never count as queer, and other people who vibrate to the chord of queer without having much same-sex eroticism, or without routing their same-sex eroticism through the identity labels lesbian or gay" (13).

The sentence, like so many in this essay, is a master class in performativity. The locution "everyone knows" alludes to the emerging distinction between homosexuality and queerness as if it were self-evident, and creates a desire to be "in the know." Redefining queerness as an affective disposition makes space for people who do not identify as gay or lesbian; at the same time, it puts other exclusions in place. I read these words as a young—but not particularly shy—lesbian, wondering whether or not I belonged in the new world of queer. Ultimately, Sedgwick reconciles queerness with homosexuality by suggesting that shame-based practices emerge from and live near lesbian and gay social worlds.[9] She writes: "Many of the performative identity vernaculars that seem most recognizably 'flushed' . . . with shame-consciousness and shame-creativity cluster intimately around lesbian and gay worldly spaces: to name only a few, butch abjection, femmitude, leather, pride, SM, drag, masculinity, fisting, attitude, zines, histrionicism, asceticism, Snap! culture, diva worship, florid religiosity, in a word, *flaming*" (13-14). This breathless tribute to queer culture is at once *scenic*, in the sense attributed to Henry James, and *sceney*, in the sense attributed to queer theory. Rather than attempt to describe or define queerness, Sedgwick shows it off, letting these flaming creatures make her argument for her. In this way, Sedgwick not only critically engages Butler—she upstages her. Drag, perhaps the most recognizable figure of *Gender Trouble*, pales by comparison. While this list begins rather quietly with butch abjection, it quickly builds momentum, the exclamation point in "Snap! culture" and the final *flaming* italics lighting the way.

Sedgwick's competitive display of shame-proneness and of her insider knowledge of queer culture would not be all that remarkable—another border skirmish in queer studies—were she content to beat Butler at her own game. But Sedgwick's ambitions are grander and stranger than that. "Queer Performativity" constitutes a first move in an attempt to seize queer studies by the root—a process Sedgwick later described as taking a "distinct step to the side of the deconstructive project of analyzing apparently nonlinguistic phenomena in rigorously linguistic terms" (*Touching Feeling*, 6). This sentence comes from the introduction to *Touching Feeling*, the book that represents Sedgwick's writing on affect from the 1990s. In this context, she describes the trajectory of this work as a "departure from the deconstructive/queer lineage." She expands:

> *Touching Feeling* wants to address aspects of experience and reality that do not present themselves in propositional or even in verbal form alongside others that do, rather than submit to the common sense that requires a strict separation between the two and usually implies an ontological privileging of the former. What may be different in the present work, however, is a disinclination to reverse those priorities by subsuming nonverbal aspects of reality firmly under the aegis of the linguistic. I assume that the line between words and things or between linguistic and nonlinguistic phenomena is endlessly changing, permeable, and entirely unsusceptible to any definitive articulation . . . Many kinds of objects and events *mean*, in many heterogeneous ways and contexts, and I see some value in not reifying or mystifying the linguistic kinds of meaning unnecessarily. (6)

While she refuses the "common sense" that prioritizes reality over representation, Sedgwick also questions the impulse to reverse this hierarchy—

to insist that linguistic expression should be privileged, and that nonlinguistic phenomena should be examined "in rigorously linguistic terms." The critical common sense about the priority of language was, like the field of queer studies itself, of relatively recent vintage. And it was never that common: few people outside the interpretive humanities were willing to grant this kind of status to language.

Still, the pull of the deconstructive/queer lineage is strong for Sedgwick: her departure from it requires a disciplinary and a historical defection. Sedgwick turns to psychology in "Queer Performativity," analyzing the work of a figure she calls "the most important recent theorist of affect," Silvan Tomkins (7). She also turned to Cold War America, a period from the 1940s to the 1960s that she, along with her collaborator, Adam Frank, would soon go on to call "the cybernetic fold."[10] Midcentury psychology and cybernetics were distant from Sedgwick's preoccupations, and those of queer studies in the early 1990s. Tomkins appears a rather unlikely protagonist in this context, considering what Sedgwick and Frank identify as the lack of "a concertedly antihomophobic project" or even of "any marked homosexual interest" in his work (99). Furthermore, Tomkins's psychology is, from the start, seen as idiosyncratic and singular. Unlike the more familiar midcentury figure of Austin, Tomkins's work, with its emphasis on the biological substrate of feeling, is difficult to assimilate to the routines and assumptions of critical theory in the early 1990s. As it turns out, however, it is Tomkins's difference from the present, and his indifference to the "queer/deconstructive legacy," that makes him valuable. Tomkins is a key figure for Sedgwick because his work is "sublimely alien": for this reason, he provides "a different place to begin."[11]

If Sedgwick's turn to Tomkins seems to take her far afield, another citation in the essay suggests that this flanking action may in fact be a return. In "Queer Performativity," Sedgwick also cites another midcentury figure, the Canadian American sociologist Erving Goffman: in suggesting that the subtitle of his 1963 book *Stigma* might serve as a new name for the field of queer studies, Sedgwick invokes another "sublimely alien" figure. However, in Goffman, Sedgwick names someone whose influence was crucial, if unrecognized, all along. Goffman's work on mental asylums, prisons, impression management, the performance of gender, and the making and breaking of social norms is tied by many threads, both genealogical and conceptual, to the field of queer theory.[12] As salient and formative as his research and his methods were, they did not survive what Sedgwick describes as the "subsuming" of "nonverbal aspects of reality firmly under the aegis of the linguistic." Many of Goffman's key insights about the microdynamics of social power were taken up and translated into terms more congenial to the deconstructive/queer legacy. Queer critics undertook such borrowings without giving credit, and often seemingly without the knowledge that they were borrowing. As Gayle Rubin and others have argued, empirical research by scholars of sexuality laid the foundation for the emergence of queer theory as a discipline centered in the humanities around 1990, but these debts were often unacknowledged. Sedgwick's discovery of the new territory of the cybernetic fold is better described as a *rediscovery* of a landscape that was not unknown so much as willfully forgotten.

THE SOCIAL SCIENCE ROOTS OF QUEER THEORY

From the 1950s to the 1970s, scholars in the social sciences conducted empirical studies of marginal sexual communities and practices. In the period dedicated to what has been called the "new" or "appreciative" studies of deviance, these researchers turned their attention to practices and communities formerly seen as sick or criminal.[13] Erving Goffman, Mary McIntosh, Evelyn Hooker, John Lofland, David Matza, Howard Becker, John Gagnon and William Simon, Esther Newton, John Kitsuse, Edwin Lemert, Edwin M. Schur, and Laud Humphreys reframed deviance as a relational dynamic rather than as a set of inherent traits. While only some of this work was explicitly homophile or partisan, as a whole it tended to counter the stigma of homosexuality, drag, and anonymous sex. These researchers transformed the meaning of sex by treating it as a social phenomenon, turning even the most unfamiliar and "outlandish" behaviors and desires into grist for the sociological mill.

Seeing sex as social also meant seeing the enormous variety in the arrangements that had and could organize sexual desires and activities. This attention to the variability of sexual categories and practices explains why this work was instrumental in the birth of a "social constructionist paradigm" of sexuality. As Gayle Rubin writes, "Social construction was little more than the application of ordinary social science tools to sexuality and gender. What seemed so radical was in many respects a conventional set of approaches to an unconventional and highly stigmatized set of subject areas."[14] These comments appear in a 2011 essay ("Blood under the Bridge") in which Rubin reflects on the history of the feminist sex wars and the context for her landmark essay "Thinking Sex" (1984). Rubin's comments about the social treatment of sex appear in the opening section of the essay "The Fight against Forgetting." It is an apt phrase to describe a great deal of Rubin's work, which she has devoted to recovering the suppressed bibliography of empirical and constructionist work on sexuality (in history, anthropology, and sociology) that informs queer studies.

Rubin's frustration with this fact is audible in her 2002 essay "Studying Sexual Subcultures: Excavating the Ethnography of Gay Communities in Urban North America": "Because the idioms of previous decades may seem dated, their theoretical subtlety and originality is often underestimated. Much of what we now take for granted in the anthropology of sexuality and homosexuality owes a great deal to an odd assortment of urban sociologists, historians of homosexuality, and brave, pioneering ethnographers who went where almost no one had gone before and undertook considerable risks to their careers to do so."[15] Rubin's work has been crucial in reconstructing this genealogy, as has the work of scholars including Steven Epstein, Janice Irvine, Chad Heap, Jeffrey Weeks, Jeffrey Escoffier, John D'Emilio, Arlene Stein, Kenneth Plummer, John Gagnon, William Simon, Joshua Gamson, Dawne Moon, Lisa Duggan, Kath Weston, Kristen Schilt, Peter Nardi, Beth Schneider, Adam Isaiah Green, and Trevor Hoppe.[16] These scholars have traced continuities between postwar social studies of deviance and queer studies, focusing on the reframing of sexuality as collective and social; the separation of role and behavior; a recognition of variety in the social organization of sexuality; a moral leveling that emphasized the existence rather than the judgment or reform of practices; a link between sexual stigma and other forms of social stratification; the treatment of stigma as a social dynamic rather than as inherent to particular physical or social traits; attention to the microphysics of power; and theories of the social construction of sexuality.

While scholars of sexuality in the social sciences have amply acknowledged this legacy, those in the humanities have largely failed to do so. There are many reasons for this historical erasure, which remains in place even in a moment of détente between the humanities and the social sciences. In identifying the roots of the field, queer scholars have tended to cite more proximate antecedents, from psychoanalysis to philosophy to linguistics. In addition, the field shares a critique of the social sciences with the humanities at large. From the moment of its founding, queer scholarship opposed the methodology, epistemology, and ethics of the social sciences, equating empiricism with positivism, and associating social scientific method with objectification, social control, and state violence. Such associations are particularly strong at midcentury: both during WWII and after, the social sciences were conscripted into government service at an unprecedented scale. Research was flooded with federal grant money and employment opportunities, consolidating an image of science pursued in the shadow of the national interest.[17] For these reasons, the field of queer studies has been slow to recognize its debt to postwar social science.

With her turn to affect studies, Sedgwick took a deep dive into an unexpected archive. This return to the cybernetic fold led her to adopt a fresh perspective on many key issues in the field, and to embrace approaches that had previously been sidelined. In justifying her return to Tomkins, Sedgwick calls out the antiscientific bias in queer theory and in Left critique more broadly as a form of dogmatic parochialism. She does not, however, acknowledge the close genealogical links that already exist between queer theory and midcentury social science. Nevertheless, Sedgwick's citation of Goffman points to this missing lineage. *Underdogs* is an attempt, from the position of a scholar steeped in the "deconstructive/queer legacy," to pursue queer's connections to postwar social science. In particular, I am concerned with the study of social outsiders in the field of deviance studies that was the context for Goffman's *Stigma*. Despite the social transformations that have taken place since the 1950s, the concepts and methods of deviance studies have proved remarkably durable, and have had a significant afterlife in the field of queer studies. The insights of midcentury social science were always there in canonical queer theory, hiding—like the reference to Goffman in "Queer Performativity"—in plain sight.

REMEMBER THE FIFTIES?

Sedgwick expresses some qualms about her choice of shame as the key to queer subjectivity in "Queer Performativity." In an embarrassed preamble, she reflects on shame's prominence in pop psychology and self-help. Sedgwick, however, avows her kinship with these degraded and feminized discourses: "My sense of the force of the affect shame is clearly very different from what is to be found in the self-help literature, but there it is: Henry James and the inner child it must be" (6).[18] More troubling than psychology's crossover success, however, is its history as a legitimate discipline. It is Sedgwick's venture into the terrain of the social sciences that demands justification. The fact that Tomkins wrote his major works during the height of the Cold War (he published the first two volumes of *Affect, Imagery, Consciousness* in 1961 and 1962) makes Sedgwick's championing of him even more contentious. This period is known for the growth of Big Science, the rise of a surveillance state complicit with social science, and the use of behaviorist "cures" for homosexuality. To queer theorists, Cold War social science—and psychology especially—was a known enemy, the point of convergence for all the things these critics opposed: positivism, objectivity, normativity, social control, expertise, liberalism, and the expansion and professionalization of the disciplines. In the midst of the AIDS crisis, many critics saw links between the 1950s and the 1980s: in both eras, the government, social scientists, and health-care professionals colluded to enforce restrictive sexual and social norms.[19]

But if the Cold War was a target of queer critique, it was also an inevitable touchstone for the field. The immediate postwar period was the backdrop for the childhood and adolescence of queer theory's founding generation, including Sedgwick (b. 1950). This fact is reflected in the field's signature intellectual and aesthetic preoccupations. The term *queer* itself, though it began to accumulate connotations of nonnormative desires at the end of the nineteenth century, was in heavy rotation by midcentury, doing service both as a playground slur and a blackmailer's term of art. The themes of surveillance, paranoia, and the closet that dominate canonical queer theory bear the stamp of the McCarthy era. Similarly, the version of resistance promulgated in the field recalls the mix of ambient disobedience and wildcat strikes that characterize life in a "totally administered society."[20] The impress of this era is visible in Sedgwick's earlier work, *Between Men* (1985) and *Epistemology of the Closet* (1990), which elaborated the violence of male bonds and homophobia in canonical Western literature from Shakespeare to Proust, with a particular focus on Victorian and modernist literature. However, the world depicted resembled America in the 1950s, as imagined by Alfred Hitchcock, saturated by secrecy and double-dealing.[21] At times, Sedgwick referred to a rather different midcentury, the queer worlds of urban bohemia, artistic coteries, and "sleaze" subcultures.[22] With the mention of figures such as J. R. Ackerley, Kenneth Anger, W. H. Auden, Divine, Jean Genet, Jack Smith, Gore Vidal, John Waters, and Andy Warhol, Sedgwick invokes a more variegated terrain of the Cold War period, one marked by the violent enforcement and the widespread flouting of sexual norms.[23]

Silvan Tomkins's appearance in this crowd is rather unexpected. However, despite his lack of interest in queer culture, Sedgwick and Frank champion Tomkins for the project of "antihomophobic inquiry."[24] They see in Tomkins's work a refreshing distance both from the normalizing violence of Cold War psychology and from the deadening protocols of contemporary theory. In distinguishing Tomkins from his historical moment, they point to the lack of a "core self" (98) in his account of subjectivity. This resistance to depictions of interiority has a long history in queer representation, where the refusal to be a person has been a key strategy for evading surveillance. Sedgwick and Frank also applaud Tomkins's love of taxonomies, and his almost endless ability to generate them. Promoting Tompkin's use of taxonomy is a surprising move for Sedgwick and Frank, since taxonomy is often understood as a tool of a pathologizing scientism. Instead, they are enamored by Tomkins's habit of listing, which they describe as calming and inspiring, addicting and soothing. This quality of his work earns him a comparison to Proust, for whom, they write, "the highest interest of such taxonomies is ever in making grounds for disconfirmation and surprise" (98).[25] While taxonomy might be used to stabilize identity, grouping traits to confirm the existence of determinate kinds of people, in their account it has the opposite effect, opening new possibilities for being and relation. Sedgwick and Frank also note Tomkins's distance from behaviorism, and celebrate the descriptive richness of his system of affects. They cite generous chunks of this "rich claustral writing" (95), for instance, a long passage about possibilities for affective complementarity that they compare to the writing of Gertrude Stein: "If you like to be looked at and I like to look at you, we may achieve an enjoyable interpersonal relationship. If you like to talk and I like to listen to you talk, this can be mutually rewarding. If you like to feel enclosed within a claustrum and I like to put my arms around you, we can both enjoy a particular kind of embrace" (96). And so on.

Such examples clarify Tomkins's distance from mainstream—behaviorist, top-down, quantitative—social science and from the punitive forms of control and containment associated with it. But Sedgwick and Frank also acknowledge the impress of the postwar period in Tomkins's work. Tomkins was anomalous in his moment, but he was also of his moment, the period of the cybernetic fold. Exploring the mixture of analog and digital models in Tomkins's affect theory, Sedgwick and Frank describe this moment as a phase in the history of technology when the human capacity to imagine artificial intelligence outstripped the actual computing capacity of existing machines. They describe a less familiar version of midcentury social science, one elaborated under the sway of systems theory, integrating "ethology, neuropsychology, perception and cognition, social psychology, and . . . a prescient series of rereadings of Freud" (99). They see the characteristic strength of this moment as an ability to "discuss *how things differentiate*: how quantitative differences turn into qualitative ones, how digital and analog representations leapfrog or interleave with one another, what makes the unexpected fault lines between regions of the calculable and the incalculable" (106). Sedgwick and Frank's use of the word *fold* (territory; enclosure; bend, crease, ply, or coil) to describe this period suggests their surprise and pleasure in the discovery of Tomkins's work and of this alternate version of midcentury social science. There is something thrilling, even sublime, in such an unexpected find, like stumbling on a portal into a proximate but unknown land. What begins as an attempt to defend Tomkins from charges of essentialism turns into an argument on behalf of a prior historical moment's power to disrupt the present.

It is ultimately Tomkins's distance from the present rather than from the past that makes him so significant for Sedgwick and Frank, because the antagonist of this essay is not Cold War social science but rather what Sedgwick and Frank refer to simply as theory. Sedgwick wrote "Queer Performativity" and "Shame in the Cybernetic Fold" as one of theory's acknowledged masters, but she was on her way out: these pieces mark her increasing distance from this role. Sedgwick described this transformation as a turn from "paranoid" to "reparative" thought. She pursued it by breaking with the interpretive protocols with which she was most familiar, and by finding "other places to begin." But she also pursued it by means of what Sedgwick and Frank call "dialectical struggle" (99), and even occasional bare-knuckled attacks—which is how "Shame in the Cybernetic Fold" opens: "Here are a few things theory knows today."[26] Sedgwick and Frank preempt criticism of Tomkins's work as naive or essentialist by painting a picture of theory as supercilious, jaded, and dour—a characterization that, in the years since this essay's publication, has only become more familiar. Alluding to Tomkins's elaboration of a set of determinate affects, Sedgwick and Frank write, "You don't have to be long out of theory kindergarten to make mincemeat of, let's say, a psychology that depends on the separate existence of eight (only sometimes it's nine) distinct affects hardwired into the human biological system" (94).

At once defensive and defiant, Sedgwick and Frank alert their readers to the obvious drawbacks of Tomkins's thinking, pointing to both a rigid scientism and to inconsistency. But their critique is actually directed at the "'scientism' of theory," which, they write, "can become visible in this light as a different product of almost the same, very particular technological moment as Tomkins's. The fact that one, today, sounds cockamamie and the other virtual common sense, or that one sounds ineluctably dated and the other nearly fresh as print, may reveal less about the transhistorical rightness of 'theory' than about the dynamics of consensus formation and cross-disciplinary transmission" (94–95). The scientism of science, Sedgwick and Frank argue, is all too easy a target for theory, which, as they describe it, is characterized by intellectual arrogance, black-and-white thinking, and dismissiveness. In this view, the structuralist/poststructuralist tradition of critical theory is actually an inheritor of Cold War scientism, whereas Cold War science is much more variegated and surprising. If the choice of Tomkins might at first seem arbitrary or idiosyncratic, this challenge to theory in his name makes clear just how high the stakes are. Sedgwick and Frank aim not only to redefine performativity, or to transform queer studies, but more broadly to question the fundamental grounds of the interpretive humanities.

Despite their suggestion of riches hidden in the cybernetic fold, this is a somewhat thin account of this period in the history of the social sciences. Sedgwick and Frank offer a parsimonious definition of the cybernetic fold (computing imaginary > computing power), and ignore a broader landscape that might include Black sociology, the antipsychiatry movement, sociological best sellers, Marxist sociology, the second Chicago school, and other sources of radical sociology.[27] In addition to Tomkins, Sedgwick and Frank mention Paul Goodman and Gregory Bateson, but there were many other examples of midcentury researchers who broke away from their disciplines. A short list of midcentury "maverick" social scientists might include Howard Becker, Daniel Bell, Horace Cayton, St. Clair Drake, E. Franklin Frazier, Harold Garfinkel, Nathan Glazer, Erving Goffman, Alvin Gouldner, Jules Henry, Herbert Marcuse, C. Wright Mills, David Riesman, Dorothy Smith, William F. White, and Irving Zola. One might also mention in this context Alfred Kinsey: the example of the Kinsey Reports suggests how even research that embodies many troubling features of Cold War science (statistical reduction, ethically questionable research design, major grant funding) can have contradictory effects. Despite its putatively normalizing framework and its scientistic approach, Kinsey's reports on male and female sexual behavior in 1948 and 1953 challenged the norm of universal heterosexuality.[28] Many of these examples of postwar research are alien, even "sublimely alien," to the presumptions of contemporary theory, and to mainstream Cold War social science as well. And some of it is remarkably free of heterosexual teleology, despite its explicit thematization of homosexuality.

Sedgwick's use of the word *cockamamie* to preempt criticism of Tomkins evokes a midcentury archive that is otherwise absent from this article. *Cockamamie* acquired its meaning of *implausible, ridiculous,* or *absurd* across the period of the cybernetic fold. The word first appeared in the 1930s and 1940s, a probable corruption of the term *decalcomania* (the name for the Victorian fad for transferring decorative images from paper to glass and porcelain). While the term literally described paper strips children used to transfer images to their skin (or temporary tattoos), it was also applied, particularly in the context of Yiddish-inflected urban dialect, to an outlandish person.[29] In a 1956 interview, Shelley Winters referred to the Hollywood movies she was cast in as "like cockamamies." The *New York Times,* underlining Winters's hardscrabble Jewish upbringing, offered a gloss: "This word, translated from the Brooklynese, is the authorized pronunciation for decalcomania. Anyone there who calls a cockamamie a decalcomania is stared at."[30] By the 1960s, the word appeared more regularly as an adjective, describing something that is unlikely or improbable, for instance, in this quote from a collection of Ed McBain's Eighty-Seventh Precinct stories published in 1962: "You walked into the precinct with a tight dress and a cockamamie bunch of alibis" (OED). Across the middle of the twentieth century, *cockamamie* traveled from ethnic enclaves to the all-American alienation of hard-boiled fiction, all the while carrying associations of criminality and defiance. *Cockamamie* recalls Broadway or the Bowery much more than the technocratic world of Cold War social science, systems theory, or cybernetics. It also suggests midcentury homosexuality, as the writers of *The Simpsons* episode "Homer's Phobia" acknowledged when they named the antique store where a gay clerk voiced by John Waters works Cockamamie's.[31] Like *queer, cockamamie* suggests taboo, social marking, strangeness, impossibility, in a word, *stigma.*

Both *queer* and *cockamamie* evoke a midcentury underworld, the shadowy territory that constituted the "field" for the sociological study of deviance, including Goffman's 1963 book *Stigma.* Goffman was asked to teach a course on social deviance at Berkeley in the spring of 1961. He drew on a mix of memoirs, case studies, drugstore fiction, and newspaper items about the folkways of a miscellaneous band of social outsiders and rebels, underdogs and outcasts, many of which made their way into *Stigma*'s footnotes. Despite the fact that Goffman is the major modern theorist of stigma, Sedgwick's reference to him and in particular to the phrase the "management of spoiled identity" nonetheless strikes a recherché—not to say cockamamie—note. The difference, of course, is that Sedgwick spends no time elucidating Goffman's relevance for her project, whereas she embraced Tomkins, providing context for his work and later publishing an edition of his writing on affect.

Goffman's concept of "spoiled identity," with his indication of permanent damage, was hard to square with Sedgwick's sanguine account of performativity. In that context, shame was much more appealing, with its volatility and erotic charge. But in the framework of deviance studies, it was "spoiled identity" and indelible stigma that was at stake. If the associations of marking and scapegoating made stigma an indispensable concept during the AIDS epidemic, the downbeat tone and noir iconography of deviance studies was at odds with the energy of radical queer activism circa 1993. What did the lives of hobos, hustlers, and con men have to do with the takeover of media spaces, with spectacles of eroticism, mourning, and rage, with queer lives lived in public and without apology? What could the empirical study of the careers of marijuana users, juvenile delinquents, and circus performers have to do with the linguistic construction of gender, the undoing of the homo-hetero divide, or the radical critique of identity? Despite the obvious differences, the connections are profound. Queer theory inherited many of its key concepts and frameworks from the empirical study of the lives of sexual and other deviants: its focus on the figure of the social outsider; its stigma-centric, anti-identity, coalitional model of politics; and its careful attention to the everyday effects of inequality. From the 1950s through the 1970s, scholars in sociology, anthropology, and history generated accounts of social construction; of stigma as contingent and relational; of the dramaturgical or "performed" self; and of power as the product of small-scale, ordinary social interactions. As significant as these concepts were for queer theory, this work has rarely been acknowledged by contemporary scholars in the humanities.

The field of queer studies is known for its tendency to suppress or disavow its antecedents.[32] Many streams, both activist and academic, fed into queer studies: the legacies of AIDS activism, the feminist sex wars, third world and Black feminism, and trans politics, among others, have yet to be fully acknowledged or integrated into the field. In the context of these broader exclusions, it is not obvious why the failure to recognize the contributions of midcentury deviance studies is a problem. Given the fact that postwar social science was even less diverse than the founding generation of queer theory, returning to these roots might seem like a retrenchment rather than an expansion of sexuality studies. Deviance studies after WWII was characterized by nationalism, parochialism, and its assumption

of a White, middle-class standard of behavior. It reflected widespread seg-
regation in US education and society, as well as continuing gender, racial,
and class hierarchies in the university. Even though deviance studies provided a way for formerly illegitimate subjects to enter scholarly discourse,
the field was nonetheless marked by its embrace of a hegemonic view of
difference as otherness. While investigating this lineage may cause discomfort or anger, and prompt contemporary critics to distance themselves
even further from this troubling past, it is vital to recognize and address
the links between the deviance paradigm and the methods and politics of
queer studies.[33] Far from having an isolated or anomalous influence on the
field, the impact of deviance studies is significant and widespread, showing up everywhere in the history of the field, and notably in the work of
critics who would seem to oppose it. Because of this deep influence and
staying power, a confrontation with the legacy of deviance studies is necessary. Exploring this history is important in adressing critiques of the
field, particularly by queer scholars of color who have called attention to
the false universalism in queer's ambition to represent all forms of marginality. While I do think deviance studies laid crucial groundwork for this
well-documented feature of queer thought, my aim here is not entirely or
even primarily critical. Deviance studies shapes contemporary racial, gender, class, and geographical exclusions in queer studies, but it also shapes
its vision of collective liberation, characterized by coalitional thinking
and an elevation of society's most stigmatized individuals, practices, and
communities. Things *have* changed. The contemporary field reflects the
takeover of the expert investigation of stigmatized people by those people
themselves, as well as a greater recognition that individual experiences of
stigma should be viewed as symptoms of interlocking systems of oppression. However, despite these changes, the image of deviance developed in
midcentury social science remains deeply embedded in queer studies and
its vision of social transformation.

Kadji Amin makes an argument for the need to "*rehistoricize*" the origins of queer theory in his 2017 book *Disturbing Attachments*.[34] Amin imagines this project as an "attachment genealogy," by which he means a critical investigation of the field's characteristic affects and rhetorics through
attention to its multiple and excluded legacies (14). For Amin, the period
of the early 1990s is decisive, since this is when the mix of utopian longing, celebration of marginality and resistance, and countermorality that
defines queer political feeling was solidified. *Disturbing Attachments* reck-
ons with this history, considering what happens to the hopes of first-wave

queer theory once the idea of "an articulable list of basic ethical values expressed consistently by an identifiably queer political culture" has been challenged by expanding geographical, racial, and historical boundaries. Amin writes, "the future of the field of Queer Studies—as well as its relevance for scholarship on prior historical periods, racialized populations, and areas outside the United States—requires a reckoning with the field's affective haunting by the inaugural moment of the U.S. 1990s . . . That is, by engaging *queer*'s *multiple* pasts—including those prior to its explicit deployment as a political and theoretical term in the 1990s—scholars might expand and multiply the affective histories that give queer meaning" (17).

Amin undertakes this historical reckoning through an in-depth analysis of the career and reception of Jean Genet. Genet is an icon of queer radicalism sent over from the deviance studies central casting office. Petty criminal, prisoner, prostitute, and homosexual: as Amin notes, Genet "resonates, more than any other canonical queer author from the pre-gay liberation past, with contemporary queer sensibilities attuned to a defiant nonnormativity" (2). The fact that Amin's argument about the expansion of queer studies precedes through an extended engagement with Genet and his reception makes clear how important the concept of deviance is to the version of queer ethics developed around 1990. Behind the glamourous outcast, hero, saint, and hustler is a more pedestrian group of oddballs and misfits, pickpockets and pensioners, who made their way into the pages of sociological studies, dime-store fiction, and popular journalism in the decades before gay liberation.[35] If Genet's avant-garde credentials made him an appealing point of origin for the antirealism of queer theory, his links to the underworld, though they were often conflated with formal rebellion, situated him in a milieu exhaustively studied by twentieth-century social scientists. Given that homosexuality was inseparable from that milieu, deviance could never be entirely disentangled from the representation of gay and lesbian lives.[36] But if social scientific studies of the same were dead on arrival in the poststructuralist and antifoundationalist moment of queer theory, it took longer—it would in fact take the structural realignment of the field—for the dark allure of Genet to fade. If Genet comfortably embodied all the values of queer as articulated in its earliest version, he looked quite different in a larger, more worldly frame. How, Amin asks, could queer studies come to terms with the deflation of the "*romance of the alternative*" (2) once Genet was revealed not only as a heroic avatar of sexual dissidence but as also deeply embedded in histories of colonialism, pederasty, and racial fetishism?

Amin's tough question to contemporary queer studies far outstrips the methodological, conceptual, and political resources of midcentury deviance studies, which set the pattern for the parochialism and individualism of queer studies. But it is a question that nonetheless still gets posed in the terms of deviance studies: as Amin states early in *Disturbing Attachments*, the central idea for the book emerged after "Genet spoiled my own investments in him" (4). The word *spoiled* stands out here, as it does in Sedgwick's "Queer Performativity," a sign of the persistence of deviance as a living framework for queer studies. The book is not a lament for the loss of a unified queer ethics, although Amin admits that he suffered a loss over the dissolution of that dream. Instead, he is concerned with new possibilities for queer studies that emerge in the wake of the deflation of one version of queer radicalism. He writes, "Deidealization is not the wholesale destruction of cherished ideals, but a form of the reparative that acknowledges messiness and damage" (11). Given that queer ideals emerged from a messy, damaged past, they are ripe for spoiling.

Underdogs takes as its focus an outmoded and tarnished mode of scholarship. The point is not to restore its reputation, which was never the best, or to recommend it as a practice in the present. Rather, this encounter with the past is meant to illuminate the sources—intellectual, ethical, methodological—of a contemporary formation. Deviance studies persists within queer studies as its all but avowed precursor, the repository of both its most stubborn faults and its utopian potential. It may seem an odd place to begin the work of attachment genealogy, but I hope to show that it is, despite appearances to the contrary, a significant point of origin for the dream of radical antinormativity that Amin sees at the core of first-generation queer theory. In particular, the tradition of microanalytic studies of interaction I examine here is salient. It allows for a precise accounting of social experiences, especially those of exclusion and marginalization, even as the conditions of stigmatization shift. Scholars of deviance attended to dynamics of stigmatization as they affected individuals; these tools are still crucial, even as the stigmatized cast of characters has changed. For some, both deviance studies and queer studies will be forever limited by their attention to individual experience and in the lack of a structural account of oppression. Yet, despite its focus on the individual, work in queer studies is still understood as aiming toward a collective good. Even though these aims were apparently lacking in deviance studies scholarship, this book attends to that field's collective and political dimensions.

UNDERDOG METHODS

Tracing the persistence of the deviance paradigm in the 1990s and after requires a return to the 1950s, the moment when the version of deviance that
underwrites queer studies took shape.[37] It requires, as I argue, the study
not only of deviant subjects but also of the people who studied them—that
is to say, not only Jean Genet but also Erving Goffman. The risk of deflation
is acute in this work, since it makes visible the split identity of queer scholars as people who identify as outsiders (to sexual norms, to the academy)
but who are also insiders—implicated in converting deviance into a de-
liverable in the modern research university. This split identity has made
it difficult for queer scholars to reckon with our position as knowledge
workers and with the field's status as a positive knowledge project. Tracing
the field's roots in deviance studies is important in coming to terms with
the institutional identity of the field and in addressing the ethical difficulties entailed in the scholarly study of marginal and stigmatized subjects.

    After WWII, scholars in the field of deviance studies explored society's
margins, focusing ethnographic attention on the haunts and habits of
troublemakers and misfits, outcasts and rebels. Although it is marked by
the moment of cybernetics, the field of deviance studies absorbed many
other influences, from Émile Durkheim's studies of social norms and Chicago school style ethnographies of urban disorder to social problem films,
existentialism, and the antipsychiatry movement. Situational and interactionist accounts of social life, attentive to the smallest units of verbal
and nonverbal communication, were particularly significant in analyzing
the making and breaking of rules at the microscale. Deviance studies focused its attention on social outsiders, using what Laud Humphreys referred to, citing Eugene J. Webb, as "oddball measures." Humphreys, observing the activities of men seeking anonymous sex in public restrooms,
was interested in employing "the least obtrusive measures available—the
least likely to distort the real world."[38] For him, this meant going undercover as a participant in tearoom sex, which gave his research some of its
oddball quality. But, as he stressed, "these research methods are actually
only uncommon applications of such tested measures as physical traces,
the running record, and simple observation" (21–22). Humphreys's research is typical of deviance studies in its choice to treat outlaw or unac-
ceptable behavior as ordinary. The methods used by these scholars often
depended on fine-grained, real-time observations in situ of small-scale
gestures, glances, and interactions. While this kind of observational re-

search was a core method for sociology, in the work of deviance studies scholars it was practiced in the underworld and on a scale so small as to be considered odd. It is this combination of stigmatized subject matter and almost absurdly detailed observation that constitutes the underdog methods of the time.

Those who researched deviance were often marked by association with the social stigma that they set out to study: the history of the scholarly study of deviance includes the stories of those who became outsiders in the profession. Rather than focus on the specific differences that set people apart from the mainstream, these scholars instead sought to account for processes of marginalization. The first paragraph of Howard Becker's classic 1963 text *Outsiders* is exemplary in its attention to the making of deviants:

> All social groups make rules and attempt, at some times and under some circumstances, to enforce them. Social rules define situations and the kinds of behavior appropriate to them, specifying some actions as "right" and forbidding others as "wrong." When a rule is enforced, the person who is supposed to have broken it may be seen as a special kind of person, one who cannot be trusted to live by the rules agreed on by the group. He is regarded as an *outsider*.[39]

Becker's definition of *outsider* comes swathed in qualifications. From the scare quotes around *right* and *wrong* to the use of the phrase *regarded as* to introduce the key term in his book, Becker suggests the guesswork in the attribution of rule breaking, and the arbitrariness of the moral qualities that attach to it.

Stigma: On the Management of Spoiled Identity strikes a similar note. Goffman relied on literary and popular accounts as well as his own keen social observations to build this influential theory of stigma. He defines stigma as a form of disqualification that results from the failure to meet the expectations associated with one's social role. Elaborating on the concept of "spoiled identity," Goffman writes,

> While the stranger is present before us, evidence can arise of his possessing an attribute that makes him different from others in the category of persons available for him to be, and of a less desirable kind—in the extreme, a person who is quite thoroughly bad, or dangerous, or weak. He is thus reduced from a whole and usual person to a tainted,

discounted one. Such an attribute is a stigma, especially when its discrediting effect is very extensive.[40]

Goffman's definition centers social expectations, emphasizing the narrow
range of appropriate behavior and how out of scale the consequences are
for failing to stay within that range. The traits that come to count as stigmas
are undermotivated: as Goffman writes, "not all undesirable attributes
are at issue, but only those which are incongruous with our stereotype of
what a given individual should be" (3). Despite the distinction drawn in
Stigma between "we normals" and stigmatized others, the model is universalizing, since any trait could be the basis of a stigma and the choice
is a matter of convention, or collective judgment. Because of the wholly
social nature of the process of stigmatization, "a language of relationships,
not attributes, is really needed" (3). Goffman is less interested in particular traits than in the social relationships and processes that convert them
into signs of stigma. His interest in homosexuality is situational: it is one
of many attributes that can be stigmatized, but it does not hold his interest more than other traits that are. However, the utility of this account in
refusing gender essentialism and heteronormative teleology is clear. Goffman anticipates key concepts in the field of queer theory, from the focus
on performance to the primacy of social relations in the making of the self.
    Because of his idiosyncratic methods, trenchant analyses of postwar
social conventions, and attention to sites of power (the mental hospital,
the clinic, the prison) analyzed by his near-contemporary Michel Foucault, Goffman is sometimes framed as a hero of the Left. However, this
judgment has always been in tension with accounts that emphasize his
failure to address large-scale structures of inequality, and to denounce the
social dynamics he described. The ambiguity of Goffman's politics and
the volatility of his reception are fodder for Alvin Gouldner in his 1970
polemic *The Coming Crisis of Western Sociology*. He writes,

> Goffman's avoidance or rejection of conventionalized hierarchicaliza-
> tions has ... important ambiguities to it. On the one side, it has an impli-
> cation of being *against* the existing hierarchies and hence against those
> advantaged by it; it is, to this extent, infused with a rebel vision critical
> of modern society. On the other side, however, Goffman's rejection of
> hierarchy often expresses itself as an *avoidance* of social stratification
> and of the importance of power differences, even for concerns that are
> central to him; thus it entails an accommodation to existent power ar-

rangements. Given this ambiguity, response to Goffman's theories is often made selectively, the viewer focusing on the ambiguity congenial to him, and thus some among the rebellious young may see it as having a "radical" potential.[41]

Gouldner indicts Goffman's focus on the minute particulars of the social order, and his disregard for structures of hierarchy. Such immanent, fine-grained analysis appears badly in need of a fulcrum: although careful inspection of what is close at hand has its value, it is only by finding a point of view outside of the system—for instance, through attention to political economy, militarism, or the history of racial capitalism—that one can perceive its gross injustices. According to Gouldner, Goffman's failure to achieve such a perspective makes his analysis of contemporary arrangements not only ineffective but complicit. As he argues concerning Goffman's method more broadly, "A dramaturgical model is an accommodation congenial only to those who are willing to accept the basic allocations of existent master institutions, for it is an invitation to a 'side game'" (386). Furthermore, the fact that such analysis can look and sound like critique makes it doubly dangerous, since it leads "rebellious youth" to believe they are challenging the social order when they are in fact supporting it.

In *The Coming Crisis*, Gouldner suggests that Goffman is compromised by his accommodation to new forms of soft power. But he also suggests that this failure sets a corrupting example to young people. The impugning of Goffman's masculinity and the implication of improper influence are made more explicit in Gouldner's account of how Goffman's dramaturgical model of social life fits into a new context of consumerism, permissiveness, and the inversion of traditional values:

> "Pop art" declares an end to the distinction between fine art and advertising, in much the same manner that dramaturgy obliterates the distinction between "real life" and the theater. The "Mafia" become businessmen; the police are sometimes difficult to distinguish from the rioters except by their uniforms; heterosexuality and homosexuality come to be viewed by some as akin to the difference between right-handedness and lefthandedness; the television program becomes the definition of reality. The antihero becomes the hero. (390)

Gouldner argues that Goffman's air of detachment "celebrates" a "camp" "way of life" and that dramaturgy as an interpretive frame refuses to take

the bull of "utility and morality" by its two horns and instead offers "an interior decoration that provides a new look to . . . older furnishings" (388).
Such were the weapons in Gouldner's arsenal. In his 1968 essay "The Sociologist as Partisan," an early and influential attack on deviance studies,
Gouldner offered a related critique of Becker's sympathy with the underdog (as against midlevel enforcers such as police and teachers) as a veiled
identification with overdogs, or the architects of the welfare state. Gouldner links Becker's political shortcomings to his cool stance of detachment,
remarking on his failure to practice "passionate or erect partisanship" in
favor of a "flaccid" and "limp" style.[42]

If Gouldner's strong-man posturing sounds dated—not for nothing
was he called the Norman Mailer of sociology—it is worth noting how
often similar critiques have been (and are still) directed toward Michel
Foucault.[43] Foucault's focus on the minute and situational operations of
power and his insistence that power cannot be cleanly separated from resistance has resulted in charges of everything from quietism to radical
chic. This negative judgment of Foucault's "capillary" approach to the
question of power recalls a long history of attacks on microsociology for
its banality, inefficacy, and political irrelevance. Like Goffman and others,
though, Foucault looked to the microscopic not to avoid power, but because he saw power everywhere. This was not only a means to reveal the
inequalities embedded in everyday life; it was also an attempt to bring a
social and institutional analysis to the level of the subject, and to "what
we tend to feel is without history—. . . sentiments, love, conscience, instincts."[44] Macro approaches to large-scale social structures might leave
the humanist subject intact. Such immanent approaches turned an inex-
haustible attention on it instead, bearing down with ruthless scrutiny.

Foucault's work, in addition to being seen as politically suspect, is also
regularly seen as dangerous to impressionable youth. As David Halperin
has shown, attacks on Foucault's pessimism and the inefficacy of his version of politics were especially acute in relation to his "darkest and most
radically anti-emancipatory book, *The History of Sexuality, vol. I*."[45] But the
subject of this book also matters, not just Foucault's approach to it, since
sexuality is regularly seen as a "side game," unrelated to hard economic
realities, geopolitics, or the "master institutions." Throughout this history,
the dismissal of the gay topic and the suggestion of methodological and
political weakness are difficult to disentangle. Even though Goffman and
Becker never made homosexuality a central concern for their research,
that research was dismissed in terms that made sexuality's rhetorical sa-

lience clear. Foucault's centering of modern sexuality as a site of power thus illuminated an association that had been a long time in the making.

Foucault and Goffman were extraordinarily attentive to small-scale operations of power, such as the kindly advice of a doctor or the extension of humanizing sympathy by a normal toward the stigmatized. They argued that such benevolent and banal manifestations of social power are not distinct from power in its most enduring, violent, and effective forms. This shared emphasis points to the importance of the antipsychiatry movement as a context for both thinkers. The clinic and the asylum are both emblems and enactments of normalization and of the double binds that are produced in institutions of care.[46] Despite their shared preoccupations, approaches, and reception, Foucault has been understood as a key precursor (and often the founding figure) of queer studies, whereas Goffman's influence—and the influence of deviance studies scholarship more broadly—has been acknowledged much more rarely, and almost exclusively by scholars in the social sciences. Given the obvious debts, documented in citations, acknowledgments, and even in impassioned, closely argued articles and books, why is there still such widespread amnesia about the deviance studies roots of queer theory?

THE PERSISTENCE OF DEVIANCE

This willed "forgetting" can be understood as part of the inevitable repressions that attend the founding of a field. But there are other challenges to the recognition of Goffman's specific influence and the more general influence of the field of deviance studies. Reading classic texts of deviance studies today can be disconcerting. Employing midcentury language that now sounds actively stigmatizing (rather than part of a study of stigma), deviance studies scholars adopted the tone of the scientific observer; they did not identify themselves with the communities they studied, and refused partisanship in favor of a stance of neutrality. Social studies of deviance originated in the work of urban reformers and academic sociologists concerned with patterns of settlement and symptoms of social disorder. These analysts considered social problems such as crime, suicide, and homosexuality in the context of poverty, migration, and tenement housing. These origins are evident in the prioritizing of social equilibrium or management, deviance scholars' treatment of social groups as permanently stigmatized, and in the burden of representation that outsider figures perform in their work.[47] The idea of the norm and the margin as articulated in deviance studies research owes a debt to the scholar's bird's-eye view of the city as a racialized patchwork of more and less diseased or deviant zones. Postwar studies of deviance tended to focus on individuals, zooming in on their unique pathways through the social world. Researchers described the fate and stratagems of particular figures, like the marijuana user, the stutterer, the jazz musician, the juvenile delinquent, and the ex-mental patient. In this discursive explosion, the rise of new social groups unapologetic about their difference from White bourgeois America is evident, if not fully acknowledged. If deviance studies scholars mostly fail to address the structural oppression their subjects faced, they nonetheless attended to their negotiation of race, class, and gender norms.

The field of deviance studies is divided from the present by intervening changes in the social order. The increasing self-determination across the twentieth century of social groups formerly understood as deviant effectively dismantled many of the epistemological frameworks of the field. This process had already begun in the work of Marxist and Black sociologists in the early part of the century, and also, to some extent, in the work of the Chicago school. As discontent with ruling norms and dominant institutions began to spread in the 1960s, deviance studies became part of an insurgent formation in the academy. Liberal and disaffected scholars began to align themselves, sometimes explicitly, with society's underdogs.[48] The "new deviance studies," as it was sometimes called, persisted into the early 1970s but fell apart with the rise of the new social movements. New identity-based subfields displaced deviance studies as the key site for the exploration of social difference.[49] Debates about the viability and political significance of deviance studies played out across the 1970s, often in the pages of the journal *Social Problems*. If Gouldner critiqued Becker and Goffman from the perspective of Marxist sociology, arguing that their analyses were insufficiently attuned to broader economic and political forces, a new set of critiques argued against the deviance paradigm based on formerly deviant populations' right to self-determination, and the progressive breakdown of a single dominant standard of behavior.

In a 1972 essay, for instance, Alexander Liazos memorably indicted the study of "nuts, sluts, and preverts" arguing that "all is not well with the field of 'deviance.'"[50] Despite the attempt to "humanize" social outsiders and point to larger dynamics of deviance, "the emphasis is still on the 'deviant' and the 'problems' he presents to himself and others, not on the society within which he emerges and operates" (104). In particular, Liazos was concerned with the focus on individual acts of violence and how it enabled inattention to *"covert institutional violence"* (104) like war and poverty. In his 1979 address to the Society for the Study of Social Problems, "Coming Out All Over: Deviants and the Politics of Social Problems," John Kitsuse addressed the "embarrassment" of scholars of deviance in the face of the wide-scale political protests and calls for self-determination by the formerly stigmatized.[51] Noting the "dramatic assertiveness with which deviant groups have rejected and denounced the accommodative adjustments" cataloged by scholars of deviance, Kitsuse asks, "How does the conception of deviants who live lives of quiet desperation square with the political activities of deviant groups that are daily reported in the media?" (5)[52]

These critiques suggest why the field of deviance studies is rarely allied with contemporary projects of Left critique, and has migrated into departments of law and criminology.[53] However, despite its declining fortunes, the deviance paradigm has proven to be remarkably durable, and has profoundly affected the method and politics of queer studies. With its focus on the variegated and potentially universal category of the social outsider or underdog, research in deviance studies gives us a model of social exclusion that resurfaces in key moments in the history of sexuality studies. This model of shared marginality and collective stigma appears in the urban ecology of Chicago school sociologists and of social problem research more broadly, particularly that focusing on sexual disorder. It forms the basis for postwar social science collections like *Sexual Deviance* (1968) by John Gagnon and William Simon. Looking for deviance can help us to rethink Foucault's work and explain his focus on individual stigmatized figures such as the masturbating child, the hysterical woman, the pervert, and the Malthusian couple.[54]

In a reflection on the impact of Gayle Rubin's canonical 1984 essay "Thinking Sex," Steven Epstein offers a persuasive argument about the utility of the deviance concept for queer studies. Epstein argues that Rubin's essay was "anointed as a classic because of how it took the insights of empirical studies of sexuality—particularly, historically informed ethnography—and drew out their intellectual and political implications in a way that facilitated an astonishingly interdisciplinary engagement."[55] "Thinking Sex" is grounded in empirical studies of sexuality, particularly in the postwar field of deviance studies and in the interactionist tradition exemplified by Gagnon and Simon. The influence of the deviance paradigm in particular is legible in the aspect of the essay that has been most influential in queer studies: Rubin's formulation of a "radical politics of sexuality" that focuses on the shared condition of sexual stigma.[56] Rubin's attention to the practices and experience of miscellaneous sexual subcultures recalls the ethnographic research of Chicago school sociologists, detailed by Chad Heap and others.[57] Rubin represents the sex hierarchy as a "charmed circle" of "Good, Normal, Natural, Blessed Sexuality" surrounded by the "outer limits" of "Bad, Abnormal, Unnatural, Damned Sexuality." This image makes visible the granting of social status and material goods to natural, normal, nonexploitative, egalitarian sexuality and situates other kinds of sexuality in the margins. Rubin's model evokes the Chicago school's "ecological" view of the city, in particular Ernest Burgess's "concentric zone" model of urban growth, which postulated deep ties between space, place, and sexual deviance. Rubin fuses an empirical approach borrowed from deviance studies with a now more familiar theory of social marginality, derived from Foucault, which focuses on the immanence of power. According to Epstein, Rubin's fusing of these two traditions is responsible for the near hegemony in queer studies of a model of politics that is based on a coalition of nonnormative and stigmatized subjects.

This coalitional model reached its apogee in the work of Michael Warner around 1990. His vision of a broad community of deviants in revolt against the "regimes of the normal" in his introduction to *Fear of a Queer Planet* was crucial to the development of queer theory.[58] This understanding of deviance as the key to queer community runs throughout Warner's early work, and underwrites his sense of the ethical and social ties that bind the otherwise miscellaneous people gathered under the name queer. Deviance studies also plays a key role in Cathy J. Cohen's 1997 critique of the false universalism of queer studies. Cohen calls out the centering of White, economically advantaged gays and lesbians in queer politics, and proposes that the field renew itself by making shared marginality "the basis for progressive transformative coalition work."[59] Cohen's influential essay "Punks, Bulldaggers, and Welfare Queens" recalls the syntax of Liazos's "Nuts, Sluts, and Preverts." In her invocation of these specific, stigmatized figures, Cohen indicts the power of a racist and homophobic society to label as deviant those with less social and economic power. But she also points to the political potential that inheres in a community of the stigmatized. Although midcentury scholars of deviance rarely argued explicitly for social transformation in the ways that queer scholars do, they nonetheless imagined a community of stigmatized outsiders that grounds such a political vision.

This political vision persists even in targeted critiques of deviance studies. In his 2004 book *Aberrations in Black: Toward a Queer of Color Critique*, Roderick Ferguson implicates canonical sociology in the continuing marginalization of queer people of color in the modern university, and calls for a reorientation of queer studies toward the foundational thought of Black feminism.[60] Even though the kind of microanalytic, interactional deviance studies that I consider in this book was never at the center of the profession, it is nonetheless marked by the racial and sexual normativity that Ferguson sees as essential to the sociological tradition. Ferguson situates the deviance paradigm within the long history of capitalism, describing the process by which heteropatriarchy produces spectacular and racialized figures, such as the prostitute in the nineteenth century, that condense a range of social anxieties. Ferguson's critique of canonical sociology also holds true for many of the scholars I consider in this book. And yet because of the ambiguous lure of deviance itself, these midcentury scholars leave their mark on Ferguson's own thinking. Ferguson laments the normalizing effect of this production of "difference as deviance" (111). Nonetheless, the book opens with a meditation on a few specific figures. Ferguson describes his project as an attempt to inquire about the people who are not pictured in an archival photograph of a segregated railway station in Manchester, Georgia. He writes, "I know this railroad station. It is a ten-minute walk from the house I grew up in. I know as well that there are subjects missing who should be accounted for—the transgendered man who wore Levi's and a baseball cap and chewed tobacco; the men with long permed hair who tickled piano keys; the sissies and bulldaggers who taught the neighborhood children to say their speeches on Sunday morning" (viii). In critiquing the failures and exclusions of canonical sociology, Ferguson indicts the social processes that produce aberrations in Black, and Blackness as aberrance. Yet the political community he imagines is still made up of individuals who make visible specific dynamics of stigmatization.

MUTUAL ADVENTURE OF OUR SPOILED IDENTITY

The visibility of difference in a deviance framework risks turning stigmatized individuals into forensic evidence, spectacles, or allegories of suffering. But risking visibility is also necessary if the aim is to specify the dynamics of social life. On occasion, Sedgwick herself risked erasing sexuality's imbrication with the material dimensions of lived experience by framing it in contrast to other forms of identity cast as more visible and permanent. Race and gender thus formed a stable backdrop to the more volatile performativity of sexuality. However, in her discussions of deviance and deviant sexual subcultures, Sedgwick attends most specifically to homosexuality's material traces. In the dialogue "Divinity," cowritten with Michael Moon, Sedgwick elaborates connections between fatness and homosexuality through a reflection on the films of John Waters, with particular attention to his love of "sleaze" and the mixture of abjection and glamour in his films. Sedgwick and Moon reflect at length on the dynamics of stigma, invoking the way that body size, gender nonnormativity, and homosexuality inflect each other in the appearance and performance style of Divine.[61] As opposed to Sedgwick's expansive and abstract accounts of queerness, here she focuses on a historically determinate and embodied homosexuality notable for its Whiteness. The essay features Sedgwick's most extended engagement with Goffman's work and with the phrase "spoiled identity," which recurs throughout the essay (and appears in one especially striking formulation, when Sedgwick describes her relationship with Moon as the "mutual adventure of our spoiled identity").[62]

"Divinity" also returns to Judith Butler through a discussion of cross-dressing as a trope in recent critical theory. But in this context, the critique of the limits of antiessentialism is paired with a reflection on queer theory's midcentury inheritances. Adopting the first-person plural, Sedgwick writes that, in discussions of cross-dressing, "we fear a conflation of the question of what might be called phylogeny with that of individual ontogeny. The origin of this conflation probably has something to do with the double disciplinary genealogy of constructivism itself: on the one hand, through a Foucauldian historicism designed to take the centuries vertiginously in stride; on the other, through an interactional communications theory whose outermost temporal horizon is, in practice, the individual life span" (226). Sedgwick is unusually explicit in calling out "interactional communications theory," so central to the elaboration of deviance studies in the 1950s and 1960s. But she also highlights the danger in failing to keep Foucauldian discourse analysis separate from individualistic human sciences produced in conjunction with communications theory during this time. In conflating the two, one may misunderstand the scale of action and agency. What results from this mixture of phylogeny and ontogeny is a voluntarist and individual account of resistance—a familiar critique of Butler's theory of gender performativity. But one can also appreciate the value in this essay of ontogeny as method, which is of course central to Sedgwick's as well as Moon's work in literary studies. With its focus on

the specifics of individual experiences and bodies, "Divinity" offers a textured account of the midcentury moment, including Moon's memories
of growing up "in rural Oklahoma in the fifties"; queer subcultural references from women's prisons to Judy Grahn to Rock Hudson; and an anecdote about Divine having to get "a police escort to get to and from school"
(224). The focus on individual experience in this essay yields both a granu-
lar account of some aspects of queer history, as well as an attention to the
facts of stigma and violence.

THE PROBLEM OF SEXUALITY

In his tribute to Rubin's essay "Thinking Sex," Epstein emphasizes her
inheritance of social science traditions, thus highlighting aspects of the
essay that tend to get passed over by queer scholars in the humanities: a
focus on particular communities; the role of urban space in the organization of sexual life; institutions; social mechanisms of stigmatization; and
attention to social practice and ritual. Epstein's account of Rubin's work fits
within a tradition of social science critiques of contemporary queer studies
for prioritizing discourse and representation at the expense of practices,
material conditions, and institutions. Jeffrey Escoffier articulated one of
the sharpest versions of this critique: "Queer theory . . . focuses too exclusively on the discursive aspects of knowledge or power and not enough on
political and economic domination or the historical-social structures of re-
pression. Ironically, our age demonstrates an awe-inspiring sophistication
about cultural representations but is otherwise by a marked grave under-
estimation—perhaps even ignorance—of the social."[63] Escoffier originally
wrote these words in 1990 in *OUT/LOOK*, during the year that we now
associate with the birth of queer theory. Over thirty years later, one might
still point to the preponderance of textual and cultural readings in queer
studies, although studies of sexuality are more integrated into the social
sciences now than before. The example of Rubin's work as well as more recent work in queer studies by scholars trained in the social sciences makes
clear that these approaches are not always opposed or even distinguish-
able.

Still, there are important reasons why scholars in the humanities resist a social and empirical view of sexuality. Traditionally, the centering
of sexuality as an object of study has caused consternation not only because of its illegitimacy but also because of its elusiveness. Sexuality is
regularly understood in contradictory and overlapping ways as a practice,

a feeling, an orientation, an unconscious complex, a historical artifact, and as the basis for community formation and politics. Scholars trained in literary studies, aesthetics, psychoanalysis, and critical theory tend to approach sexuality primarily through the categories of desire and representation, whereas empirical research on sexuality tends to emphasize social practice and collective life.[64] In social scientific studies of sexuality, sex can be treated alongside other social phenomena, but the emergence of sexuality as a topic for literary studies depended on showing its difference from other realms of human activity. In an influential statement of this position in *The Critical Difference* (1985), Barbara Johnson writes, "It is not the life of sexuality that literature cannot capture; it is literature that inhabits the very heart of what makes sexuality problematic for us speaking animals. Literature is not only a thwarted investigator but also an incorrigible perpetrator of the problem of sexuality."[65] Johnson published these words in the same year Sedgwick released *Between Men*. Attempting to avoid both the positivism of the social sciences and the psychologism of existing scholarship on sexuality, Sedgwick claimed that the "centrality of sexual questions in this study is important to its methodological ambitions as well."[66] More explicitly than Johnson, Sedgwick set out to show the importance of literary criticism as both investigator and perpetrator of the problem of sex. In a discussion of sexual violence, for instance, Sedgwick argued for the need to resist stabilizing methods in the face of "real" social problems: "The signifying relation of sex to power, of sexual alienation to political oppression, is not the most stable, but precisely the most volatile of social nodes . . . Thus, it is of serious political importance that our tools for examining the signifying relation be subtle and discriminate ones, and that our literary knowledge of the most crabbed or oblique paths of meaning not be oversimplified in the face of the panic-inducing images of real violence, especially the violence of, around, and to sexuality" (10). It was the crabbed and oblique image of sexuality, rather than the image of sexuality as ordinary sexual practice, that was centered in queer theory circa 1990.

Furthermore, the antiempiricism of humanities disciplines during this period made it difficult to recognize the contributions of deviance studies to the academic study of sexuality. Social science researchers shifted the view of homosexuality from an individual pathology to a social formation. While this was a crucial step in objectifying sexuality and turning it into an object of study, this move has been seen in retrospect by humanities scholars as a negation of its psychic complexity. The value of empiricism is linked to an equally divisive question about the value of description. Scholarship in deviance studies is characterized by a descriptive rather than a prescriptive relation to its objects: Goffman's account of stigma is focused on tracing the everyday dynamics of stigma rather than on combatting stigma, or transforming the conditions that give rise to it. Scholars in deviance studies addressed many of the same questions that queer scholars do: power, social stigma, antisocial behavior, nonnormativity, and the performance of social roles. But these scholars saw deviance as a fact of social life rather than as an ethical aspiration or a model of political resistance. This focus on deviance as a social fact survives in the work of even the most politically radical scholars in the social sciences. Rubin makes an explicit argument for the political value of descriptive scholarship in "Thinking Sex." Writing in the context of the feminist sex wars, Rubin argues on behalf of the value of sexological research. She writes, "Sexology and sex research provide abundant detail, a welcome posture of calm, and a well developed ability to treat sexual variety as something that exists rather than as something to be exterminated." Rubin's controversial suggestion was that the work of sexologists—widely seen in queer and feminist circles as pathologizing and as stabilizing of social hierarchies— might provide a better "grounding for a radical theory of sexuality" than "the combination of psychoanalysis and feminist first principles to which so many texts resort."[67]

Rubin pushed back against the feminist project that aimed to produce better (less patriarchal, more egalitarian) forms of sexuality, arguing instead for the need to shelter already existing but vulnerable sexualities. She thus refuses entirely the utopian project of imagining a better sexuality into being and instead defends practices and communities that already exist. Since the rise of queer studies, it has been difficult to acknowledge the political value of stabilizing identity. But as I argue in *Underdogs*, we can understand this missed connection as a disciplinary as well as a political conflict. What queer humanities scholars have understood as the political failures of deviance studies should also be understood in terms of methodological and epistemological differences between the humanities and social sciences. The rise of queer theory took place during a resettlement of this division, in the moment that has come to be known as the "linguistic turn." In its wake, critics have distanced themselves from scholarship that lends reality to precarious worlds or asserts the ordinariness of queer life. Such an approach can be seen as complicit with both Cold War liberalism, and contemporary neoliberalism. Is it really necessary to give US gays and lesbians a firmer standing in the social world, one might ask, now that sexual and gender differences are no longer a necessary impediment to economic, political, and social hegemony? Stigma, as a framework, may seem less useful than ever in capturing the tectonic shifts in queers' social standing. However, sweeping narratives—whether neoliberal celebrations of "postgay" life or queer critiques of "homonormativity"—fail to grapple with the unevenness of these developments and the contingency of the social world. The concept of stigma may carry associations of individual suffering no longer relevant in the era of gay marriage. It also trails the history of midcentury social science with its essentialism, Whiteness, and enthronement of expertise. Despite these problems, this framework remains relevant, still able to account for persistent and disqualifying forms of social denigration. A focus on the dynamics of social stigma makes it possible to be specific about multiple forms of marginalization and how they continue to matter. Despite advertisements for a new world of gay and lesbian inclusion, it is clear that sexual and gender stigma still have powerful effects. Investigating the history of this concept can help us assess the potential, in the present, for a coalitional politics of stigma.

MAKING THE CASE

In *Underdogs*, I have attempted, through readings in empirical studies of sexuality, to see how far one might pursue Rubin's point about the methodological and political value of description. As someone trained in the humanities, and in the arts of interpretation and critique, I have found myself engaged while writing this book with modes of thought and representation that appear alien and, at times, alienating. In undertaking this work, I have often sought out difficult cases, taking up examples and figures that do not fit well with contemporary assumptions about the ethics and politics of knowledge production. My aim was not simply to provoke or to contradict protocols simply for the sake of it, although I confess a desire to test the boundaries of critical doxa.[68] But I was motivated primarily by impatience with the limits of my own thinking. In particular, I wanted to test certain assumptions of my own: about the superiority of interpretation and narrative to other forms of description; about the violence of observational methods and of vision in general; about the value of empathy; about the stabilizing function of the social sciences; and about the exceptional status of queer thought. While my work in queer studies might be understood as challenging to traditional forms of knowledge or the disciplinary structure of the university, I was troubled by how well it fit into the framework of Left cultural studies and, as a result, missed whole areas of experience. This desire to push the boundaries, as well as a deep interest in everything that is dismissed as "dated," has led me to consider forms of thought that are troubling, even to me. I have undertaken this work in the spirit of experiment. My aim is not to prescribe a new set of methods but rather to challenge taken-for-granted agreements about the value, meaning, and effects of our own research practices.[69]

The first chapter focuses on Erving Goffman, treating *Stigma* as a crucial precursor for queer studies. Goffman's attention to the dynamics of social power, as well as his focus on inequality, difference, and stigma, makes him an indispensable figure for contemporary social thought. Indeed, it is difficult to find subject areas in the contemporary social sciences and humanities that are not influenced by Goffman: the majority of his books have remained in print continuously since their original publication, and he is one of the most cited scholars of all time. Yet, as many critics have pointed out, Goffman did not give birth to a school, and his reception remains uneven. Many fields that do bear his stamp are nonetheless highly critical of his scholarship. Some of these conflicts can be understood as a product of disciplinary differences, since Goffman's observational approach to social difference is at odds with the critical hermeneutics most often practiced in the humanities. Other conflicts are the result of the historical difference between his moment and the post–civil rights era. Yet even accounting for these tensions, there are other features of Goffman's approach that make him a challenging figure for contemporary critics: his comparative, abstract, and synthetic approach to social stigma; his microscopic focus on individual interaction rather than large-scale structures of domination; and his attention to behavior rather than to experience. In particular, his refusal of political partisanship is a bitter pill for contemporary critics. Goffman accounted for problems in the social world, but had little or nothing to say about how to change them. Although he was interested in questions of power, he tended to frame social inequality, exclusion, and violence as fixtures of social life, approaching them as a neutral observer rather than as an outraged witness.

Although I group Goffman with other empirical scholars of sexuality, his work cannot be called empirical in any traditional sense. Many of Goffman's key sociological insights are based on evidence drawn from novels, short stories, biographies, memoirs, lightly fictionalized case histories,

and human-interest stories clipped from the newspaper. Goffman approaches texts in the same way that he approaches scenes of interaction.
In the introduction to *Frame Analysis*, he notes that "any raw batch of occurrences" can be subject to behavioral analysis—no matter its "status in
reality."[70] Although many of these batches are taken from literature, Goffman's work is not typically literary. He does not see literature as a store-
house of human potential, experience, or feeling; he looks to literature to
account for the complexities of social life, but has little time for traditional
humanist categories of consciousness and motivation. Goffman does not
dig deep, looking for motivation or psychological conflict; instead, he
reads texts as records of behavior, making scenes of interaction available
for visual description and analysis.[71] Despite its distance from the present,
Stigma is an important precursor for queer studies because of how it takes
the insights and archive of postwar deviance studies and "thins them out"
through recourse to an observational and antipsychological approach.
This refusal to elaborate on the interior life of his subjects recalls a crucial
strategy of queer theory. Early critics in the field resisted the pathologizing of homosexuality through a wholesale rejection of the psychological
framework that had given rise to it.

Chapter 2, "Just Watching," extends the emphasis on observation by
considering exchanges between animal ethology (or the study of animal
behavior) and observational approaches in the social sciences. Across the
middle of the twentieth century, borrowings between biologists and human
scientists resulted in hybrid forms, from "animal sociology" to "human
ethology." Although the reputation of this work has been tarnished because of its links to sociobiology, I distinguish between the comparison
of human and animal nature and the application of methods borrowed
from field naturalism to the observation of human interaction. Looking at
a moment of interdisciplinary exchange regarding communicative behavior at the Macy Conferences on Group Processes, I trace connections between European ethologists and American sociologists, particularly those
studying interaction and nonverbal communication. The research methods I consider might be seen as troubling for several reasons: because of
reliance on human-animal comparisons; because of the dehumanizing
and reductive effects of visual observation; because of lack of attention to
human meaning and agency. I argue by contrast that naturalistic methods
and a focus on visible behavior could have other effects: by ignoring the
interiority of their subjects, these researchers dissipated the stigma associated with some forms of difference.

In this chapter, I consider two cases of human subject research conducted under the influence of animal sociology. I address animal ethologist Nikolaas Tinbergen's late-career research on children with autism. Tinbergen won the Nobel Prize in 1973 for his work on fish, gulls, and wasps, but by that point he had begun to use the methods he had learned through animal observation on children in everyday settings in Oxford. In the book that he wrote with his wife Elisabeth Tinbergen, *Early Childhood Autism: An Ethological Approach* (1972), Tinbergen comments on the fact that psychologists make so little use of the basic scientific practice of observation. This research was deeply flawed. The Tinbergens saw autism as purely environmental, and so indulged a tendency to blame the mother for improper care; they refused the biological roots of autism, a finding that later research has repeatedly challenged. They also corresponded for many years with Dr. Martha Welch, the main proponent of holding therapy as a cure for autism, which advocated prolonged sessions of maternal intimacy. However, this practice has since been denounced, and is widely understood as both unhelpful and coercive. Still, in seeing autism as a matter of environment and assimilating it to other childhood behaviors deemed normal, the Tinbergens refused essentializing views of autism. Instead, they developed a contingent and nonpathologizing account, using observational methods to avoid the pitfalls of biologism.

The sexuality studies researcher Laud Humphreys took a similarly observational approach in his 1970 book *Tearoom Trade: Impersonal Sex in Public Places.* The book is a classic example of naturalistic, interactional microsociology. Humphreys conducted his fieldwork by observing men engaging in sex acts in public restrooms (also known as "tearooms") in the Midwest in the 1960s. His work on these casual encounters was a form of participant observation, though his dual role was unknown to the men he studied: Humphreys posed as a "watchqueen," that is to say someone who is simultaneously a voyeur and a lookout, watching by the entrance for both unsuspecting patrons and police. Humphreys's characterization of his methods as "underdog" has both to do with its discrediting association with sexual deviance and with the fact that naturalistic microsociology was never a dominant method. The impersonal nature of the "sexual encounters without involvement" that Humphreys observes is reflected in the impersonal methods he uses to document them. Floor plans and "systematic observation sheets" record the microbehaviors—gestures, glances, and sex acts—that take place in the tearoom. *Tearoom Trade* is widely known as a negative example because of Humphreys's violation of the codes of research ethics. The book is compromised by several of Humphreys's choices, including his surreptitious gathering of biographical and social data about the men in the tearooms. But in this chapter, I analyze Humphreys's ecological view of their tearoom activities, arguing that this method, which might be understood as dehumanizing or objectifying, is in fact destigmatizing.

In the third chapter, "A Sociological Periplum," I revisit a textual crux in the history of sexuality studies: Joan Scott's influential reading of Samuel R. Delany's memoir, *The Motion of Light in Water*, in her 1991 essay "The Evidence of Experience." Scott's essay articulates a powerful critique of traditional empiricism, and is an important document of the linguistic turn, when scholars in the social sciences turned to interpretive paradigms drawn from the humanities to challenge the positivism of their disciplines. Scott offers a dual reading of Delany's memoir, focusing on a scene when Delany describes first entering the Saint Mark's Baths in 1963. Delany recounts a conversion experience, in which the sight of men's bodies in the bathhouse explodes his previous understanding of homosexuality as an isolated and minor experience, showing him a social and sexual world to come. Scott suggests that, while Delany's reaction might be seen as an example of naive empiricism, his account in fact underlines the uncertainty and contingency of experience. By following the example of literary critics, and focusing on representation instead of truth, Scott argues, we can understand how social knowledge is made, not discovered. Scott's essay, which was reprinted in the 1993 anthology *The Lesbian and Gay Studies Reader*, became a flashpoint in early queer studies, as scholars in the field claimed that Delany's understanding of the "reality" of the baths was even more provisional than it appeared in Scott's reading. Through this exchange, and because of the significance of his 1999 account of the lost sexual culture of the Times Square porn theaters, *Times Square Red, Times Square Blue*, Delany became a key figure in the antifoundationalist field of queer theory. In this chapter, I present another version of Delany: as a social historian and empirical researcher, invested in documenting marginal sexual worlds. By situating Delany as an inheritor of the deviance studies tradition, I attempt to historicize queer theory in relation to the linguistic turn, and suggest that a fuller appreciation of Delany's documentary poetics will allow us to broaden the purview of the field.

In "Doing Being Deviant," the final chapter, I continue the work of historicizing queer theory by exploring the attitude of its early practitioners toward work in the social sciences. I assess the politics of contemporary queer studies, considering its long-standing difficulties with the ordinary and the everyday. Addressing recent debates in the field regarding the politics of antinormativity, I trace how queer studies turned the descriptive study of deviance into a normative injunction to be deviant. I argue that the field of queer studies has fundamentally misunderstood the politics of deviance studies, which aimed not to disrupt social norms but instead to recognize and create space for marginal communities and practices. I argue that strong claims about the stabilizing function of empirical methods should be understood in the context of disciplinary rivalry between the humanities and the social sciences. Queer studies has often understood itself as outside of disciplinary regimes of knowledge, and opposed to the university. But a more realist account of the field's history and current entanglements will allow us to come to terms with the paradoxes of institutionalization and the material basis of our knowledge. Work in this vein is already happening under the rubric "queer methods." In an afterword, I weigh the possibilities for a politics of stigma in an era of gay and lesbian assimilation.

SCENES OF SHAME

When I first read "Queer Performativity," I agreed with Sedgwick about the need to *begin with stigma*. Regarding the "experimental, creative, performative force" of stigma, I wasn't so sure. Are all forms of stigma useful for politics? What, I wondered, about ongoing experiences of stigma, and recalcitrant feelings of shame? What about the bad feelings that persist into adult life, resist our efforts to transform them, and continue to circulate in queer communities? Some feelings, surely, are not ripe for transformation. As if refusing an extravagant gift, I demurred from Sedgwick's characterization of shame as "a near-inexhaustible source of transformational energy." Would it be possible to pursue a form of inquiry that wasn't about *managing* stigma, or *transforming* it, but simply *acknowledging* it? It was, after all, Sedgwick's acknowledgment of the scene of childhood shame, rather than her belief in its transformation, that changed things for me. I explored this possibility in an article I wrote in graduate school about Radclyffe Hall's punishingly sad 1928 novel *The Well of Loneliness*. It is hard to generate political energy from the bad feelings represented in this book, I argued. "The novel's subtitle," I wrote, "ought simply to be: 'Spoiled Identity.'"[72]

I can see now that I overstated my difference from Sedgwick, kicking up a fuss in order to be part of the conversation. "Queer Performativity" celebrates shame's transformative potential while acknowledging that its actual transformation is never guaranteed. Sedgwick writes, "therapeutic or political strategies aimed directly at getting rid of individual or group shame, or undoing it, have something preposterous about them: they may 'work'—they certainly have powerful effects—but they can't work in the way they say they work." Underlining the significance of shame in making individual and group identity, she continues: "The forms taken by shame . . . are available for the work of metamorphosis, reframing, refiguration, *trans*figuration, affective and symbolic loading, and deformation: but unavailable for effecting the work of purgation and deontological closure" (13, emphasis in original). In other words, shame *is* transformative, but we can never be sure *how* it is transformative. One might therefore add, *Careful what you wish for.* In conjuring such unruly, pervasive, and harmful feelings, it is possible to repeat the violence that you are hoping to ameliorate; antihomophobic inquiry that makes homophobia too central can be complicit with homophobia. Sedgwick draws strength from the example of queer activism, which had shown clearly that a term of abuse could do powerful political work. However, she also acknowledges that reworking shame is permanently risky business.

Disagreeing with Sedgwick helped me to formulate an approach to queer literary history that centered negative and painful feelings. If at one time I thought this was a difference in politics, or temperament, I can now see how it emerges from the disciplinary history that I have canvassed in this introduction. We might understand Sedgwick's imagined rewrite of the subtitle of Goffman's *Stigma*, away from management toward creative force, as a sign of the times, the updating of a pre-Stonewall text about secret deviants in light of a new wave of queer activism. We can also understand it as an attempt to translate an empirical and descriptive account of stigma into an interpretive and prescriptive framework. Whether you believe that scholarship's goal is to describe how people respond to unequal conditions in the world, or is to contribute, in whatever way, to changing those conditions, this difference is not necessarily best understood as a matter of courage, resourcefulness, or commitment. Instead, it also points to a fundamental disagreement about what scholarship is. Sociology has been critiqued for its static, descriptive view of the world; queer scholarship has been critiqued for its inflated sense of its own power to change that world. There are advantages and disadvantages to both approaches. Descriptive scholarship offers a portrait of how the world works, but in doing so it risks accommodating itself to social conditions, and treating as permanent a situation that is in fact temporary. Prescriptive scholarship points to potentials that have not yet been realized in the world, and therefore is a source of both resistance and hope. But scholarship that focuses on the future risks giving an incomplete, distorted, or "hopeful" portrait of the present, including of its own material and social determinants.

My attraction to "Queer Performativity," it now seems to me, was because of its staging of this tension between the descriptive and the prescriptive, or, in J. L. Austin's terms, the constative and the performative. This dilemma resonates with such force because of Sedgwick's ability to think through antinomies, to pose without resolving contradictions. I also think it is because of the way Sedgwick incorporates the deviance studies legacy in this essay. "Shame *is performance*," Sedgwick writes, and later, on the same page, "shame is itself a form of communication" (5). This account of performativity draws on performance as it emerges in the writing of Henry James, as a translation of the space of the stage into the intimate theater of voice and novelistic point of view. But it also draws on the sense of the *scene* as it circulated in the social scientific contexts of the 1950s and 1960s: in Goffman's dramaturgical theory, especially as articulated in *The Presentation of Self in Everyday Life*; in the collection of knowing journalistic observations on midcentury morals, *The Scene before You*; or in Gagnon and Simon's collection *The Sexual Scene*. It was Sedgwick's essay that first pointed me to this other scene of queer studies, which has become a kind of obsession over the last couple of decades—as if I were uncovering a secret parentage. This process has convinced me that deviance studies is not only a point of origin for queer studies, but that it is also a living presence in the field today. The deviance paradigm remains crucial in queer studies because it is the carrier of the material and social specificity of gay, lesbian, and transgender lives. Although its portrait of gay life was distorted and incomplete, it was driven by a method—interactional microsociology—which allowed, and allows, for the representation of as yet unacknowledged experiences of stigma. Which is why this book begins with *Stigma*.

1 · The *Stigma* Archive

One finds that the performer can be fully taken in by his own act; he can be sincerely convinced that the impression of reality which he stages is the real reality. When his audience is also convinced in this way about the show he puts on—and this seems to be the typical case—then for the moment at least, only the sociologist or the socially disgruntled will have any doubts about the "realness" of what is presented.

Erving Goffman, *The Presentation of Self in Everyday Life*[1]

In a 1994 essay "A Queer Encounter: Sociology and the Study of Sexuality," Steven Epstein offers an early appraisal of the influence of empirical studies of sexuality for the emergent field of queer studies. Noting that "queer theory and sociological theory confront one another with some suspicion, and more profoundly with misrecognition," Epstein traces the continuities and the disjunctions between postwar studies of sexual life and the humanities field of queer theory.[2] With a focus on deviance studies, symbolic interactionism, and labeling theory, Epstein argues that these scholars departed from behaviorism and biologism to reframe sexuality in the realm of ordinary social life. Despite such debts, Epstein observes that younger scholars tend to come to social construction theory "directly from the work of Foucault, bypassing the social sciences" (194). The problem, he suggests, is that deviance studies scholars assumed the permanent marginality of sexual minorities; their account of the dilemmas of social underdogs and outsiders did not survive the advent of a liberationist era. "Applied to lesbians and gay men," Epstein writes, "the sociology of deviance was the sociology of the closet" (194). Queer theory, by contrast, was premised on "the centrality of marginality" (189). "Just as queer *politics* emphasize outsiderness as a way of constructing opposition to the regime of normalization as a whole," he continues, "so queer *theory* analyzes putatively marginal experience, but in order to expose the deeper contours of the whole society and the mechanisms of its functioning" (197, emphasis in original).

Erving Goffman's 1963 *Stigma: On the Management of Spoiled Identity* is the book he wrote most closely identified with deviance studies. Although it doesn't focus on homosexuality, its attitude toward marginality is most easily assimilated to what Epstein characterizes as "the sociology of the closet." The book seems to maintain a clear distinction between norm and margin and to focus on the adjustment of the stigmatized to prevailing conventions. As such, *Stigma* seems far from the oppositional politics of queer theory, and yet, surprisingly, the book is an essential source text for the field of queer studies. Goffman's interests—shame, institutions, passing, failure, agency, and power—link him to key concerns in the field. The influence of his 1959 book *Presentation of Self in Everyday Life* on Judith Butler's theory of gender performativity in *Gender Trouble* (1990) is rarely remarked. Goffman's interest in total institutions and in the broader abuses of the mental health field link him closely to the antipsychiatry movement and to the career of Michel Foucault. He also shares with Foucault an interest in the microdynamics of power, and in normalization as a ubiquitous form of social control.[3] Goffman directly inspired foundational texts like Laud Humphreys's *Tearoom Trade* (1970) and Esther Newton's *Mother Camp* (1972). He also stands in the background of performance studies and affect studies, fields that are foundational to queer studies, and *Stigma* in particular has a central if vexed presence in critical disability studies.[4] Scholars in the interdisciplinary humanities have started to recognize this influence, focusing on the intellectual history of the postwar period. Didier Eribon brought attention to the salience of Goffman's thinking about shame and stigma for contemporary queer life in *Insult and the Making of the Gay Self* (2004 [1999]).[5] In *Tame Passions of Wilde* (2003), Jeff Nunokawa considers Goffman in relation to Foucault and Butler: he sees in Goffman's attention to individual agency an alternative to Foucault's "pessimistic structuralism," and, in his focus on "farcical" or failed social performances, a drag on Butler's political optimism.[6] In his 2013 book *Camp Sites: Sex, Politics, and Academic Style in Postwar Culture*, Michael Trask traces the links between dramaturgical sociology (including Goffman's) and postwar US queer culture. Trask performs a historical leap to the midcentury analogous to Sedgwick's turn to the cybernetic fold; he traces a link between the focus on performance in 1950s sociology and on artifice in queer theory, and sees in both a resistance to the discourse of authenticity embraced by the student activists of the 1960s.[7]

Despite these connections, Goffman may seem an unlikely precursor for queer studies. Homosexuality appears in his work as merely one example of the kinds of disadvantaged traits that can be stigmatized. Furthermore, Goffman's attention to the "small change of social interaction" and his refusal of politics make him a challenging figure for any field of inquiry dedicated to social transformation.[8] Many critics have faulted Goffman for his failure to account for the structures of power that determine everyday experience. In paying attention to minute happenings in the realm of social interaction, they argue, he neglected the large-scale inequality and violence that structure it. Goffman meticulously described the everyday and microscopic effects of social marginalization, but cultivated a pose of neutrality toward these outrages. He repeatedly insisted that he was an analyst, not an activist. A former student recalls a blunt but not atypical statement in a methods class Goffman taught at the University of Pennsylvania: "I'm not into politics." (In case you missed that: "I am not interested in serving any population or making anyone live better.")[9] He adopted the stance of the bystander, observing acts of cruelty with the eye of a satirist rather than a reformer. Although Goffman did not see anything natural about the social order and was keenly attuned to its points of vulnerability, he accepted its stability as a fact. For this reason, he was skeptical about the ability of "militant" groups to organize social life on radically different lines: "When the ultimate political objective is to remove stigma from the differentness, the individual may find that his very efforts can politicize his own life, rendering it even more different from the normal life initially denied him" (*Stigma*, 114).

In formulating his theory of stigma, Goffman drew on accounts of the lives of those who are "engaged in some kind of collective denial of the social order": "Prostitutes, drug addicts, delinquents, criminals, jazz musicians, bohemians, gypsies, carnival workers, hobos, winos, show people, full time gamblers, beach dwellers, homosexuals, and the urban unrepentant poor" (143–44). These are categories of people familiar from mid-century deviance studies. Unlike others in the field, however, Goffman didn't maintain a steady focus on an individual category, refusing to pay sustained ethnographic or any other kind of attention to individual kinds of identity. Instead, he exploited the miscellaneous nature of these outsiders and underdogs, comparing unlike figures relentlessly in order to generate concepts for his theory of stigma. Using this method, he refused to credit the integrity of identity. On the one hand, this led him to disrespect and diminish the full human qualities of individual actors. On the other hand, it led him to free up the kind of individuals most often represented in the human sciences, undermining the deadly seriousness of many treatments of the socially marginal. Goffman seemed to rip the stuffing from the key characters in deviance studies by stripping them of the moral fiber most often used to condemn their behavior. He also used the technique of excessive listing in order to pile up examples of deviants and thus to suggest a baroque and antic quality in the entire enterprise. Through these methods of hyperbole and irony, Goffman made the subject matter of deviance studies and the energies of alienation available for resignification.

In the last paragraph of *Stigma*, we can see Goffman making a concerted plea for the value of comparison in demoting content in order to attend to concept:

> I have argued that stigmatized persons have enough of their situations in life in common to warrant classifying all these persons together for purposes of analysis. An extraction has thus been made from the traditional fields of social problems, race and ethnic relations, social disorganization, criminology, social pathology, and deviancy—an extraction of something all these fields have in common. These commonalities can be organized on the basis of very few assumptions regarding human nature. What remains in each one of the traditional fields could then be re-examined for whatever it is that is really special to it, thereby bringing analytical coherence to what is not purely historic and fortuitous unity. Knowing what fields like race relations, aging, and mental health share, one could then go on to see, analytically, how they differ. Perhaps in each case the choice would be to retain the old substantive areas, but at least it would be clear that each is merely an area to which one should apply several perspectives, and that the development of any one of these coherent analytic perspectives is not likely to come from those who restrict their interest exclusively to one substantive area. (146–47)

Goffman's discussion of the "extractions" made from substantive areas for the purposes of efficient analysis seems to ally him with the top-down, instrumental approach of Cold War social science. Yet, paradoxically, his lack of concern for the specificity of sexuality links him to the anti-identitarian field of queer theory. Unlike scholars in gay and lesbian studies, queer scholars did not focus on any one "substantive area." Instead, drawing from the history of sexuality, feminist thought, and critical race studies, queer scholars sought to find commonalities among all those arrayed along society's margins. Eve Sedgwick describes this aspect of queer thought in "Queer and Now" (1993): "A lot of the most exciting recent work around 'queer' spins the term outward along dimensions that can't be subsumed under gender and sexuality at all: the ways that race, ethnicity, postcolonial nationality crisscross with these and other identity-constituting, identity-fracturing discourses."[10] Sedgwick along with many of her peers in the first generation of queer theory shared with Goffman a commitment to the miscellaneous, centrifugal force of identity. This resulted both in a hesitation about focusing solely on the lives of gay men and lesbians and a striking ability to register the role of the contingent and aleatory in the constitution of the self. (See Sedgwick's Axiom 1 in *Epistemology of the Closet*: "People are different from each other."[11]) In queer theory, unlike in Goffman's work, there was an attempt to blend this approach with more timely and pressing approaches drawn from critical race theory and other fields, such as intersectionality. This combination of a strict refusal of gay and lesbian identity politics with a drive outward toward other forms of difference resulted both in queer theory's remarkable reach and success, and in charges of false universalism.

Goffman's war against substance was waged not only against identity but also against the idea of the person. One of the values of extraction and comparison as methods is that they yield an account of stigma that "can be organized on the basis of very few assumptions regarding human nature." Goffman does not understand "human nature" as a tool to dignify and enrich the lives of the stigmatized. Instead, he sees the extension of humanity to social outsiders as part of the burden that they have to bear—the burden of well-meaning concern, advice, and sympathy. In protest against this kind of liberal understanding, Goffman considers the lives of the stigmatized from the outside. Although he draws on a wide variety of sources, many of them literary and autobiographical, Goffman ignores these stories' psychological content and narrative form. Instead, he treats them as "strips of behavior," or brief sequences of social action, which constitute the raw material for analysis.[12] The dynamics of stigma are visible in gesture, tone of voice, spacing, and body posture: he considers human action as a set of empirically observable performances, rather than as the disclosure of an essence.

Scholars have criticized Goffman for his "black box" psychology and for his denuded, game-like view of the social world.[13] These elements of his work have led critics to see him as an avatar of Cold War social science, with little concern for the vulnerable subjects whose lives he mined for concepts.[14] But, as I argue, the blank, empty selves that circulate in Goffman's writing are designed to repel the incursions of both lay observers and of social scientists. Goffman's refusal of interiority sidesteps the forms of surveillance that do not stop at visual observation but aim, in Foucault's words, to "trace the meeting line of the body and the soul."[15] Goffman's stripped-down psychology and his atomizing view of the social world are not intended to stabilize the social order, nor to integrate outsiders into a smoothly functioning nation. Rather, they are an attempt, in George Gonos's words, to "defeat humanism in the sanctuary of its most endeared and protected subject, everyday face-to-face relations."[16] Inserting Goffman into a history of queer theory makes clear the political stakes of his antihumanism, as well as the more serious investments of critics sometimes seen as postmodern tricksters or cynics. What these critics continue from Goffman is a refusal of the human that is intended to ward off the scrutiny of an institutional gaze that finds both anchor and alibi in the core of the person.

In "A Queer Encounter," Epstein argues that postwar sociology contributed to the project of displacing the normal. But, he suggests, these efforts were limited by a naturalized understanding of the relation between norm and margin—an understanding that was finally challenged by the field of queer studies. Epstein writes,

> A presumed goal of the sociology of deviance . . . was to study the processes by which people become labeled deviant, so as to reveal, by contrast, the ideological construction of "the normal." In practice, however, sociologists have tended to relegate the study of "sexual minorities" to the analytical sidelines rather than treating such study as a window onto a larger world of power, meaning, and social organization. The challenge that queer theory poses to sociological investigation is precisely in the strong claim that no facet of social life is fully comprehensible without an examination of how sexual meanings intersect with it. (197)

Epstein aptly describes the intellectual and political ambition of queer theory, which sought to challenge the categories—homo/hetero, male/female—that made sexual minorities legible, but also lesser. In accounting for the shift from deviant studies to queer studies, Epstein also indicates the social changes, in particular the loss of a single prevailing norm, that made that intellectual transition possible. But changes were afoot much earlier.

Goffman didn't explicitly contest the relation between norm and margin. To the extent that Goffman expressed partisanship with social underdogs, he did so in terms characteristic of liberal second-wave deviance studies. Yet the profound negations of Goffman's sociology void the sympathy that grounds such scholarship. Goffman's view of the social world relies on the professional detachment of the social scientist but also includes the corrosive distance of the "socially disgruntled." He combined objectification and alienation, recasting the scientist's scrutiny as a view from the margins. For Goffman, there were only sidelines: deviance was, in his view, the truth of social life. Yet this perspective, although it is consonant with the radical antinormativity of queer theory, nonetheless remains difficult to acknowledge or to integrate, since it was fundamentally world destroying rather than world building.

GOFFMAN'S METHOD

Goffman identified the focus of his research as "ordinary persons doing ordinary things."[17] He described the embodied and the ephemeral aspects of everyday reality, considering gesture, clothing, spacing, facial expression, manner, and tone of voice; he was remarkably sensitive to uses of language and to the contingencies of interaction, particularly to those mistakes that open minor gaps in the social fabric. Goffman turned his attention to the local, bounded situation, small-group dynamics, and face-to-face interaction—the world of the "interaction order."[18] In the introduction to *Frame Analysis* (1974), his culminating statement on method, Goffman writes, "My perspective is situational, meaning here a concern for what one individual can be alive to at a particular moment, this often involving a few other particular individuals and not necessarily restricted to the mutually monitored area of a face-to-face gathering" (8). Goffman's focus on the situation is indebted to his training in empirical methods and ethnographic sociology at the University of Chicago. There he absorbed the interactionist tradition of George Herbert Mead and Charles Cooley, and was influenced by Durkheim's account of social ritual. Gary Alan Fine identifies Goffman as a member of the second Chicago school, and argues that he added observational detail and ethnographic richness to Mead's insights about the nature of social interaction.[19] Goffman's attention to the details of social scenes also recalls his early interest in documentary film. Before finishing his undergraduate degree, Goffman worked at the National Film Board of Canada in Ottawa, identified with the filmmaker John Grierson and an early site for the development of direct cinema.

Goffman is difficult to categorize in the major traditions of sociology.

He tended to favor sketches over systems, and even his attempt to offer a synthetic account of his method, *Frame Analysis*, launches a series of fugue-like portraits of a potentially endless number of frames (or analytic contexts). Although he is considered one of the founding figures of microsociology, Goffman's links to both ethnography and empiricism are tenuous, since he rarely engaged in traditional fieldwork and treated fictional and literary texts (as well as fabricated anecdotes) as evidence. For this reason, Goffman has been understood by some critics as a poststructuralist fellow traveler, a postmodern ironist at odds with his discipline.[20] But Goffman does not doubt the reality—only the naturalness—of social life. A key statement can be found in the introduction to *Frame Analysis*. Goffman identifies the central question to be answered in sociological inquiry: "What is it that's going on here?"[21] To get answers, he analyzes "strips of behavior," or "arbitrary slice[s] or cut[s] from the stream of ongoing activity."[22] *Any* strip of behavior can be analyzed in this way, whether it is fictional or nonfictional, authentic or faked, printed or staged, rehearsed or for real. While frames add complexity and complicate the ontological status of the original event, they do not cancel it out. Goffman imagined dizzying complexity—irony, fictionality, reflexivity, and self-reflexivity—as integral to behavior: but he did not question the existence of behavior as a ground for those reframings. Although Goffman engages questions of method, he points out the danger of focusing on method to the exclusion of research: "Methodological self-consciousness that is full, immediate, and persistent sets aside all study and analysis except that of the reflexive problem itself, thereby displacing fields of inquiry instead of contributing to them" (12).

There is perhaps no more skilled reader of social scenes than Goffman. Throughout his career he demonstrated a virtuosic ability to analyze fine details of social interaction. In his first published essay, "Symbols of Class Status" (1951), Goffman reads minor behavioral, linguistic, and social cues as evidence about status and status dissimulation, while musing about the possibility of achieving even greater analytic purchase. Discussing the difficulty in parsing the individual "particles of behavior" (300) that constitute social performances, he writes: "We tend to be impressed by the over-all character of a person's manner so that, in fact, we can rarely specify and itemize the particular acts which have impressed us. We find, therefore, that we are not able to analyze a desired style or behavior into parts which are small and definite enough to make systematic learning possible" (300). Goffman's career might be understood as the fulfillment of this dream: he broke social performances down into smaller and smaller units in order to make the most banal and fleeting encounters available for systematic study. This reduction in scale made Goffman one of the key figures in the founding of microsociology. His ability to perceive these minor details of communication also made him crucial in the development of studies of interaction. His ability to combine painstaking attention to microscopic elements of behavior, communication, and interaction made everyday social scenes newly available for analysis, and worked to alienate midcentury readers from their lifeworlds.

In a tribute essay, Pierre Bourdieu describes Goffman as a "meticulous student of the real": his contribution was that he "introduced sociology to the infinitely small, to the things which the object-less theoreticians and concept-less observers were incapable of seeing and which went unremarked because they were too obvious, like everything which goes without saying."[23] Goffman's abilities as both an observer and a theorist are remarkable, even singular. His observations of social scenes were always full, even to the point of overflowing, of concepts; as a theorist, which he no doubt was, he insisted on the importance of having an object—theory should be about *something*. Even though his work had a dubious empirical foundation, he had the social scientist's belief that the only theory worth having was grounded theory. Goffman's eye for detail has earned him comparisons to novelists including Kafka, Flaubert, and Proust. Yet he was less interested in building up fictional worlds than in deflating them. His aim was not to give the illusion of real life, but rather to pick apart brief sequences of thought and action and to show how they worked. While he offered extraordinarily precise accounts of social interaction, his method is not empiricist in any traditional sense. Goffman took an early detour from social scientific method. His dissertation, planned as an ethnography of rural Shetland Islanders, got sidetracked as he began hanging around the hotel observing the workplace relations in the restaurant (his analyses of these interactions form the basis for *The Presentation of Self in Everyday Life*). Throughout his career, Goffman combined observations of everyday life with "research" drawn from a remarkably miscellaneous collection of materials, including novels, memoirs, biographies, case histories, and newspaper clippings. This practice has undermined Goffman's authority among sociologists, but it has not gained him any favor from literary critics either. He does not respect the literary qualities of texts, but instead mines them for insights into the dynamics of human interaction. Goffman ignores the distinction between text and world, enlisting literature as well as other narrative and fictional forms in the service of describing social dynamics. He attends to the microdynamics of interaction, whatever their provenance; he analyzes the tonal nuances of scenes taken from "real life" and reads literature for its account of social behaviors.

In "Some Frames for Goffman" (2009), Louis Menand situates the sociologist in a postwar moment that Menand identifies as the "heyday of hermeneutics."[24] At a moment when New Criticism was dominant in literary studies and structuralism was emergent in the social sciences, Goffman denatured scenes of everyday life through his extremely detailed, small-scale analyses. This practice can rightly be understood as hermeneutic, since Goffman's ultimate aim was to draw out the meanings of social scenes. But Goffman's method was not *only* hermeneutic, since it was influenced by other traditions at some distance from the interpretive humanities: animal ethology, psychological behaviorism, kinesics (or the study of gesture), linguistics, game theory, and dramaturgical accounts of social action. Across his scholarship, Goffman repeatedly violated a basic principle of qualitative, interpretive, and humanistic scholarship: if you want to understand what people are experiencing, you should talk to them, and listen carefully to what they have to say. Most often, he resorted to watching people, looking at their behavior, and drawing inferences based on these observations. Goffman attended to the meaning of people's actions, but not their motives. By combining a practice of close reading informed by hermeneutics with an observational style that is behavioral (without being behaviorist), he offered an account of the complexity of social life from the outside.

Goffman's minute attention to the details of everyday life reflects a pervasive culture of surveillance in Cold War America. The period was marked by attention to state and military secrets, the tracking of American citizens, and a vastly expanded capacity for data collection and storage. The unblinking gaze of the microsociologist, often assisted by film cameras and new sound recording technologies, formed part of a media ecology that included satellites, hidden cameras, one-way mirrors, wiretaps, and FBI dossiers.[25] These examples suggest all the ways that observation was a tool of the state, but observation can also be a weapon of the weak.[26] Alongside this litany of surveillance technologies, we might point to less menacing examples, such as observational cinema, Mass Observation, and cruising.[27] In "Some Frames for Goffman," Menand mentions *Candid Camera*, which premiered in 1947 and sought to expose the cracks and flaws in the smooth surface of reality.[28] Goffman betrayed a similar fascination with the everyday "glitches" that threaten the stability of the social order. Goffman's interest in performance is driven by a fascination with failure, for it is in moments of breakdown that the tacit structures guiding interaction come into view:

> To be at ease in a situation is to be properly subject to these rules [of relevance and irrelevance], entranced by the meanings they generate and stabilize; to be ill at ease means that one is ungrasped by immediate reality and that one loosens the grasp that others have of it. To be awkward or unkempt, to talk or move wrongly, is to be a dangerous giant, a destroyer of worlds. As every psychotic and comic ought to know, any accurately improper move can poke through the thin sleeve of immediate reality.[29]

Goffman describes such tears in the social fabric as colossal in their effects, but they are more easily described as microscopic and anodyne.[30] Although there is a tendency to dismiss small-scale analysis as politically irrelevant, it is well suited for capturing dynamics of social hierarchy that escape other frameworks. The situational deviance and information management that Goffman explores in *Stigma* are especially useful in addressing the experiences of the closet and disability, particularly invisible disability. This tight focus on the minutiae of social interaction informs Foucault's work. Goffman's faith in the outsized effects of glitches in social life anticipates Judith Butler's utopian political project outlined at the end of *Gender Trouble*, which imagines the breakdown of the binary gender system as a result of the improper and unaccountable performance of gender.[31] Like these acknowledged critics and provocateurs, Goffman drew on his minute observations of social life not to consolidate the existing social order but rather to destroy it.

According to Goffman, social disqualification is an excellent training in social observation. In *Stigma*, he argues that the stigmatized individual "may be led into placing brackets around a spate of social interaction so as to examine what is contained therein for general themes. He can become 'situation conscious' while normals present are spontaneously involved within the situation, the situation itself constituting for these normals a background of unattended matters. This extension of consciousness on the part of the stigmatized persons is reinforced ... by his special aliveness to the contingencies of acceptance and disclosure, contingencies to which normals will be less alive" (111). This condition of being highly "situation conscious" suggests a link between the "socially disgruntled" and the professional social scientist. Goffman did not make a hard-and-fast distinction between the professional scrutiny of the researcher and the scrutiny of those engaged in everyday acts of social judgment. The "we" that is impressed by the "over-all character of a person's manner" but longs to "specify and itemize" the components of their performance blurs the line between sociologists and ordinary social actors. If Goffman's account of the competencies of lay observers dignifies their efforts, it also implicates the professional analyst of behavior in feats of anxious self-making. There is evidence that Goffman himself was highly "situation conscious": he systematically blocked efforts to photograph, record, or interview him, and asked for his archive to be sealed after his death. Rather than see Goffman simply as the avatar of Cold War social science or as a normal looking to reinforce his status, we can see that his pose of objectivity served as a cover for other less socially approved ways of looking: the anxious scanning of the social climber, the libidinal curiosity of the bystander, or the high-stakes scrutiny of the committed gambler.

THE USES OF STIGMA

In *Stigma*, Goffman provides an overview of the concept from the Greek branding of slaves and criminals to the Christian concept of stigma as a sign of grace. His focus, however, is on the fate of the stigmatized in the twentieth century: his emphasis therefore falls on the modern definition of stigma, which refers more to "the disgrace itself than to the bodily evidence of it."[32] He defines the stigmatized in relation to the normal, using "we" throughout the book to refer to the category of the normal. Goffman understands stigma as a social, public dynamic: it is an interaction that takes place "while the stranger is present before us" (2). He sees "attributes" not as fixed marks or indelible stains so much as aspects of interaction ("evidence can arise" of stigma during an interaction). Analyzing the experiences of this miscellaneous collection of underdogs, misfits, and castoffs, Goffman describes those who do not meet normative expectations for behavior or appearance as socially disqualified, "reduced in our minds," as he writes, "from a whole and usual person to a tainted, discounted one" (3). Stigma is a damaging reduction of the person to one trait. Stigma arises not from that trait; rather it is an effect of role discrepancy, and it arises when an individual possesses traits that do not fit with her expected social role. Goffman attends to the situation of those whose repeated experience of situational impropriety transformed them from the momentarily embarrassed to the socially excommunicated.

Goffman generates his theory of social exclusion through reading a wide range of sources, many of them literary. I am not the only one to remark on the richness of Goffman's footnotes. In his essay "Resemblances," Phil Manning writes that "Goffman stitched into the footnotes of all his books an amazingly eclectic set of references, these ranging from studies of pig farming in Queensland to snippets from the *San Francisco Chronicle*, in a manner quite unlike contemporary scholarship."[33] Alan Bennett comments, "Whole novels take place in [Goffman's] footnotes."[34] In *Stigma*, Goffman draws on materials from the 1950s and early 1960s, many of them from the popular press. He is committed to seeing the commonalities among different forms of social exclusion; out of a miscellaneous collection of vastly different texts, he produces a set of powerful and useful concepts: passing, covering, minstrelsy, and others.

Stigma focuses on narratives by and about criminals, alcoholics, homosexuals, drug addicts, people with a range of physical and mental disabilities, and homeless people, as well as immigrants and ethnic minorities. Goffman's definition of deviance reflects a broader tendency to group together those traditionally seen as victims of society with those in open rebellion against it. Alongside rebels who flout social expectations, Goffman considers "in-group deviants" (who are stigmatized by groups of which they are also members), "disadvantaged" ethnic and racial minority groups, and "members of the lower class who quite noticeably bear the mark of their status in their speech" and are as a result treated as "second class citizens" (145–46). Despite Goffman's interest in the relational and contingent nature of stigma, these groups are treated as stable and self-evident. Goffman adopts the categories of midcentury deviance studies, but voids their contents, seeing in them examples of more general social processes. In *Stigma*, Goffman draws on the assumptions, methods, and frameworks of deviance studies, relying most problematically on social scientists' top-down, static view of the socially different as specimens of otherness. Despite his avowed stance of distance, Goffman observes the dynamics of social denigration from an ant's point of view, noting even the slightest gesture or tone of voice. Thus, he is able to offer a highly specific account of the operations of hierarchy and exclusion as they happen. However, this extremely detailed and close-up view does not rely on a rounded portrait of or empathetic identification with the human subject. Instead, he relentlessly "thins out" this account, withholding the data of feeling and intention, thereby refusing the protocols of psychological portraiture.

Goffman catalogs a remarkable number of ploys on the part of what he calls "normals" to exclude, diminish, ignore, sentimentalize, and condescend to those who do not meet their expectations for behavior or appearance. His view of social life is breathtakingly abstract. At the same time, it is concrete and specific in its focus on particular social scenes and particular moments of social interaction. His definition of stigma emphasizes copresence and perception. Like Durkheim, Goffman understands stigma as a dynamic social situation where fitness is defined in the context of the community rather than in absolute terms. As his description of the stigmatized person as "bad, dangerous, and weak" implies, Goffman is blunt in his account of the effects of stigmatization, and he does not offer a positive account of difference. Indeed, Goffman is far from offering such an account because he himself has no sense of value in difference. This indifference, or even hostility, to coloring outside the lines appears to mark him perhaps more than anything as a figure of his moment. However, his stark, cold gaze on social life hardly elevates existing social norms. Without idealizing either norms or deviance, Goffman highlights a paradox of scholarship on stigma: in describing the conditions of stigmatization, one risks repeating them. But at the same time, he scrupulously avoids a related danger: by refusing to celebrate difference or even to credit its contents, he undermines the stigma that attaches even to characteristics that are intermittently or selectively valued.

Goffman's definition of stigma as role discrepancy undermines essentialist understandings of difference, suggesting that all forms of social hierarchy are relational and contingent. This view is valuable because it suggests that stigma is not yoked to particular traits or behavior, nor is it permanently fixed to individuals or groups. A person who is stigmatized in one context may be seen as unexceptional in another; once stigmatized behavior or traits may become acceptable or even enforced as new norms down the line. According to this view, stigma is a system, a way of sorting persons into categories of normal and deviant along the lines of preexisting social hierarchies. However, defining stigma as behavior out of place excludes categories of people from consideration: behavior may meet social expectations and still be deemed "quite thoroughly bad, or dangerous, or weak" (3). This situational lens fails to address forms of discrimination that are not based on behavior, those deep and persistent forms of domination that disregard a person's qualities. Goffman speaks, for instance, drawing on an article by G. J. Fleming, about the reaction to the "'good English' of an educated northern Negro" (44) visiting the American South—but not about, for instance, the experience of Southern Blacks exposed to discrimination or economic oppression on a regular basis. In an excerpt drawn from Finn Carling's 1962 memoir of living with cerebral palsy, *And Yet We Are Human*, Goffman considers the example of a "dwarf" who must play "the part of the fool in company." Carling writes: "Only when she was among friends, she could throw away her cap and bells and dare to be the woman she really was: intelligent, sad, and very lonely" (cited in Goffman, 110). Goffman's examples tend to be characterized, as these are, by "high contrast"; they also tend to feature exceptional figures, people who stand out from their category or environment. Goffman's topic is role deviance, and he largely ignored stigma that is an effect of role congruence. Goffman was aware of the fact that entire categories of humanity were deemed lesser or worse, yet through his focus on anomalous experience he tended to work around the edges of these mass disqualifications.

In the body of *Stigma*, Goffman outlines abstract concepts and then points to his examples, in most cases a collection of texts by and about social others. We can see evidence of Goffman's relentlessly comparative method in a single footnote. In a section of the book titled "Professional Presentations," for instance, Goffman describes the difficult balance between "revealing and concealing" (109) difference that the stigmatized experience; in order to be perceived as having an authentic form of identity, they should engage in neither minstrelsy nor passing. While a stigmatized person is, on the one hand, warned against acting out "before normals the full dance of bad qualities imputed to his kind," he is also

> encouraged to have distaste for those of his fellows who, without actually making a secret of their stigma, engage in careful covering, being very careful to show that in spite of appearances they are very sane, very generous, very sober, very masculine, very capable of hard physical labor and taxing sports, in short, that they are gentlemen deviants, nice persons like ourselves in spite of the reputation of their kind. (110–11)

To illustrate this impossible and contradictory demand, Goffman offers the following list of citations: "On Jews, see Sartre, *op cit.*, pp. 95–96; on Negroes, see Broyard, *op. cit.*; on intellectuals, see M. Seeman, *op. cit.*; on the Japanese, see M. Grodzins, 'Making Un-Americans,' *American Journal of Sociology*, LX (1955), 570–582."[35] There are several moments like this one in *Stigma*: Goffman outlines an abstract concept, and then, in a footnote, points to his examples that range indiscriminately over populations, time periods, and nationalities, ignoring geographical distinctions as well as forms of self-identification. The gargantuan reach of these footnotes and their blatant disdain for context is evident in a few examples: "For another study of the mental defective" (15n31), see A; "An example from the experience of a blind person may be found in" (33n67) B; "On similar techniques employed by a man with hooks" (137n12), see C. It is not only in such omnibus footnotes that Goffman performs his work of comparison. His method depends on the comparison of microgestures extracted from accounts that differ significantly in their context and particulars.[36] For Goffman, it is the structure of a face-to-face interaction that matters, and that can be meticulously diagrammed, regardless of personal or geo-political or historical differences.

This synthetic method is at a great distance from contemporary approaches to difference that emphasize the local, the particular, and the singular. Linda Alcoff, for instance, in *Visible Identities: Race, Gender, and the Self* (2005) writes: "I believe that the topic of identity is best approached in very specific context-based analyses. This locality and specificity is necessary because identities are constituted by social, contextual conditions of interaction in specific cultures at particular historical periods, and thus their nature, effects, and the problems that need to be addressed in regard to them will be largely local."[37] Despite their shared interest in interaction, Alcoff's insistence on context runs directly counter to Goffman's free-ranging, abstract investigation of the physics of interaction. He investigates social encounters with an eye for the particularity of their unfolding in time and space, but depends on an idea of time and space denuded, stripped of the kinds of geographical and historical texture that we tend to value today. These scenes are all the more troubling because they are incompletely stripped of context—that is to say, Goffman leaves intact general social categories and identities; without further specification, such categories can easily turn into stereotypes. However, in his reduction of individual to type, Goffman shows his work. In his footnotes, meager as they are, we can find the traces of histories and narratives that make visible the particularity that he has excluded from his account. His primary method of abstract synthesis is supplemented, and perhaps even challenged, by the trace of the embodied, affective experience of social others, both fictional and real, archived in his notes.

Goffman's mining of hundreds of texts from many different genres, disciplines, and areas of life allowed him to offer a synthetic account of stigma that, despite its conceptual abstraction and ignorance of context, is nonetheless highly responsive to the lived experience of stigmatization. Goffman's practice of "sociology by epitome," along with his catholic reading habits, may help to explain the lasting power of *Stigma*. Incorporating the evidence of multiple, far-flung narratives, Goffman captures the anxieties of a social world on the verge of transformation. The apparent ease with which Goffman alludes to the categories of normal and stigmatized as if they were self-evident and stable marks this book as a product of the 1950s. But there are also signs that the world described is about to end: tensions appear not only in Goffman's mention of militant or unrepentant deviants, but also in the general sense, registered both substantially and formally, of the contingency and fragility of Goffman's own distinctions. This sense of fragility results in part from Goffman's creation of a kind of fantasy space in which every identity is replaceable by every other identity. While this might seem like professional disregard for anyone's experience, it appears in Goffman as something strange and even intoxicating—like a masked ball. This giddy fungibility of all identity thus generates excitement for the anti-identitarian critic today and can seem to anticipate queer theory at its most heady. However, it is in tension with Goffman's flat invocation of the categories of deviance studies, and his apparent reliance on the ideological categories of White, middle-class America in the 1950s. These moments are no doubt troubling in Goffman's work, and yet it is his deep refusal to acknowledge the claims of identity, whether in social scientific, stereotypical, or more authentic contexts, that remains the deepest challenge of his work. Assimilating the insights of *Stigma* remains most difficult for those critics invested in the importance of identity, which is continuously undermined by Goffman's method.

Goffman is alive to the significance of categories, without which there could in fact be no theory of stigma as he understands it. However, those categories are only significant to the extent that they are negotiated within the context of unfolding interaction. This hyperawareness of details of social scenes is a form of contextualism, but not in the sense that Alcoff intends it: the details that Goffman attends to are so highly mobile, aleatory, and contingent as to scuttle most working definitions of context. This nondeterministic view of identity gets perhaps its most full airing in his presidential address to the American Sociological Association, "The Inter-

action Order." In this essay, Goffman responds to critiques of microsociology for paying scant attention to social structure. Goffman argues that life
in the interaction order is "relatively autonomous" and that social actors
do not simply express transparently the larger social forces that operate
in and through them.[38] He considers the way that the main four "critical
diffuse statuses" (age-grade, gender, class, and race) intersect with other
kinds of statuses, personal features, and the contingency of a given social
scene, and argues that the constant sorting (or processing) that takes place
in social encounters can serve unexpected functions.

Goffman writes,

> It is in these processing encounters, then, that the quiet sorting can
> occur which, as Bourdieu might have it, reproduces the social struc-
> ture. But that conservative impact is not, analytically speaking, situa-
> tional. The subjective weighting of a large number of social attributes,
> whether these attributes are officially relevant or not, and whether
> they are real or fanciful, provides a micro-dot of mystification; covert
> value given, say, to race, can be mitigated by covert value given to other
> structural variables—class, gender, age, comemberships, sponsorship
> network—structures which at best are not fully congruent with each
> other. And structural attributes, overtly or covertly employed, do not
> mesh fully with personal ones, such as health or vigor, or with prop-
> erties that have all of their existence in social situations—looks, per-
> sonality, and the like. What is situational, then, about processing en-
> counters is the evidence they so fully provide of a participant's real or
> apparent attributes while at the same time allowing life chances to be
> determined through an inaccessible weighting of this complex of evi-
> dence. Although this arrangement ordinarily allows for the surrepti-
> tious consolidation of structural lines, the same arrangement can also
> serve to loosen them. (8)

Key to Goffman's understanding of the fixity of identity as well as its potential disruption is the structure of the situation. The importance of this concept for Goffman can hardly be overstated. It is in some sense misleading
to call it a concept; it is more apt perhaps to call it the fundamental unit of
society. Although some social factors are surely beyond its reach, Goffman
was committed to exhaustively cataloging the characteristics, dynamics,
and relations that had to be negotiated within it. The form of the situation

is strict, determining the kind of moves that are possible. Though rule-bound, it is open-ended, for within this structure an almost endless number of moves can be made.

Goffman is alive to the significance of those categories and forces most often invoked by sociologists, social class and race. He also attended to some of the factors made newly salient by the rise of the new social movements, such as disability, gender, and homosexuality. But he also saw the importance of much more miscellaneous categories, noting the influence of qualities seen as purely personal such as looks and health. On a first reading of this passage, Goffman seems to take on the reductive methods for which sociology is known, pointing to a timely piece of spy-craft, the microdot. This technology reduced documents to miniature pieces of film, which could be covertly removed from secure facilities and delivered to enemy governments. But rather than advocating reduction, Goffman offers a challenge to sociologists, and indeed to all social observers, to pay attention to what is concealed within the minute and apparently insignificant. Goffman takes his subject matter, the infinitely small, what has been rendered imperceptible and unobtrusive, through a shift in scale. His task as a sociologist is not to make microdots or even to transport them like an agent in the field. Instead, he remains an intelligence officer, back at his desk, committed to the task of blowing up these microdots in order to make them visible once again. Under this kind of scrutiny, any fragment of behavior will reveal its constituent parts, which include both the ways that general forces in society inhere in everyday interactions and the way that everyday interactions fail to correspond in any predictable measure to general social forces. Thus, the sorting process that Goffman considers may produce structural privilege and domination, but these effects are unpredictable. It is in the open mesh of personal and structural characteristics and in the "inaccessible weighting" of evidence that the possibility of a reshuffling of social roles appears, for a moment, possible.

In a section on information control and personal identity in *Stigma*, Goffman offers the concept of a "positive mark" or "identity peg"—a trait used for recognition. Goffman describes a mark that allows people to be pegged or allows others to hang things on them (one of his examples is the fingerprint). But as he goes on to define personal identity this idea develops: "By personal identity" he means the mixture of "positive marks or identity pegs" with the "unique combination of life history items that comes to be attached to the individual with the help of these pegs for his identity. Personal identity, then, has to do with the assumption that the individual can be differentiated from all others and that around this means of differentiation a single continuous record of social facts can be attached, entangled, like candy floss, becoming the sticky substance to which still other biographical facts can be attached. What is difficult to appreciate is that personal identity can and does play a structured, routine, standardized role in social organization just because of its one-of-a-kind quality" (57). In this account, Goffman captures not only the conditions of everyday life in an information society, but also more general features of personal identity in modernity. His understanding of the stickiness of personal identity describes a general condition of living with highly advanced techniques of information management. But Goffman also makes it clear that that these general conditions are exacerbated in the case of social others. The "social facts" that stick to all individuals are stickier in the case of persons whose distinguishing characteristics and "typical life stories" mark them as social outsiders. No distinguishing characteristics are quite as sticky as the disqualifying marks of stigma.

In his article "Goffman as a Systematic Social Theorist," Anthony Giddens writes, "Through [Goffman's] career he resolutely refused to tread upon two terrains that would seem to stretch invitingly open to him. On the one hand, with the exception of his work on total institutions, which in any case is expressed mainly in terms of their effects upon individual identity, Goffman maintained a strict separation between his work and that of sociologists interested in the macro-structural properties of social systems. On the other hand, various comments and allusions throughout his writings notwithstanding, he refused to be drawn into any kind of elaborated account of the psychology of the self."[39] In the context of Goffman's argument about typecasting and the danger that people might be equated with their attributes, we might understand the bounded nature of his investigations as strategic. Giddens continues, "Goffman's attempt to distinguish the interaction order as a clearly delimited field also gains plausibility from his disinclination to confront questions of motivation. If Goffman's writings are 'flat,' lacking that vertical dimension which an enriched treatment of institutions would provide, they are also in a certain sense 'empty' in respect of the motivation that leads actors to behave as they do in day-to-day life" (277–78). In his "flat" and "empty" accounts of everyday life, Goffman turns the self into a placeholder—merely a mark. In this sense, he can both describe the stickiness of identity and offer an account of the self nothing can stick to.

The resistance of that "empty" self is limited, however, and the social effects of stigmatization are distributed unevenly. Structure emerges in Goffman as repetition over time. In a well-known passage in *Stigma*, he reflects on the emptiness of the categories of stigmatized and normal and on the way that some individuals become typecast. He writes:

> Stigma involves not so much a set of concrete individuals who can be separated into two piles, the stigmatized and the normal, as a pervasive two-role social process in which every individual participates in both roles, at least in some connections and in some phases of life. The normal and the stigmatized are not persons but rather perspectives . . . The lifelong attributes of a particular individual may cause him to be typecast; he may have to play the stigmatized role in almost all of his social situations, making it natural to refer to him, as I have done, as a stigmatized person whose life-situation places him in opposition to normals. However, his particular stigmatizing attributes do not determine the nature of the two roles, normal and stigmatized, merely the frequency of his playing a particular one of them. (137–38)

Toward the end of *Stigma*, Goffman derealizes the categories of normal and stigmatized, making it clear that they have no fixed content. Being stigmatized is a matter of having to play the role of the stigmatized too often—but it is no less definitive on that account. Characteristically, Goffman makes no effort to rescue this typecast character; he merely comments, with ice water in his veins, that he himself has participated in the production of this person as one of the permanently stigmatized.

UNDERDOG CONFESSIONS

Goffman's interest in the relations between various kinds of social outsiders was widely shared in the 1950s and early 1960s. *Stigma* includes in its footnotes several collections of case histories from this period. Sometimes fictional, sometimes factual, these collections include vignettes that, implicitly or explicitly, compare miscellaneous forms of failure and social exclusion. In 1961, Philip Toynbee, a literary reviewer at the *Observer*, published one such study, *Underdogs: Eighteen Victims of Society*.[40] Toynbee placed advertisements in several major newspapers in England in which he asked people to send in their "underdog confessions." In his introduction, he reports that he received over five hundred replies in the first two weeks; in the end, he selected eighteen underdog stories to publish. The fact that Toynbee was overwhelmed with underdog confessions in response to his appeal might support Foucault's claims about the incitement to discourse and the embrace of confession as a dominant genre of modernity. But the existence of this underdog archive might also lead us to challenge Foucault's understanding of the power dynamics of the clinic and of the case study. Like several of Goffman's sources, *Underdogs* is made up of self-authored case histories. These capsule stories of social suffering, failure, and alienation are not written by a psychologist, medical doctor, or criminologist, but by the subjects themselves. These examples of "own stories" or "case histories written by themselves" frustrate our expectations about the politics of authorship and authority. These instances of self-proclaimed underdogs serving up digest versions of themselves in the genre of "social problem" literature suggest something other than a simple internalization of oppressive social forces. Instead, they indicate the plasticity of the case-study form, the felt need to articulate experiences of social suffering, and the significance of narrative in representing the specific dynamics of stigmatization.

The book is focused on the question of what makes someone an underdog. The question is not only what social features might mark someone as an outsider, but also what attitude or emotion is an appropriate response to stories of social victimization. *Underdogs* includes "confessions" by people in a variety of situations: some of these were later organized into social movements, others were not; some seem extremely familiar as examples of social exile, others are much more difficult to classify or to see as deserving of underdog status. The case histories include accounts of poverty, homelessness, disability, domestic violence, homosexuality, and illegitimacy, as well as confessions from a pederast, a mother of four young children during wartime, and a ghostwriter with frustrated literary ambitions. Each contributor must make her case about why her story deserves attention, and why she might legitimately be considered a victim of society. But as Toynbee notes, in many cases, it is difficult to say whether an individual is suffering from social inequality or from some unfortunate conditions of human existence in general. He writes, "to most of us cruel husbands and charmless women seem to be an incurable aspect of the human condition as we know or can foresee it" (12).

Because of the lack of clear distinction between naturally occurring and human-authored forms of suffering, it can be difficult to judge which underdog stories might form the basis for social collectivity. Like Goffman, Toynbee interests himself both in generally recognized categories of domination and in those that seem merely personal, a matter of individual character or luck rather than social structure. Could such a disparate group of outsiders, failures, or losers ever constitute a meaningful social group? It's not clear, though a letter to the editor of the *Daily Telegraph* that Toynbee reprints in the introduction seems to suggest that it might. The act of inviting people to see themselves as underdogs constitutes, in this reader's mind, a threat to English masculinity and to the future of the nation.

> This book should become a twentieth-century classic, the contemporary equivalent and reversal of Samuel Smiles's Victorian manual *Self Help*, a park-bench-side book for those who want to go down in the world and are looking for the most up-to-date forms of maladjustment and failure. In the past, the worship of the criminal and the underdog has mostly been confined to intellectuals and rich Bohemians. Now there are ominous signs that it is beginning to permeate the mass of the nation and gain approval in the highest quarters . . . There is a frenzied search for new varieties of the under-privileged, from misunderstood working-class undergraduates to perverts of every kind. It is a raging disease which will end in complete identification with the object of idolatry. It will be our fate to become what we love. Then the symbolic figure of England will be a half-witted, impotent, armless, half-caste pickpocket, continually grumbling about his mistreatment by one-armed foreign rivals. (Cited in Toynbee, 10–11)

Despite the biting, cynical tone of the author, and his fatalistic predictions for English society, he nonetheless registers the rumblings of social change still in process. This statement is consistent with many of the period noting a voluntary embrace of debased social qualities; but rather than being merely an affectation of those with nothing better to do, this identification downward threatens in this view to become a mass social movement. In this sense, the letter accurately captures a shift that was taking place. For it was an alliance between the working class and students, which involved a broad identification with the margins, that made possible the new social movements. This challenge to the nation and to the very concept of "normal man" took place partly in the name of downward mobility, and swept up dissenters, outcasts, the criminal classes, and "perverts of every kind." In contrast to the moral exemplar featured in Smiles's *Self Help*, this letter offers an image of society's most downtrodden—but also its most alienated and disaffected—member. What emerges is a grotesque, a figure that combines all forms of deviance, and thus becomes an image of what the nation cannot abide. Though unreal and thoroughly ideological, this figure anticipates the strange alliances just out of view at this moment in the 1950s. Such combinations as well as the corrosive attitudes that emerge from them did constitute a potent threat to the nation as it was. They also point, if obliquely, toward the queer collectivities of the future.

Like Goffman's *Stigma*, *Underdogs* brings together a range of experiences of social exclusion, some of them soon to be validated by mass social protests, and others too personal or idiosyncratic to ever form the basis of such a movement. As in *Stigma*, the major axes of sociological inquiry, race, ethnicity, and gender are present, but they are identified along with a much wider variety of differences. Toynbee's aim in collecting these narratives is to shed new light on unrecognized forms of suffering, and to raise the question of what can make an individual into an underdog. His emphasis on unexpected forms of discrimination leads Toynbee to emphasize outliers in the field of difference. As he writes in his introduction, "The resulting book, then, is in no sense a comprehensive survey of our underdogs; it is not even a representative selection from the main complaints which have been made. But it does contrive, I think, to deal with the familiar in a new way and to reveal a great deal of suffering which we seldom contemplate."[41]

Toynbee organizes highly diverse narratives in relation to a general category, the underdog. In each of his cases, the designation is up for grabs; each writer spends some time defining what it means to be an underdog and arguing that his or her experience is adequate qualification for underdog status. The authors speculate about the relationship of their form of disadvantage to others. In one example, the anonymous author N. O. Goe begins his confession, called "The Stricture," with a reflection on the relative obscurity of his condition.

This title, which so interestingly looks as though it might be that of a poem by Donne or a story by Henry James, simply means what The Concise Oxford Dictionary says: "STRICTURE (Path.) morbid contraction of some canal or duct in the body." The matter is, in fact, very down to earth, and in every sense of the word, vulgar; and some may well think it trivial. But while I agree that, compared with other disadvantages, such as physical deformity, the lack of one or more of the five wits, or a sexual deviation, the stricture scarcely ranks high, nevertheless it can cause a certain sense of shamed inferiority, as well as bodily discomfort, and may have a considerable influence on a person's life. (147)

By framing this medical condition in terms of the dynamics of stigma—what makes the stricture a difficult condition to live with is primarily "a sense of shamed inferiority," even more than "bodily discomfort"—one sees the definitional flexibility that underdog status allows. Having a stricture does not necessarily lead one to identify with others with strictures; rather, his connection is to a less specific, expansive group, the members of which are negatively rather than positively defined—those, who through unexpected turns in their life course, have been converted into underdogs.

For Toynbee, the capaciousness of the category *underdog* constitutes its value. He points out that this category captures better the way in which social exclusion need not be tied to moral or constitutional unfitness. He writes, "A book of this kind could only have been produced, with any hope of welcome, in a society which no longer equates failure with moral error, or criminality with wickedness" (14). Disarticulating pathology from underdog status allows Toynbee's authors to describe themselves as underdogs but not as wholly other. Underdog, as its name would suggest, is not a fixed category of identity, but rather a position vis-à-vis dominant society. For Toynbee, to see the contributors as underdogs is a mark of social progress: evidence of an unwillingness to ascribe blame, and even as a kind of secular grace. He writes, "What has certainly happened in the last hundred years is that more of us have adapted the famous heart-cry of John Bradford. There, but for some accident of upbringing or circumstance, go we ourselves. And the fact that almost all of us sometimes regard ourselves as underdogs is not necessarily a foolish indulgence or due to a fit of meaningless depression. We are given, at these moments, an opportunity to ally ourselves in spirit with those who are more constantly unfortunate" (14). In contrast to the standard perspective of deviance studies, which imagines passive victims awaiting rescue from above, Toynbee envisions a form of coalition based on lateral thinking across difference. Partial identification—rather than pity for the wholly other—is the form of response that Toynbee imagines to these stories of failure. In his formulation of the category of the underdog, Toynbee invokes three crucial elements: the expansion of the concept of otherness; depathologization; and flexible and capacious forms of solidarity. All three were essential to the forging of a mass movement based on a fracturing of a national norm and an embrace of difference in general.

The fact that the category of underdog might include potentially anyone who feels excluded is both the strength and the weakness of this term. The radical expansion of the category of the underdog makes possible new forms of identification and creates new possibilities for coalition. But it always carries the risk of blurring the difference between greater and lesser forms of adversity, or even of blurring out any concrete meaning for the term.[42] Focusing on the fate of underdogs also makes it hard to imagine the possibility of social transformation: underdogs are excluded by definition; if they were, somehow, to transform their conditions and become overdogs, the social structure would remain intact. Neither *Underdogs* nor *Stigma* poses a direct challenge to society's starkest inequalities. Because of the profound reach of class, racial, and gender oppression, they appear throughout these accounts, but are not always at the center of analysis. Instead, both books depend on a deviance model of power, one that emphasizes the costs of nonnormativity rather than oppression. This deviance model of power in combination with influential accounts of the normal and the pathological in the history of medicine have become familiar to us in recent years because they are fundamental to the notion of power that operates in queer and disability studies.

We might read these books as cautionary examples about the politics of analogy; the difficulties of taking on near-universal categories of otherness; and of disregarding pervasive (rather than exceptional or novel) forms of inequality. Similar debates have clustered around the term *queer*, another quasi-universal category of social marginality. However, while these texts might be read as cautionary tales about the dangers of comparison, they also suggest the utility of a general theory of stigma grounded in specific accounts of social marginality. The emergence of queer theory as explicitly focused on the study of margins clarifies, retroactively, the political significance of Goffman's method. His grouping together of social outsiders by extracting what their situations in life have in common becomes, in queer studies, a means of rallying "collectivities of the shamed."[43] As critiques of queer studies have intensified, pointing to its class privilege, its Whiteness, and its tendency to subsume all forms of difference into the term queer, this political strategy has come under fire.[44] However, despite these critiques, queer with its image of shared marginality continues to have a significant hold on the contemporary political imagination.

GENDER MOMENTS

Goffman's use of a general category of otherness that included many forms of difference links him to the emergence of queer theory decades after he wrote *Stigma*. It is also his attention to performance as the foundation of social life that makes him such an important precursor to the field. Queer theory rose to prominence in the early 1990s fueled by the concept of performativity. Derived from the scholarship of J. L. Austin and Jacques Derrida and inspired by the scene-stealing activism of ACT UP and Gran Fury, performativity had both a respectable philosophical lineage and street credibility. The theory of performativity countered the discourse of gender and sexual essentialism and at the same time helped to explain activist and everyday interventions in the fabric of reality. But the idea of performativity as repetition with a difference also acknowledged the force of existing social arrangements. In *Gender Trouble*, Judith Butler insists on the linguistic constitution of the subject, challenging traditional accounts of agency that imagine a subject "understood to have some stable existence prior to the cultural field that it negotiates" (182). Drawing on Nietzsche to refute the idea of a "doer behind the deed" (181), Butler thus offers an antifoundationalist account of the subject that nonetheless recognizes the transformative energies of dissident gender performance. The idea of a self that is linguistically constituted resonates with the thoroughly social self Goffman describes. Butler resists the association, however. She recognizes neither Goffman nor a host of other scholarship in the social sciences on "doing gender" as relevant to her project.[45] She writes, "This is not a return to an existential theory of the self as constituted through acts, for the existential theory maintains a prediscursive structure for both the self and its acts" (181).

Butler's refusal of the existential lineage in her formulation of gender performativity is a key moment in the history of the linguistic turn, when, according to Eve Sedgwick, "nonverbal aspects of reality" were "subsumed" "firmly under the aegis of the linguistic." Several decades later, in a moment when the hegemony of the linguistic has ebbed, what seemed like a dialectical step forward at the time looks more like a missed connection.[46] Although Butler does not mention Goffman in *Gender Trouble*, she did address his work explicitly in an article published a few years earlier in *Theater Journal*, "Performative Acts and Gender Constitution: An Essay in Phenomenology and Feminist Theory" (1988). This essay engages traditions of performance from theater studies and the social sciences, fields that Butler increasingly downplayed as she developed a linguistic theory of performativity. The essay is multidisciplinary in its approach to gender, drawing on, as Butler writes, "theatrical, anthropological, and philosophical discourses, but mainly phenomenology" (520). Butler's explicit aim in the piece is to differentiate her account of gender performativity from related accounts developed in these disciplines, particularly the phenomenological doctrine of constitution and anthropological notions of ritual and performance in everyday life. Despite the critical and distancing focus of the essay, Butler deploys metaphors of theatricality much more freely than elsewhere in her work, as in the following gloss on the concept of an act: "The act that one does, the act that one performs, is, in a sense, an act that has been going on before one arrived on the scene. Hence, gender is an act which has been rehearsed, much as a script survives the particular actors who make use of it, but which requires individual actors in order to be actualized and reproduced as reality once again" (526).

Even here, Butler's discussion of Goffman is confined to a brief reference. He is held up as a representative of the pitfalls of the concept of theatricality, and the expressive account of gender that follows from it. Butler argues that gender should not be "understood as a *role* which either expresses or disguises an interior 'self'"; instead, gender "constructs the social fiction of its own psychological interiority" (528). *The Presentation of Self in Everyday Life* is adduced as an example of such a limited and limiting account of theatricality. According to Butler's reading, Goffman's description of social life depends on a stable, interior self that acts in and on the world; such a view underestimates the power of norms, particularly of linguistic norms, and aggrandizes individual agency. Butler writes, "As opposed to a view such as Erving Goffman's which posits a self which assumes and exchanges various 'roles' within the complex social expectations of the 'game' of modern life, I am suggesting that this self is not only irretrievably 'outside,' constituted in social discourse, but that the ascription of interiority is itself a publically regulated and sanctioned form of essence fabrication" (528). Butler argues that Goffman assumes a preexisting gendered self that takes up and discards social roles at will; at the same time, by subscribing, through this notion of the self, to the stabilization of gender, Goffman implicitly participates in "a social policy of gender regulation and control" (528). By missing the radical potential of gender performativity as distinguished from the performance of gender, Goffman contributes to the perpetuation of the status quo.

Butler reiterates a familiar critique of Goffman, arguing that his mode of describing the social world is an endorsement of its violence. Butler recasts this critique in the terms of an antifoundationalist argument about identity as inherently stabilizing social hierarchies. Because Goffman believes in the notion of a self, he therefore supports the current arrangements of gendered control. However, this view underestimates the complexity of Goffman's account of individual agency. It ignores in particular his interest in "essence fabrication," which, in its imputation of fakery to the basis of the self, constituted its own potent form of antifoundationalism. Goffman's view of the self is far from substantial; instead, his view of authentic human subjectivity was corrosive and vertiginous. While in his early work he understands the self as a dramatic effect, in later writing he shifts to understand it as an effect of patterned social relations. At all points it is thoroughly social and relational.

The evisceration of the self as an expressive or authentic core is not only a repeated argument in Goffman's writing. It also formed the basis for an important feature of his methodology, as he makes clear in the introduction to the 1967 collection *Interaction Ritual*:

> I assume the proper study of interaction is not the individual and his psychology, but rather the syntactical relations among the acts of different persons mutually present to one another. None the less, since it is individual actors who contribute the ultimate materials, it will always be reasonable to ask what general properties they must have if this sort of contribution is to be expected of them. What minimal model of the actor is needed if we are to wind him up, stick him in amongst his fellows, and have an orderly traffic in behavior emerge? What minimal model is required if the student is to anticipate the lines along which an individual, *qua* interactant, can be effective or break down? That is what these papers are about. A psychology is necessarily involved, but one stripped and cramped to suit the sociological study of conversation, track meets, banquets, jury trials, and street loitering.
>
> Not, then, men and their moments. Rather moments and their men.[47]

Goffman, far from "ascribing interiority," as Butler argues, distances himself from psychological accounts of the subject; while he sees individuals as implicated in social games, by prioritizing the rules of those games ("syntactical relations") rather than the desires of those who play them, he undermines rather than amplifies individual agency. Goffman strikes a note of resignation as he explains that since actors "contribute materials" to social situations, some minimal notion of the self is needed in order to account for interactions. The "self," for Goffman, is a methodological necessity, more like a game piece, counter, or stick figure than a fleshed-out psychological self. By identifying the goal of such specification as an "orderly traffic in behavior," Goffman makes clear that one of the key social frames for the behavior of these actors is the context of his own interpretive study of them. This extreme self-reflexivity, as well as a willingness to "strike the set" and dispense with any interpretive frame, runs throughout Goffman's work.[48]

The key elements of Butler's theory—her suggestion that selves are radically ungrounded and thoroughly constituted by social norms; that identity is "constituted in time" (519); her entire account of "the mundane way in which bodily gestures, movements, and enactments of various kinds constitute the illusion of an abiding gendered self" (519)—are suggested strongly both in Goffman's account of self and role and in his specific reflections on gender. His work on the "presentation of self" and his discussion, late in his career, of the social reproduction of gender inequality focus on the way that identity is constituted in time, through the repetition of gestures and social acts, and on the mundane social performances that make cultural gender roles appear as essence. Furthermore, Goffman offers an ecological view of the self that places it in dynamic context, understanding individual behavior to be situated not only in time but also in space. His focus on concrete social interaction and particular social spaces does not preclude attention to language and textuality, as is suggested by his reference to the syntax of social interaction as well as the extreme reflexivity of his account of individual agency ("if we are to wind him up . . ."). On the one hand, then, Butler's dismissal of Goffman might be seen as a predictable moment of strategic misreading. On the other, it is significant because it constitutes a missed connection between a socially grounded account of performance and a linguistically oriented account of performativity.

Although any mention of Goffman drops out in the revisions for *Gender Trouble*, what does survive is a discussion of Esther Newton's *Mother Camp*. Newton's drag ethnography drew heavily on Goffman's understanding of stigma, of "front stage" and "back stage" presentations, and on the performance of social roles. The topic of Newton's ethnography as well as its political stance against compulsory gendering makes it a more obviously salient example for Butler. However, Goffman's crucial meth-

odological influence in *Mother Camp*—legible in the account of gender as
determined by social location—is missing. Drag is an important topic for
Butler and for queer theory, but Goffman's ecological perspective drops
out of view in both.

The complex relations between the self, agency, and the influence of
the social world play out in Goffman's discussion of gender: not women
and their moments, but moments and their women. In his late book *Gender Advertisements* (1979) and in the essay "The Arrangement between the
Sexes" (1977), he considers the question of institutional reflexivity, which
is the term he uses to explain how "irrelevant biological differences" between the sexes are "elaborated socially."[49] This attack on the naturalness of expression does not depend on a straightforward linear account of
the social construction of gender; instead, Goffman emphasizes the way
that social and cultural norms retroactively produce the illusion of natural sexual difference. Considering the "cultural matter" of "toilet segre-
gation" in the 1977 essay, Goffman argues that this practice is "presented
as a natural consequence of the difference between the sex-classes, when
in fact it is rather a means of honoring, if not producing, this difference"
(316).[50] In *Gender Advertisements*, Goffman launches a broad argument
against the "doctrine of natural expression," which underlies not only our
understanding of gender but also of "intent, feeling, relationship, information state, health, social class, etc."[51] He writes, "What the human nature of males and females really consists of, then, is a capacity to learn to
provide and to read depictions of masculinity and femininity and a willingness to adhere to a schedule for presenting these pictures . . . One might
just as well say there is no gender identity. There is only a schedule for the
portrayal of relationship" (8).

While Butler focuses on the stylized repetition of gendered acts, Goffman, influenced by Durkheim, considers the consolidation of gendered
existence as a matter of social ritual. Foregrounding ritual means emphasizing performance, but it does not presuppose, as Butler intimates, an autonomous, willing self. Goffman instead suggests that institutions com-
mand social performance by compulsorily gendered actors. He writes,
"deep-seated institutional practices have the effect of transforming social
situations into scenes for the performance of genderisms by both sexes,
many of these performances taking a ritual form which affirms beliefs
about the differential human nature of the two sexes even while indica-
tions are provided as to how behavior between the two can be expected to
be intermeshed" (325). Goffman's focus on the centrality of the scene in

"the practice between the sexes of choreographing behaviorally a portrait of a relationship" (*Gender Advertisements*, 8) means that he understands sexual difference as unfolding in socially conditioned time and space.

Goffman treats the difference between the sexes as a portable social ritual. No matter what the setting, Goffman suggests, gender roles can and will be recreated as if according to script. In "The Arrangement between the Sexes," he writes,

> Gender, not religion, is the opiate of the masses. In any case, we have here a remarkable organizational device. A man may spend his day suffering under those who have power over him, suffer this situation at almost any level of society, and yet on returning home each night regain a sphere in which he dominates. And wherever he goes beyond the household, women can be there to prop up his show of competence. It is not merely that your male executive has a female secretary, but (as now often remarked) his drop-out son who moves up the hierarchy of alternative publishing or protest politics will have female help, too; and had he been disaffected enough to join a rural commune, an appropriate division of labor would have awaited him. And should we leave the real world for something set up as its fictional alternative, a science fiction cosmos, we would find that here, too, males engage in the executive action and have females to help out in the manner of their sex. Wherever the male goes, apparently, he can carry a sexual division of labor with him. (315)

Through his account of the reproductive work of social scenes, and his conjuring of several highly particularized examples, Goffman explains how the force of institutional gender difference ("division of labor") is also a pop-up roadshow, a spectacle of difference that can be staged anywhere. Here, as elsewhere, Goffman draws equally from fictional and factual examples, identifying both realms as equally saturated by the ideology of gender. The particularity of these scenes is important, since each new apparently improvised scene gives the look and feel of spontaneity and nature to what is a highly scripted social performance. There are clear points of continuity between Goffman's view of gender as performance and Butler's later better-known account. What is less easily remarked is the clear continuity in the political vision shared by Goffman and Butler, which consists in their belief that exposing artificiality to view will loosen the hold of categories deemed to be natural. Though contemporary critics may see Goffman's investments in the transformative power of knowledge as naive, or even quietist, it is a view that strongly marks the writing of the first generation of queer theory.

UNIVERSALIZING STIGMA

Goffman did not call out the injustice of the social world, nor did he offer a road map for social transformation. At the outset of *Stigma*, he maintains the distinction between the normal and the stigmatized. But the distinction crumbles across the course of the book. In a memorable moment toward the end of *Stigma*, Goffman suggests that the category of the normal may be an empty set: "In an important sense," he writes, "there is only one complete unblushing male in America: a young, married, White, urban, northern, heterosexual Protestant father of college education, fully employed, of good complexion, weight, and height, and a recent record in sports" (128). By studying spoiled identity, Goffman sought to spoil social life, and to make the condition of the stigmatized central, even universal.

In his early essay "On Cooling the Mark Out: Some Aspects of Adaptation to Failure," Goffman considers strategies employed to help people adjust to the diminished circumstances that follow on various forms of failure. Borrowing terms from the criminal underworld, Goffman describes the necessity of consoling (or "cooling out") the mark or target of a con after it has become apparent that he has been victimized. In order to keep the mark from going to the police or some other authority, the cooler is assigned to help the victim adjust to his new reality—in essence, to recognize his failure and be reconciled to it. From this specific story of the con, Goffman moves to a general theory of social management and adjustment. He argues that cooling the mark out is "one theme in a very basic social story."[52] What is at stake in moments of failure is a profound shift in social role; the individual confronted with his shortcomings must shift his perception of himself and give up on certain cherished illusions about his place in the world. "For the mark," Goffman writes, "cooling represents a process of adjustment to an impossible situation—a situation arising from having defined himself in a way which the social facts come to contradict. The mark must therefore be supplied with a new set of apologies for himself, a new framework in which to see himself and judge himself" (10). Goffman describes a number of characters who must be consoled in common social situations: customers who are dissatisfied or have complaints; employees who are passed over for a promotion or fired; suitors who are rejected in situations of "decourting"; and spouses who are being dropped in a divorce. More difficult is the job of the priest or doctor who must persuade terminally ill individuals "to accept quietly the loss of life itself" (10).

Death is both the most extreme case of the role adjustment that individuals go through and a model for all failure. Goffman writes, "A mark who requires cooling out is a person who can no longer sustain one of his social roles and is about to be removed from it; he is a person who is losing one of his social lives and is about to die one of the deaths that are possible for him. This leads one to consider the ways in which we can go or be sent to our death in each of our social capacities" (18). The fact that death is the model for failure—from receiving substandard service in a restaurant to getting fired to being deported to actually dying—indicates both the profound impact of failure as well as its universality. Even those individuals that manage to avoid failure in their lives will find it necessary to adapt to the loss of youth and health in old age, and the eventual loss of life. Goffman indicates the universality of disappointment and the concomitant necessity of role adjustment and social appeasement in his invocation of the psychotherapist as "society's cooler" (17). In describing social disappointment as universal—as universal as eventual death—Goffman indicates, if faintly, a collective of social outsiders, a stigmatized majority. At the same time, he suggests the kinds of distinctions that might continue to matter in forging collectivities—such as the difference between the universal conditions of alienation and physical vulnerability and the influence of history, caste, and class. The fact that we will all die some day does not change the fact that, at this moment, some of us are alive while others are dead.

Goffman describes the way that failure and success can bring people from different milieus into contact with each other. He writes:

But perhaps the most important movement of those who fail is one we never see. Where roles are ranked and somewhat related, persons who have been rejected from the one above may be difficult to distinguish from the one below . . . No doubt there are few positions in life that do not throw together some persons who are there by virtue of failure and other persons who are there by virtue of success. In this sense, the dead are sorted but not segregated, and continue to walk among the living. (20)

Goffman's account of a universal but unnoticed social death suggests an unwitting community between the living and the dead. Unlike the total institution, where social failures are secreted en masse, in this world persons mix with ex-persons, and the socially dead wander where no one knows their name.

UNDERDOG IN THE UNDERWORLD

In "Symbols of Class Status," Goffman considers the fact that status symbols do not reliably indicate the social standing of the people who display them. Signs such as demeanor, clothing, bearing, and accent, used to "place" individuals, are "better suited to the requirements of communication than are the rights and duties that they signify," and are therefore vulnerable to imitation and expropriation. Because people can appear to be other than what they are, they access opportunities that would otherwise be closed to them. Goffman is less concerned with the possibility of deception itself than he is with the "the pressures that play upon behavior as a result."[53] Those of higher rank are not immune to these pressures either; by instituting "restrictive mechanisms" (296) to safeguard their position, they undermine their claims to natural superiority. Those who aim to rise may enjoy unearned rewards, but they will also suffer inauthenticity and pervasive anxiety. In a postwar society ruled by appearances, dissimulation becomes a necessity rather than a luxury. If people *can* hide their true selves, they may find themselves compelled to do so. According to Goffman, "there are people whose daily work requires them to become proficient in manipulating symbols which signify a position higher than the one they themselves possess," pointing out that "teachers in the field of higher learning," along with other "curators" (domestic servants, interior decorators, architects, and artists), are typically "recruited from classes which have much less prestige than the class to which such services are sold" (303).

Goffman's vision of a world ruled by self-interest and gamesmanship has struck many critics as unsavory. In *The Coming Crisis of Western Sociology*, Gouldner argued that Goffman's work is symptomatic of the rise of the professional-managerial class and of a move from production to consumption in the US after WWII. On this view, *The Presentation of Self in Everyday Life* accepts rather than indicts these new conditions, and might even be read as a cynical guide to living and thriving in them. In a 2002 essay, Norman K. Denzin amplifies Gouldner's point, suggesting that

Goffman "gave midcentury academic sociology exactly what it wanted, and what it needed: Men and women in gray flannel suits performing the rites and rituals of a postwar white collar society . . . Goffman's actors did not resist, they conformed to the requirements of a local and global capitalism that erased class, race, and gender in the name of a universal human nature. Goffman's moral selves knew their place in the order of things."[54] Universal human nature in this context was never universal; instead, it rendered powerful norms of White, middle-class belonging invisible. Many critics have supported this account, describing Goffman's sociology as static and as reinforcing of social hierarchies. Citing the culture of postwar complacency, they argue that he has no account of broader social or historical forces, or of how contemporary social arrangements might change. Discussing the expansion and professionalization of the human sciences, they argue that Goffman treats his subjects as if they were specimens under glass.[55] In this framework, Goffman's account of the social world is not critical but merely cynical, his disaffection a mask for a more fundamental investment in the status quo.

Other scholars have contested this view of Goffman, attributing to him moral seriousness and a systematic critique of postwar society. Goffman is sometimes described—often via comparisons with his contemporary Foucault—as a "major theorist of power," attentive to pervasive social control, and to the effects of the unequal distribution of the ability to "give official imprint to versions of reality."[56] Others point out that, despite his rhetorical stance of neutrality, Goffman's meticulous accounts of the situation of social outsiders attested to his sympathies, and contributed to a profound shift in social attitudes. George Gonos responds directly to Gouldner's critique in a 1980 essay, "The Class Position of Goffman's Sociology." Gonos writes, "[Goffman's] sociology does indeed reflect the social changes and new experience brought about by the giant corporation. But rather than constituting an expression of the class position of its employees, it represents a critical reaction to the life-style and ideology of these new middle classes."[57] Gonos argues that Goffman does not identify with the new managerial class but instead with the small class of independent entrepreneurs and shopkeepers left behind by postwar corporatism.[58] C. Wright Mills discusses the "sad condition" of this class fragment at length in *White Collar* (1951): he notes, "the bottom of the entrepreneurial world is so different from the top that it is doubtful whether the two should be classified together."[59] While Mills's discussion of the world of small family-owned businesses and farms leans on the traditional image of the petite bour-

geoisie as narrow and conservative, Gonos offers a more positive assessment, suggesting that this group retains "such old bourgeois qualities as
independence, flair, ingenuity, individual initiative, thrift, and competi-
tiveness."[60] These qualities do not survive undistorted in Goffman's sociology, where they are embodied not by the small shopkeeper, but by the
criminal. As Gonos writes, "Goffman's sociology is constructed by viewing
society in the perspective of the lumpen-bourgeois 'operator.' Much of its
conceptual apparatus and terminology are directly appropriated from the
mental apparatus and argot of the con man" (153). In place of partisanship
with underdogs, we find in Goffman a more thoroughgoing identification
with outcasts and criminals—all those who refuse to abide by the rules of
ordinary social interaction. Gonos identifies an "underworld" (146) perspective in Goffman's sociology, seeing in his work "a flagrant deviation
from middle class morality" (146).[61]

From his early account of class passing to his later writing on mental
patients, homosexuals, convicts, alcoholics, and others caught in the gears
of projects of care and reform, Goffman attended to the vulnerability of
the socially marginal. In books such as *Asylums* (1961) and *Stigma* (1963),
he described the fate of those who, branded as different, are no longer able
to control their self-definition or protect themselves from symbolic and
actual violence. In these moments, Goffman demonstrates kinship with
the appreciative studies of deviance that flourished in the 1960s. Howard Becker, the author of *Outsiders* (1963), offers a concise account of the
stance of such revisionist scholars of deviance in his 1967 essay "Whose
Side Are We On?"[62] For Becker, the answer was unequivocal: scholars of
deviance take sides with the marginalized against institutions.[63] Goffman
sometimes joined Becker in this unequivocal embrace of the perspective
of the downcast and the marginalized. In a discussion of the limits of his
methodology in the preface to *Asylums*, for instance, Goffman writes, "To
describe the patient's situation faithfully is necessarily to present a partisan view." As a parenthesis, Goffman adds: "For this last bias I partly excuse myself by arguing that the imbalance is at least on the right side of the
scale, since almost all professional literature on mental patients is written
from the point of view of the psychiatrist, and he, socially speaking, is on
the other side."[64]

Goffman's partisanship for the underdog is complicated by his underworld perspective, his liberalism hollowed out by the profound negativity of his point of view. This underworld or "lumpen" aspect of Goffman's sociology is legible in his identification with the figure of the con

man that parasitizes the middle class, exploiting their avarice to beat them on their own turf. But it is also implicit in Goffman's methodology, in the gaze he turns on the social world. In a 1973 essay, Bennett M. Berger describes Goffman's habit of "exoticizing of the familiar." He writes: "It requires nothing less than the risk of rendering strange and problematic the very assumptions and routines which make ordinary social life possible and worthwhile. It requires the courting of anomie; a glimpse of the Void; a Faustian flirtation in which the Renaissance Devil is replaced by postmodern diagnosticians of madness."[65] This profound negativity makes it very difficult, as Berger argues, to "claim Goffman as a resource for the Left by pointing out his sympathy for the afflicted and the stigmatized, for underdogs like mental patients" (281). In one of his most searing essays, "The Insanity of Place," Goffman indicts the system of collusion that allows individuals to be scapegoated and labeled mad in order to drain off the instability of family and other social systems. He delineates the hellish situation of those so labeled, but these observations are recorded in the service of a larger analytical point about the fragility of social order. "The manic gives up everything a person can be," Goffman writes, "and gives up too the everything we make out of jointly guarded dealings. His doing so . . . reminds us what our everything is, and then reminds us that this everything is not very much."[66] Attending to the fate of the defrauded is a way of apprehending the fraudulence of all social relations; it allows Goffman to undermine the "order of things," to imagine the destruction of norms and the evisceration of personhood. Berger comments: "An *exquisite* morality: he *respects* the rule breaking of the insane because he honors their deviance with the power to threaten meaningful existence" (283, emphasis in original).

The unpredictability of the lumpen classes is notorious, and assessments of their political potential tend to reflect this volatility. Marx and Engels denigrated the lumpen proletariat as ungovernable and reactionary, more anarchic than revolutionary. Such dismissals were common throughout the twentieth century. Yet thinkers such as Mao Zedong, Frantz Fanon, and Herbert Marcuse offered more positive assessments, seeing in absolute dispossession the potential for a transformation of society. The anticolonial and Black power movements embraced the radical and anarchic qualities of the lumpen classes.

Queer theory has tended to align itself with the "nothing left to lose" politics of 1960s radicalism. Yet in reality its politics are split between the liberalism of the civil rights movement and a lumpen appetite for destruc-

tion. Goffman's combination of an *underdog* with an *underworld* view of
the social world has made it difficult to assess his politics. My aim is not to
excuse the shortcomings of Goffman's sociology. By attending to his importance for queer studies, I hope to shed light on some of its most persistent difficulties: false universalism, distance from "real" politics, and the
paradoxes of a community built around shared stigma. I also hope to show
how we have inherited from Goffman the fundamental ambivalence of an
underworld politics.

JUST LOOKING

Goffman's underworld politics has the appearance, for many critics, of
being no politics at all. His inhabitation of a cold, ironic stance toward
the social problems he so copiously diagnosed forces his readers into a
contemplation of moral questions, lit up by the glare of Goffman's intelligence. To address this interpretative crux in his work, scholars have placed
him in the context of his moment, citing the expansion and professionalization of the social sciences in the Cold War in the US. However, this
act of historicizing Goffman can seem almost like an evasion of the more
pointed and irresolvable questions his work raises for us.

There is no doubt that Goffman embodies many of the defining traits
of his moment. His work reflects the technocratic and top-down research
practices of midcentury social science. In his rampant comparison of the
lives of similar experiences lived in radically different contexts, his work is
a cautionary tale about the limits of analogy. He has also left his mark on
all forms of microanalysis. One of Goffman's few areas of demonstrated
influence, this minute form of attention to everyday life also raises difficult
issues about Goffman's method: start small, and you will never get anywhere but small. Furthermore, Goffman's ability to diagram the subtlest
social encounters depends on his ability to assume a monoculture against
which the examples he chooses stand out: White, middle-class America in
the 1950s. In addition, he relies on an even more specific version of American culture, one that is infused with the commercial spirit and characterized by pervasive manipulation and one-upsmanship. In his concern with
the surfaces of social life, Goffman's work appears to be a justification for
a new culture of appearances, advertisement, and soft skills. His emphasis
on the game-like dimensions of social life also recall the strategic thinking
that flourished during this period in military contexts, for instance, in the

playing out of imagined nuclear scenarios. Finally, Goffman's finely tuned observations more generally suggest the collusion between post-WWII human sciences and the Cold War surveillance state.

However, understanding Goffman as a representative of his era hardly accounts for what is most disconcerting in his scholarship, particularly when he addresses the fate of social others, turning his attention to the harshest dimensions of social life as it afflicts mental patients, the disabled, homosexuals, Blacks, and other oppressed minorities. It is Goffman's persistent stance of neutrality in the face of acute suffering that constitutes his most profound challenge to contemporary readers. His cool detachment and the sardonic cast of his prose led critics to see his work as mere provocation, quietism, or worse. In a memoir, former student and sociologist Gary Marx recalls a scene from the Berkeley deviance studies seminar that formed the basis for *Stigma*. Marx writes, "At the end of the last class session a Black student said 'this is all very interesting Professor Goffman but what's the use of it for changing the conditions you describe?' Goffman was visibly shaken. He stood up, slammed the book shut he had open on the desk and said 'I'm not in that business' and stormed out of the room."[67]

Goffman illuminates the violence and unfairness of the world, but fails to propose a solution. Instead, he suggests that it is the special task of the researcher to look on at this problem and do nothing. Bennett Berger describes "the peculiar melancholy of [Goffman's] ironies," the way that his "brilliant excursions often end with . . . a shrug, a twisting of the corners of the mouth through closed lips, an upturned palm of powerlessness: almost as if he were saying, in effect, I don't particularly like it, but that is the way it is."[68] Goffman invokes the narrow professionalism of his role, casting himself as a mere observer and ceding his authority to change anything in the world. Of course, Goffman does wield power; however, it is strictly within the limits of the sociological profession, or more broadly, print culture and public opinion. Goffman is careful—for many academics reading him today, too careful—to distinguish between the realm of scholarship and the realm of activism. In another anecdote reported by Marx, Goffman quips, "A university is a place to pick up your mail" (658). This purely bureaucratic notion of the university was belied by the significance of this institution in student protest and broader social change during the 1960s. But it is also belied by the transformative power of Goffman's own scholarship, a power that he not only never claimed, but refused to entertain as a possibility. Goffman's descriptions of small social worlds (particularly his work on total institutions and stigma) did have demonstrable effects in the world.

Characteristically, it is Goffman himself who offers the most damning assessment of his scholarship. In the introduction to *Frame Analysis*, Goffman not only disavows the possibility that his work would have social or political effects, he also implicates himself as a voyeur and a conservative, someone contributing to the maintenance of society as it is. This chilling passage, dropped into the middle of a statement of method, is much too weird to count as an assertion of scientific neutrality:

> Of course, it can be argued that to focus on the nature of personal ex-periencing—with the implication this can have for giving equally seri-ous consideration to all matters that might momentarily concern the individual—is itself a standpoint with marked political implications, and that these are conservative ones. The analysis developed does not catch at the differences between the advantaged and disadvantaged classes and can be said to direct attention away from such matters. I think that is true. I can only suggest that he who would combat false consciousness and awaken people to their true interests has much to do, because the sleep is very deep. And I do not intend here to provide a lullaby but merely to sneak in and watch the way the people snore. (13–14)

Goffman addresses the political critiques of microsociology, acknowledg-ing the critique both of its focus on everyday experience and on the even-ness of its attention ("to *all* matters that might momentarily concern the individual"). Goffman admits that close observation and description of everyday experience is not likely to lead to social transformation. He in fact suggests that it might, as in Marcuse's sense of affirmative culture, keep it in place. But typically, Goffman's aims are wider and more corro-sive, for he suggests that that *no* form of academic scholarship is equal to that task of remaking the world. Rather, adopting a tone of an ironic and embittered onlooker, Goffman suggests that the spell of ideology is so pro-found as to be virtually unbreakable.

This attitude toward the social world does not appear promising, to say the least, for a progressive or transformative criticism. It is precisely trans-formation, or its possibility, that appears to be systematically blocked in Goffman's writing. The indictment of Goffman's politics are hard to evade here. However, keeping in view his identification with the underworld, if not properly the underdog, I think we can also understand this moment as an embrace, however uncomfortable, of the perspective of the stigmatized. This is a form of rough justice on Goffman's part, because in taking up this perspective, he actually loses the distance of the professional critic, adopting the stance of the bare-knuckled boxer against the ropes. That is to say, his account of his own activity as a scholar is stripped of idealization and liberal bromides of education, reform, or progress. Goffman suffused his sociological writing with the bitterness of the "socially disgruntled," refusing easy solutions to intractable problems. His focus on the situation can be understood as potentially liberatory, because it suggests that the world can be made over in each instant; but in fact, what he shows us is that stigma need not be a permanent brand because it is enforced again and again, both through naked aggression and through the condescension, demands for reassurance, and pigeonholing that are the foundations of liberal tolerance. Goffman refuses to smooth over what is jagged in social life, and remains fixed on the indignities and compromises that depend on the "kind of person one is available to be." Working on the terrain of midcentury liberalism, Goffman exposed its dark underside, suggesting how little is to be gained from accommodation to the existing social order.

This refusal of liberalism, although implicit, links Goffman to the field of queer studies, as does his minimal account of the grounds for solidarity among the stigmatized. Goffman did not sympathize with his research subjects. Rather, as he suggests in a posthumously published lecture on ethnographic methods, he derived his understanding through a virtual experience of others' "life circumstances." Describing the practice of participant observation, he suggests that immersing yourself in the situation of your informants is a way of "tuning your body up." Only in close proximity to your informants are you in a position "to note their gestural, visual, bodily response to what's going on around them and you're empathetic enough— because you've been taking the same crap they've been taking—to sense what it is they're responding to."[69] Goffman's empathy is situation specific and literal minded, a quasi-mechanical entailment of a robust practice of microanalysis. His empathy depends on spatial proximity, gestural imitation, and the virtual experience of bad treatment. Goffman's anger about "what life does to" (125) people is unfeigned, because his practice involved letting it be done to him too. But the fate of that anger was unpredictable, since, as Goffman insisted, it was not anchored in more permanent conviction or in a vision of a transformed society. One might just as easily pass this crap on to the next guy as discover its underlying causes and put an end to it. But this bodily practice of identification does not pretend to an understanding of other people's real feelings. The underdogs and outsiders in *Stigma* are not shielded from the violence of the social world. But they are safe, at least, from Goffman's pity.

2 · Just Watching

When I see how, by still continuing our observations on gulls, we see
new things time and again (new only in that we had not noticed them
before, not because they are rare occurrences) and when I remember
how infinitely more complex Man is than our gulls, I am fully convinced
that even the best students of human behavior are even observationally
still at the beginning.

Nikolaas Tinbergen to S. J. and Corinne Hutt, April 11, 1970[1]

In September 1954, the Josiah Macy Jr. Foundation sponsored the first of
five conferences on "group processes" in Ithaca, New York. The foundation, which had previously organized the now better-known series of conferences on cybernetics, brought together prominent European and North
American scholars in the natural and human sciences to address communication across cultures and across the human-animal divide. Among the
participants was Nikolaas Tinbergen, the Dutch biologist credited, along
with Konrad Lorenz, with founding the field of ethology, or the biological
study of animal behavior. Early in Tinbergen's presentation, the psychiatrist John P. Spiegel interrupted him to ask for clarification about the term
"ethology."[2] Tinbergen replied that the word refers to the behavior or the
"habits" of animals, adding, "we in Europe preferred it to psychology" because "we wanted to stress that we started from an observable behavior."
The biologist Ernst Mayr jumped in to expand on Tinbergen's definition:

> There are two Greek words which, transcribed into English, are spelled
> ethos. The word ethology for animal psychology comes from ἔθος the
> habit, the custom. Since the Greek word is spelled with an epsilon, the
> word ethology must be pronounced with a short e, as in ethnology. The
> word ἦθος is closely related, but more often used in the plural to mean
> character. Perhaps it is this word ἦθος which gave rise to ethics.[3]

Tinbergen's collaborator Lorenz chimed in to suggest that ethos can
be understood as "what is intrinsically inherent to, or a property of something" (76). Anthropologist Margaret Mead followed up, noting, "for quite

some time the word 'ethos' has been used in English literature, to denote the prevailing tone or spirit of a group." She remarked that she and Gregory Bateson had planned to pursue the study of culture under the name "ethology" when this other usage "burst on our attention." Acknowledging the confusion, she landed finally on a personal difficulty: "Frequently, in the proofreading of my books, 'ethology' would be changed to 'ethnology' because it was Margaret Mead, the anthropologist, writing" (77).

In the preface to *Group Processes*, conference organizer Frank Fremont-Smith argued that significant "break-throughs . . . depend upon the integration of insights and technical skills derived from widely disparate areas of scientific investigation."[4] The five volumes of *Group Processes* transcripts attest to a remarkable diversity of fields and approaches, evident in this conversation about ethology as the study of behavior, character, ethics, and social groups. Across these meetings, researchers switched back and forth between animal and human worlds with disconcerting facility, weighing the difference between character and habit, or essence and behavior. The attempt to "integrate insights" across disciplines at the Macy events resulted in a dizzying back and forth between methods, frameworks, and examples that made short work of large swaths of human history. Speculating freely about the relation between animal habits and human ethics can strike us now as deeply troubling, both because of the failure to reckon with the complexities of culture and politics, but also because such leaps across species were important to the development of sociobiology later in the century. But the discussions at the Macy conferences represent a different moment in this history. Alongside the problematic anthropocentrism and analogical thinking in the "group processes" conferences, Tinbergen and his fellow researchers explore observational methods that rarely yield the kinds of claims about human nature made later in sociobiology.[5] Attention to visible behavior, and to concrete forms of interaction and communication, was developed in ethology and was later taken up in the human sciences. The traffic went both ways, however, since ethologists such as Tinbergen and Lorenz developed their account of communicative behavior under the influence of the social sciences, practicing a version of "animal sociology."[6] These researchers, whether they were studying animals or humans, devoted themselves to recording and describing small-scale scenes of social interaction. Writing about the influence of Ray Birdwhistell, the inventor of kinesics (a notational system for the recording and analysis of gesture), Martha Davis has called this period (1955–75) the "golden era of 'naturalistic observation.'"[7]

Often employing new recording and playback technologies, microanalytic researchers spent hours transcribing the smallest details of their subjects' actions (gesture, spacing, posture, and eye behavior).

Ethological methods were used to analyze communication in both animal and human worlds. But rather than extrapolate from observations of animal behavior to conclusions about human nature (as in sociobiology), researchers in "human ethology" applied methods designed for the observation of animals to humans. This distinction is crucial. Human ethology made use of extended observation, conducted in situ, in the field rather than in the laboratory. This research centered on visible action, or, in the words of Richard W. Burkhardt, "patterns of behavior" that could be perceived and analyzed by a well-placed observer, a matter of physics rather than metaphysics. In confining their accounts to visible behavior, and avoiding speculation about what lay behind it, ethological researchers took sides in what psychologist William R. Uttal, writing in 1999, called the twentieth century's "war between mentalism and behaviorism."[8] When Tinbergen, in his contribution to the first conference, named his paper "Psychology and Ethology as Supplementary Parts of a Science of Behavior," he was being conciliatory.[9] He and Lorenz were in a battle with the field of comparative psychology for control of animal behavior studies, which they saw as given to ungrounded claims about animal motivation, experience, and cognition, or in the contested terms of the Macy discussions, character. They insisted that animal research should be ethological: it should base its conclusions on observations of behavior (habits) in wild settings (customary places, or habitats). For the participants in the Macy conferences, and for us, the distinction is ethical.[10]

I borrow the title of this chapter ("Just Watching") from the concept of "just reading" that Sharon Marcus develops in her 2007 book *Between Women*. Marcus defines "just reading" as attending to what is "manifest on [a text's] surface"—in her argument, intimate relations between women in the Victorian novel. The "justness" of just reading refers to its minimalism (just read what is there) and its ability to see what other critics have ignored (and thus do justice to the text).[11] In proposing that we understand mid-century observational research as a minimalist and just way of looking, I am contravening some fundamental agreements in the humanities: about the ideology of objectivity; about the primacy of experience; and about the value of empathy as a tool for research. For this reason, "just watching," like the "ethics of observation," will appear to some as a contradiction in terms. To make an argument on behalf of the ethics of observation during the Cold War may seem especially perverse. In this period, observation is closely linked with surveillance, whether by satellite, hidden camera, or government dossier. However, observation was employed for many other less nefarious purposes.

Alongside concerns about observation and its links to surveillance, microanalytic researchers' focus on behavior in the context of the human sciences raises thorny ethical questions. To treat people as behaving organisms can be understood as an act of objectification that denies meaning and intention. In the strongest version of this argument, nothing done by a human being should be understood as behavior; it is always symbolic activity.[12] The refusal to speculate about what is, in behaviorist B. F. Skinner's words, "inside the skin" can look like a positivist outrage.[13] However, it can also be understood as a kind of reflexivity, a tactful refusal of projection, and an important brake on researchers' "will to knowledge." If my training in literary studies, psychoanalysis, and poststructuralist theory alerts me to the dangers of reduction and objectification, my queer training draws me to instances of the displacement of the subject. The attempt to empty out the self has been an important strategy in queer representation and thought since at least the end of the nineteenth century. As Eve Sedgwick has argued, the turning of a disciplinary gaze on sexuality entailed the emergence of the closet as an epistemological form. Since the end of the nineteenth century, silence and evasion have been crucial tools in frustrating the incursions of psychiatry, medicine, and law. Although Tinbergen's account of nesting behavior in gulls might seem distant from the epistemology of the closet, his refusal to conjure imagined inner states and, instead, to depend wholly on observation was motivated by an impulse to curb surveillance rather than to extend it. In avoiding speculation about the interior life of the animals he studied, Tinbergen sought to shield them from his own identification and thus to maintain in them what it might not be an exaggeration to call privacy.

Annamarie Jagose makes a related argument in *Orgasmology*: she claims that, although behaviorist psychology was used to cruel and violent ends in the "treatment" of homosexuality, its focus on the adaptability of behavior resonates with queer accounts of what she calls "sexuality without a subject."[14] Without excusing the harms carried out in the name of behaviorism, it is possible to trace links between behavioral or observational approaches and projects in queer ethics that attempt to render the self inoperative or unfindable. The queer refusal of personhood has an important twentieth-century history, one that ramped up alongside the consolidation of newly visible and public forms of identity. Strategies for escaping grids of intelligibility and refusing the imperatives of confession have a surprising echo in postwar behavioral research.[15]

In this chapter, I consider two examples of observational research on human behavior from the postwar social sciences. First, I consider Tinbergen's turn to "human ethology" late in his career in the study he undertook with his wife, Elisabeth Tinbergen, of children with autism. Then I turn to Laud Humphreys's uptake of observational methods in his 1970 study of sex in public bathrooms, *Tearoom Trade: Impersonal Sex in Public Places*. The research methods of both of these projects have been the subject of extensive critique. Both depend on research conducted with nonspeaking subjects; they point to the asymmetries of power, status, and knowledge that structure all fieldwork and raise stark concerns about the ethics of speaking for and about others.[16] Both Tinbergen and Humphreys have been criticized for objectifying human beings and, in the case of Humphreys's work in *Tearoom Trade*, for directly violating ethical standards of research. My aim is not to exonerate these scholars or their projects. Instead, I explore their use of observational methods and argue for the utility of this means of approaching vulnerable or stigmatized subjects. Analyzing human activity as behavior can drain it of significance, complexity, and intention.[17] But in the case of behavior understood as disordered or repellant, such approaches may also drain it of the stigma that makes it hard to see in the first place.

ACROSS THE HUMAN-ANIMAL DIVIDE

Niko Tinbergen is primarily known for his scientific and popular writing on the social behavior of insects, fish, and gulls. When, in 1973, he was awarded the Nobel Prize (along with Lorenz and Karl von Frisch), he surprised his audience by giving a speech titled "Ethology and Stress Diseases," which focused on childhood autism and the benefits of the Alexander technique.[18] Before his Nobel speech, Tinbergen had mused privately about the implications of his research for human society and conduct. Unlike Lorenz, however, he tended to confine his public statements strictly to discussions of animal behavior. Nonetheless, Tinbergen's research had drawn criticism a few years earlier in an incident that Tinbergen's biographer, Hans Kruuk, has called "one of the first salvos in the acrimonious 'sociobiology debate.'"[19] A 1969 speech at Simon Fraser University was repeatedly disrupted by activists who later published a bulletin denouncing the "fascist ideas" of this "notorious biologist": "During his talk on sticklebacks and seagulls," they wrote, "[Tinbergen] emphasized all the fascist ideas such as innate aggression, instinctive urge for territory (private property), need for living space (lebensraum), etc., the same ideas which can be found in Hitler's *Mein Kampf*. Despite the fact that Tinbergen repeatedly cautioned against extrapolating the results of animal experiments to man, he ignored his warning and proceeded to do just that" (cited in Kruuk, 296). Tinbergen took the Nazi comparison hard: he had spent two years in a German POW camp during World War II, imprisoned along with many other professors for their solidarity with Jewish colleagues fired from the University of Leiden.[20] Still, by addressing the applicability of animal behavior research to humans, Tinbergen raised alarms. His early work on animal ethology was closer to Lorenz's in centering the question of instinct. He did not make claims about human nature based on human-animal analogies, however; instead, he advocated the extension of observational methods developed for the study of animals to humans.

There are good reasons to resist the association of autistic people with nonhuman animals, as there are to resist the (also common) association of autistic people with machines, computers, and other nonliving things. Claims for the appearance of autism before its emergence as a diagnosis in the early twentieth century often include animal-human comparisons: one thinks of figures such as the Wild Boy of Aveyron as well as "wolf children" supposedly raised in the wild.[21] Leo Kanner's defining research on infantile autism features the case of Elaine C., who shows intense interest in animals but who is also said to display "animal wildness," for instance, when she "mimics" wild creatures by "walking on all fours and making strange noises."[22] Interest in animals and attributions of animal-like behavior appear throughout the literature of autism.[23] Yet more recently, interest in animals—and, in particular, acuity in observing and interpreting their behavior—has been central to the development of research, activism, and textual production by people with autism. In particular, the contributions of animal ethologist Temple Grandin to the design of livestock handling systems continue the association between autism and animality. In recent work, this link does not figure as an externally imposed judgment but rather as a claimed affinity.[24] The reassessment of human-animal comparisons in recent critical cultural studies extends beyond disability studies. If, in the 1960s and 1970s, critical intellectuals and activists saw comparisons between humans and animals as dehumanizing, a step on the way to slavery and genocide, the situation has changed utterly today. The rise of the environmental humanities, and particularly its focus on human entanglement with the natural world, has made the investigation of relations with animals central to rethinking questions of sustainability. Scholars have pursued challenges to human sovereignty through the question of the animal in queer, feminist, and critical race studies. What once looked like a failure to accord dignity to human beings now looks like a critique of the deployment of the category of the human to do violence to the planet and its inhabitants, both human and animal.[25]

Tinbergen's preoccupation with the natural world did not align him with Nazi ideology any more than it made him an avatar of contemporary animal studies. Tinbergen saw himself above all as a naturalist: as Kruuk makes clear, he was drawn early and often to wild landscapes, and was fascinated by the activities of the birds and fish and insects he found there. Tinbergen's characteristic humility is in evidence as he explains his predilection for "watching and wondering." He used this phrase as the title of an autobiographical sketch he wrote in the 1980s, in which he credits his early love of sports and the "*visible* natural world" with his success in ethology.[26] Tinbergen saw ethology as a passionate hobby that he had managed to turn into a job. "I like to be in the open," he wrote. "I am perhaps also very lazy: I like to watch animals, not to kill them."[27] The significant point of comparison for Tinbergen was not hunting but rather the rigorous pursuit of scientific knowledge. Tinbergen compared himself unfavorably to his brother Jan Tinbergen, who won the Nobel Prize for Economics in 1969, and to Lorenz, who contributed more to the conceptual foundations of ethology. It was the close connection of Tinbergen's work with Lorenz's that invited ideological critique, because Lorenz was more invested in working out questions of human nature through animal observation and had argued in print for the compatibility of evolutionary theory and National Socialism, based on the importance for both of the concept of race.[28] Ethology bears the traces of Lorenz's thought, but Tinbergen's approach was quite different. The noninterventionist methods that Tinbergen favored situated him in a tradition that included field naturalists, taxonomists, and ecologists, rather than evolutionary biologists. Also, to the extent that Tinbergen did extrapolate from his work in the field to questions of human life, he tended toward wry observation on small-scale behaviors rather than ringing pronouncements on the fate of the German *Volk*. Tinbergen was known for his observational abilities, but he rated his powers as a theorist low. In a letter, Tinbergen writes: "Lorenz tended . . . to sketch things in broad, sweeping outlines, whereas I filled in the grand outline with, if you wish, the details."[29]

Tinbergen's self-understanding is linked to the fate of natural history across the twentieth century. What had once been an epic project to identify and classify all of God's creation, nursed in the heart of empire, became by the twentieth century an odd footnote, the province of amateurs.[30] Charles Elton's 1927 book *Animal Ecology* is generally understood to mark the transition from eighteenth- and nineteenth-century forms of natural history to the twentieth-century emphasis on experiment, modeling, and quantification. Elton cleared the way for a newly professional field, defining ecology as "scientific natural history" (1), and bemoaning the "mania" for collecting and identifying specimens that yield analyses "of less value than the paper upon which they are written" (2).[31] Elton agreed that the extensive efforts of local natural history societies, collectors, and prescientific field naturalists were foundational to the work of ecologists in providing them the material for classifying animals, but wanted to maintain a strict distinction between amateur description and professional analysis. He looked forward to a future in which the task of the systematist (or taxonomist) would "become more and more that of the man who identifies specimens for other people" (165).

The situation of interdependence and rivalry that Elton describes persisted throughout the twentieth century and continues into the twenty-first, with intermittent skirmishes. The small scale and time-consuming nature of descriptive research make it especially vulnerable in the moment of climate change: mathematical modeling and big data seem more obviously suited to the scale of the catastrophe we are facing. And yet ecologists argue that descriptive research is as important as ever: they argue that intimate familiarity with organisms is necessary to promote the goal of conservation and that large-scale models do not account effectively for human intervention. In a 2005 article, for example, ecologist Harry W. Greene argues for the need to balance large-scale modeling with "descriptive ecological and ethological research," citing "a knowledge gap that is so large that, for most species, even in the best-studied regions on Earth, we cannot specify the most basic aspects of their biology."[32] He suggests that, while individual organisms might seem negligible in relation to larger patterns in nature, organisms "embody genetics, development, morphology, physiology and behavior, and they are the fundamental components of populations, communities, and ecosystems" (24). Because of the knowledge that is contained within organisms, gathering "carefully recorded observations" (25) can be as significant as theoretical and conceptual research. Still, although there is evidence of a resurgence of natural history methods, descriptive research remains devalued and underfunded, adjunct to what is seen as the more serious and consequential work undertaken at a global scale.

The anthropologist Anna Tsing, borrowing from natural history, argues that, in the era of climate disaster, attention to small-scale ecologies still matters. Against the background of massive environmental destruction, survival depends on minor practices carried out in marginal spaces. In her 2015 book *The Mushroom at the End of the World*, Tsing considers the "arts of living on a damaged planet," refusing both progressive views of history and melancholy despair about the future.[33] Chief among these arts of living is the practice of noticing. "The curiosity I advocate," Tsing writes, "follows multiple temporalities, revitalizing description and imagination. This is not a simple empiricism, in which the world invents its own categories. Instead, agnostic about where we are going, we might look for what has been ignored"—for "world-making projects," both "human and not-human."[34] Tsing opposes natural history to neoclassical economics and population genetics, two fields that profit from the scalability of their object of study. "*Noticing* is unnecessary to track these unchanging individuals . . . mathematics can replace natural history and ethnography" (28). She is looking for methods attuned to what she calls "the indeterminate encounter." Using a mix of ethnography and natural history, Tsing tracks the lifeways of Mien foragers in the mountains of Oregon and the intricate, nonscalable ecologies of matsutake mushrooms. She argues that foraging in a complex forest ecology can teach us "how to look around rather than ahead" (22).

DOING IT IN THE FIELD

Natural history exerted a powerful influence on the field of sociology at midcentury, when techniques of recording and exhaustive description were widely employed to observe human behavior and interaction. These modes of observation had their origins in Chicago school sociology, particularly in the insistence of Robert Park and his colleagues on fieldwork and community studies. But during the postwar period, researchers in the social sciences looked increasingly to the example of ethologists, and vice versa.

In accounts of group behavior, bodily comportment, and nonverbal communication, students of social life borrowed from methods developed to study nonhuman animals. Such research, conducted in situ and attending to the shaping influence of environment, offered a robust account of both the individual struggle for survival and the "social" behavior of groups. Across all this work, Tinbergen's ethos of "just watching" was crucial. What Tinbergen had referred to as laziness was in fact a rigorous doctrine of nonintervention, both practical and epistemological. Sociologists and anthropologists in the postwar period developed a concept of "naturalistic" observation.[35] Naturalistic research opposed the experimental ethos of behaviorism; adopting the attitude of natural historians toward laboratory research, it avoided changing the parameters of the behavior it sought to analyze. Naturalistic observation also distinguished itself from participant observation, adopting positions that would allow for heightened perception rather than immersion in the stream of events. These researchers wanted to watch animals, not to kill them.

Throughout his work, Tinbergen celebrates the art and science of just watching, training himself to look around rather than ahead. In his writing on method, he urges researchers to spend time watching the whole scene before they turn their attention to specific activities. In *Social Behaviour in Animals* (1953), Tinbergen's contribution to the field of animal sociology, he relates a cautionary tale about a young researcher intent on a quantitative experiment to be conducted on stickleback fish. Eager to get results, he focuses on the behavior in question, ignoring everything else.

> I was once visited by a keen student from abroad who wanted to receive training in sociological work. He arrived with one very special problem in mind: he wanted to be trained in the technique of the experimental study of releasers. I tried in vain to convince him that he could better begin with a broad reconnaissance of a species; then let him have his way, and he started to count the number of bites aimed by a territory-owning male Three-spined Stickleback at a red model as compared with a silvery model. His results seemed to be at variance with our previous work: the red models received only slightly more bites than the silver models. On doing the tests again it was found that the fish showed several signs of hostility other than actual bites (such as raising the dorsal spines, and making incipient attacks) and that these were released by red models much more often than by the silver models. Having skipped the observational study of aggressive behaviour he had been unable to

recognize and interpret these hostile movements. He then returned to just watching, and when, after some days, he resumed his tests, he got very clear-cut results. (130)

Despite his mild manner and his suggestion that he is helpless in the face of attack ("I . . . let him have his way"), Tinbergen's schooling of this keen young man might itself be seen as an act of territorial aggression. However, his methodological recommendations across his career are remarkably consistent, and Tinbergen is often as hard on himself as he is on others. The itinerary, he insists, should be determined by the setting, by the species under consideration, and by the range of behavior available for view. It is impossible to isolate and study a single behavior without familiarity with the broader patterns of activity displayed by a particular species—and there are, Tinbergen suggests, no shortcuts to acquiring that familiarity. This is a crucial and rewarding phase of research, but it requires time, patience, and sensitivity. It also requires a willingness to give up the gratifications of quick results.

Tinbergen's writing is filled with examples of heroically extended acts of "just watching." His popular book *Curious Naturalists* begins with an account of his early failures as a zoologist, or a biologist who studies the morphology and evolutionary history of animals. Instead, Tinbergen was strongly attracted to the life of the naturalist, and preferred spending his days at the seaside rather than in the laboratory. Because his work took him to the field and gave him endless opportunities to observe animals interacting in their habitats, he based his conclusions on behavior rather than biological structure. The book's first chapter, "The Bee-Hunters of Hulshorst," describes the coastal area of Holland where he had spent time as a child and where he undertook his first natural history studies of wasps. The landscape, a mix of scrub pines, heather, and sandy soil, is, fortunately, sparsely populated because it is seen as "good for nothing" by most.[36] But Tinbergen, familiar with the place since childhood and looking at it with a naturalist's eye, addresses the reader directly, warning her not to fall in with the general view of Hulshorst: "But don't think that this country was dull—far from it!" (13). Long walks reveal "many hidden treasures" (13) including honey buzzards and woodcock, edible mushrooms, and roe deer. "The Scots pine plantations, at first glance so monotonous, were full of fascinating creatures, many of them beautifully camouflaged" (13–14), and "even the bare sandy stretches had a charm of their own" (15). The charm of Hulshorst is elusive, requiring close and extended attention on the part of the child, the naturalist, and, Tinbergen suggests, the reader. That charm, furthermore, is fitful; the landscape sets the terms for interactions with humans rather than the other way around, because it is *moody*: "We lived in that country long enough to see it in a great variety of circumstances and moods, and gradually every part of it acquired significance; the whole area became charged with our experiences, which I shall never forget" (16).

Many of these experiences involve sitting for days at a time watching while nothing happens. Having discovered an area of a high concentration of wasps, Tinbergen begins watching them, observing their homing and hunting behavior. But the work proceeds in fits and starts and is filled with many dull periods. He writes, "I decided to spend a season watching the hunting wasps. This was easier said than done. There were a couple of thousand wasps about, it is true. But a first reconnaissance showed that they did their hunting over a very wide area, half a square mile or so. In spite of hours watching at the nearest apiary, I never saw a wasp come anywhere near the hives" (48). Throughout his research, Tinbergen constantly struggles to find feasible alternatives to pure observation given his realization that "it would not be possible, or at least would cost an amount of time out of all proportion, to go and watch the hunting wasps in the field" (49). Tinbergen goes on to find the wasps' hunting grounds and to successfully observe their feeding behavior, using a combination of methods, some observational and some interventionist—for instance, when he rearranged features of the landscape to see if wasps could still find their way home. But the core of his practice is field study, or watching and waiting, which takes time. At the end of the section on hunting behavior, Tinbergen writes, "It had taken us five summers to build up this picture of the life of the bee-killer—admittedly a long time. But this type of work always proceeds slowly, with setbacks caused by bad weather, lack of control over animals living in the wild, and so many other handicaps inherent to field work. Yet it would have been impossible to do these things in the laboratory; it was a matter of doing it in the field or not doing it at all" (56).

"Doing it in the field" means acknowledging the primacy of the landscape and letting the animals' patterns of behavior determine the research program. In this slow, painstaking work, the researcher does not set the conditions of the study—rather, his objects do. Nonetheless, it is still the scientist who extracts knowledge from his surroundings, rather than the other way around, a fact that gives Tinbergen pause in *Curious Naturalists*. He suggests that the work of the researcher is to monitor not only the natural world but also himself, even going on to worry over the compromised pleasures this practice affords.

> While engaged in such work, it is always worth observing oneself as well as the animals, and to do it as critically and as detachedly as possible—a tall order. I have often wondered why the outcome of such a test delighted me so much. A rationalist would probably like to assume that it was the increased predictability resulting from such a test. This was a factor of considerable importance, I am sure. But a more important factor still (not only to me, but to many other people I have watched in this situation) is of a less dignified type: people enjoy, they relish, the satisfaction of their desire for power. The truth of this was obvious, for instance, in people who enjoyed seeing the wasps misled without caring much for the intellectual question whether they used landmarks or not. I am further convinced that even my joy of gaining insight was not often very pure either; it was mixed with pride at having success with the tests. (29)

Tinbergen is right to suggest that a critical and self-reflexive view of one's own observational habits is a "tall order"—particularly in a situation of stratified expertise and authority. The naturalist watches, records, manipulates, and analyzes the behavior of the wasps; while the wasps may be said to watch his behavior and even to manipulate it, they do not record, analyze, write up, or publish the results. Nonetheless, Tinbergen imagines the field as a multidimensional space where the observer observes himself, as well as others, noting his own fleeting emotions of triumph, pride, disappointment, mastery, and failure. Although this intensive self-reflexivity does not void the imbalance of power that defines the space of the field, it makes that imbalance central and unavoidable. Despite his commitment to minimalist observation, Tinbergen did not see the field as a transparent or neutral space. Instead, it constituted a site for endless reflection on the ethics of attention, objectivity, and scientific curiosity.

WATCHING AND WONDERING

At the end of his Nobel address, Tinbergen reflects on the connection between his thoughts on childhood autism and the Alexander technique: "What have these two examples in common? First of all they stress the importance for medical science of open-minded observation—of 'watching and wondering.' This basic scientific method is still too often looked down on by those blinded by the glamor of apparatus, by the prestige of tests, and by the temptation to turn to drugs" (26). Observation was at the heart of Tinbergen's contribution to research on autism. In *Early Childhood Autism: An Ethological Approach*, the first of two books he coauthored with his wife, Elisabeth, they argue that ethology is useful not only for the study of children but for the entire field of psychology, which makes "surprisingly little use" of "the basic scientific method of straightforward observation" (13).[37] With its emphasis on observations of communicative behavior in natural settings, ethology promises to offer new insights about autism to the "psychopathological profession" (5). If Tinbergen criticized the dominance of experimental psychology, and proposed a naturalistic approach to problems in psychic life, the research that he conducted with Elisabeth offered a model of what such an approach might look like. They avoided the laboratory and the kinds of knowledge produced in experimental settings, choosing instead to go into naturally occurring environments and look around. While living and working in Oxford, they turned the city into a field for their research, venturing out into ordinary social spaces populated by their research subjects: women and children.

Their research is characterized by a gendered division of labor and resources. At the opening of *Autistic Children: New Hope for a New Cure* (1983), they write, "In our studies, started in 1970, we pooled our experiences as a lifelong student of animal behavior (N.T.) and as a lifelong childwatcher and childminder (E.A.T.) and found that this dual expertise helped us to understand a great deal about autism that experts in the field have so far been unable to explain" (2). They write, "E.A.T. has found that three semi-controlled situations in particular are admirably suited to the type of observations required: (1) meeting a mother and child during shopping in supermarkets, when, riding on a shopping cart, a child will unexpectedly come face to face with the stranger-cum-observer; (2) sitting near a mother and child on a bus: and (3) either visiting, or being visited by a family with young children" (13). Although they conceived Oxford as a field rather than a laboratory, and sought to intervene as little as possible in the scenes they observed, their choice of settings can hardly be understood as random (or truly naturalistic). The Tinbergens' account of their field sites suggests a confusion of the ordinary and the random and ignores the difference between natural and social settings. The Tinbergens' research on autism, unlike Niko's research on gulls, was marked by class, gender, racial, and national factors that determined its results. This failure to grapple with what is cultural in human parenting is only one of this research's flaws. Nonetheless, the Tinbergens' attention to behavior led them to reject a pathological view of children: they argued that the behaviors labeled autistic were on a continuum with the behaviors exhibited by other children in unfamiliar and threatening social situations.

In her article "'Birdwatching and Baby-Watching': Niko and Elisabeth Tinbergen's Ethological Approach to Autism," Chloe Silverman describes how the Tinbergens became involved in autism research as a result of their friendship with the child psychologists John and Corinne Hutt.[38] In 1970, the Hutts sent Tinbergen a copy of their book *Direct Observation and Measurement of Behavior*, a study of child behavior that was deeply influenced by ethology and which used methods of systematic observation, counting, and film recording and analysis in naturalistic settings rather than the methods of experimental psychology. The Hutts focused on the visible components of autism, attending to gestures and activities, experimenting with different recording and notational systems to try to capture what they call the "behavioral repertoire" of the child. The Hutts begin *Direct Observation* by addressing the resistance they anticipate to their use of an ethological approach. Their aim is to "show how recent thinking in ethology, the biological study of animal behavior, may contribute significantly to an objective, quantitative and descriptive science of behavior. The conjunction of *descriptive* and *science* will be an anathema to many experimental psychologists, but we maintain that for certain problems (and for the study of certain subjects) direct observation of the free behavior of the organism is the method par excellence."[39] If such an "objective, quantitative" study of behavior seems unlikely, for those who find the very concept of human behavior as an objective fact nonsensical or worse, the Hutts make clear that from the perspective of the science of psychology, ethology appears insufficiently rigorous. They also make clear that their attempt to objectively describe human activity comes not out of naive positivism but rather out of an attempt to deal ethically with the fallibility of knowledge. They cite a classic study in ethology, commenting, "One way in which the ethological approach differs from other observational approaches . . . is immediately clear: The report should not be in terms of human thoughts and desires but in terms of observables and activity statements. It may be argued that to eschew anthropomorphism when recording the behavior of anthropomorphs is an artificial exercise. The problem remains however, that we are simply not adept at inferring the motivations, intentions and emotions even of other adults" (15–16).

Early Childhood Autism begins with an inventory of the criteria used
for the diagnosis of autism, a list that is punctuated by discussions of im-
pairment and abnormality. For the Tinbergens, this attribution of organic
pathology is linked to a diagnostic framework that ignores the manifest
behavior of the children. They cite the Hutts' claim that the behavior of
autistic children is "strikingly similar to that of normal children" and go
on to argue, "all phenomena described of autistic children can often be
observed in normal children" (11). The focus on visible behavior universal-
izes autism for the Tinbergens. They see a continuity between "normal"
childhood performances of shyness, withdrawal, and aversion and those
behaviors labeled as characteristic of autism; they even go on to describe
all children's behavior as "temporarily autistic" (21). The constructionist,
universalizing view of autism pursued by the Tinbergens emerges out of
their focus on visible behavior and adaptation to environment and their
relative disinterest in diagnosis or deep psychological motive.

The hinge between the research on animal behavior and the research
on children in *Early Childhood Autism* is articulated via a discussion of
avoidant behavior and motivational conflict. Explaining Tinbergen's prior
research on gulls (primarily *The Herring Gull's World* [1953]), they argue
that communication and signaling emerge from the conflict of different
behavioral systems. For example, gulls engaging in courtship and mating
interactions alternate between approach and avoidance behavior. One
cannot characterize their actions as either fearful or aggressive; rather,
what is important to capture, according to the Tinbergens, is the "momen-
tary, fluctuating motivational state of the subjects" as well as "the way in
which the behavior of each of them is affected by that of the other" (23).
Because of the complexity of the behavior of each gull as well as the dynamism of the interaction as a whole in its context, the researcher must develop a mobile attention that can take in the entire scene rather than focusing on a particular action. Recalling a film that Tinbergen made around
this time (*Signals for Survival*), the Tinbergens suggest that film can help
to capture the complexity of events, the multiple channels of behavior that
take place at one time, and can allow attention to details that might evade
notice in a first viewing. Since motivation is overt and visible, *seeing* the
behavior is the most important way of understanding it—one need not indulge in guesswork about hidden motives and desires—and in that sense
the camera is an ideal observer. But the ultimate goal for the Tinbergens
is to cultivate ever more responsive, inclusive, and flexible forms of attention (and on these grounds they often argue against the "mechanizing of

observational, analytical and interpretive work" [24]) that can keep the researcher from "wondering while he observes."

Considering the complexity of motivation in approach and avoidance behavior in gulls, the Tinbergens pursue the animal-human comparison, writing that "an encounter between a child and a strange adult creates in the child a state of motivational conflict that is very similar to that described for female gulls in the pair-formation stage, except that of course in children the approach tendency is not sexually motivated" (26–27). Children manifest the same fluctuation between engagement and timidity, approach and withdrawal, and the Tinbergens describe avoidance behavior in concrete, overt terms ("keeping distance or moving away, avoiding eye contact, various degrees of turning away the head, various degrees of closing the eyes, etc." [27]). As in Tinbergen's analysis of gulls, they emphasize multiple systems of behavior and the irreducible qualities of concrete scenes of interaction. To underline the existence of diverse and independently functioning systems within the child, they offer an extended metaphor in which they compare the withdrawn child to a car that won't start:

> It has to be stressed once more that few practices have blocked understanding of the behaviour of these children more than the thoughtless, but unfortunately fashionable use of general terms such as "perceptual malfunctioning," "quantity of input," and "general arousal." Those who apply these terms are often not aware that they are discarding and even contradicting a great deal of relevant information, and, because of that, may be drawing wrong conclusions. To use an analogy with reference to a machine: the procedure is similar to failing, when faced with a breakdown of one's car, to distinguish between specific failures of, for instance, sparking, or flow of petrol or air, and speaking, even when the evidence is available, of "lack of input"; saying "the car can't be aroused," or ascribing the breakdown simply to "failure of motor output," to "clumsiness." (27)

In attempting to demonstrate the importance of motivational subsystems to understanding autism, the Tinbergens lean heavily on analogy, comparing children to both animals and machines. And yet the effect of these comparisons is not dehumanizing or reductionist. For the Tinbergens, reduction means the failure to see an organism or machine as a whole, and instead to reduce it to one of its parts. While their work may seem to answer to other definitions of reductionism, such as ignoring the singularity of human existence, their commitment to the complexity of systems offers a different way of valuing human life. The point of such comparisons is to *add* specificity and dynamism to accounts of autism. The Tinbergens emphasize in *Autistic Children* that the point of such comparisons is not to suggest that animals and humans are the same: rather, they "use animal examples merely to elucidate points of method" (35). Instead of a blanket diagnosis of "perceptual malfunctioning," the Tinbergens point to the operation of particular subsystems of perception and motive, suggesting that these systems are at work across populations deemed normal and those deemed abnormal, and indeed across human, animal, and inorganic worlds. Tinbergen's naturalist methods led him to develop a flexible and capacious observational ethics in his work with children. The Tinbergens' protest against the language of input and output continues the ethological critique of American behaviorism. Naturalists objected to the artificiality, manipulation, and control of laboratory experiments as well as to behaviorists' single-channel conception of the human organism. *Early Childhood Autism* rejects the black-boxing of perception, interaction, and emotion in diagnoses of autism. But rather than reach deep inside the subject for evidence of organic pathology or human essence, the Tinbergens strained to take in a whole field of behavior.

Despite the tendency of the Tinbergens' research to universalize and therefore destigmatize autism, it was nonetheless clearly marked by extreme asymmetries of expertise and power, as well as age and authority. The Tinbergens argue that one of the reasons that ethological methods are so useful in the case of children with autism is that they were designed for situations where communication is nonverbal. Since the children they observe are largely nonspeaking, they find their methods for the observation of communication among nonhuman animals are relevant (11). The constraints on consent or reciprocity in such a research situation are severe. These asymmetries structure Tinbergen's Nobel presentation, "Ethology and Stress Diseases," not only in his discussion of autism but also in his account of the Alexander technique. In the version of the talk published in *Science*, Tinbergen includes anonymized photographs of naked children and adults to illustrate posture defects and the efficacy of treatment. In relation to both autism and poor posture, Tinbergen is positioned as the expert observer discussing difficult cases, their dignity preserved and nullified by the blackout bars covering their faces.

Yet Tinbergen's position on both topics was more complicated.[40] Tinbergen speaks not just as a researcher of the Alexander technique, but also a patient and a convert. Despite initial skepticism, he writes, the treatment "sounded so extraordinary I felt that I ought to give the method the benefit of the doubt" (24). Tinbergen goes on to describe how he, his wife, and his daughter all sought this treatment, and "discovered that the therapy is based on exceptionally sophisticated observation, not only by means of vision but also to a surprising extent by using the sense of touch" (25). As a result of "gentle . . . corrective manipulation," he reports that they experience "very striking improvements in such diverse things as high blood pressure, breathing, overall cheerfulness and mental alertness, resilience against outside pressures, and also in such a refined skill as playing a stringed instrument" (25). Tinbergen is much less forthcoming about his personal interest in autism, citing merely his and Elisabeth's observation that "it looks as if this set of aberrations is actually on the increase in a number of Western or Westernized societies" (20). But in fact, Tinbergen's investment in autism was much more personal. He was concerned that one of his children might be diagnosed with autism. He was also drawn to autism as a topic because of his own chronic depression, which he saw as having many of the same effects. Tinbergen's letters are filled with accounts of his attempts to understand and to cure his depression, but also, as in the following letter to Philippa Elmhirst, with comparisons between his own physical and mental state and the experience of autism:

> From introspection I know very well how very similar to autistic a depressed person is and also how many typically autistic traits he shows, such as withdrawal, lack of initiative and enterprise and interest, toe walking, wanting sameness, stereotypies, etc. etc. Now with me (and with many autistic children when they are emerging) irritability, anger, and similar conditions are very common. Lies [Elisabeth] always says that when I begin to be irritable (where until then I had been simply cowed, withdrawn), she knows that I am coming out of one of my bouts. But my irritability is not technically speaking "aggression," it is a defensive behaviour accompanied by "don't interfere," "leave me alone," thoughts.[41]

Although in the majority of his published research Tinbergen avoided questions of deep motivation, in his more personal writings he both speculated about the experience of autism and identified with it. Discussing depression, for example, he imagines very particular mental states for children with autism—whereas in fact the only evidence for those states is his own experience. However, by choosing observation over introspection as the method for his own research, Tinbergen avoided such speculation in his published writing.

One of the most troubling aspects of the Tinbergens' research on autism is their investment in holding therapy as a cure, which developed about a decade into their research. Although in *Early Childhood Autism*, the Tinbergens were interested in the influence of parents, they didn't advocate any special techniques for curing autism; instead, they put their faith in general ideas of good parenting—attentive but not intrusive, flexible, responsive.[42] By the time they published *Autistic Children: New Hope for a New Cure*, they had become advocates of holding therapy, a practice that, as Silverman points out, was at odds with their earlier critique of aggressive parenting styles. They had also become embroiled in lengthy correspondence with both advocates and opponents of forced holding. A key correspondent was Dr. Martha Welch, the most prominent advocate of holding therapy. In her 1988 book *Holding Time*, Welch made the case that extended and nonconsensual sessions of cuddling would repair damaged bonds between parents (primarily mothers) and their autistic children.

Welch's techniques have, in the intervening decades, been widely denounced both by the field of psychology and by the autism community. As in the case of the Alexander technique, though, Tinbergen was not just an advocate of holding, he also submitted himself to it as a potential cure for his ongoing struggles with depression and other ailments. Welch and Tinbergen exchanged several letters in the early 1980s about Tinbergen's depression. Welch emphasized the effect of trauma from Tinbergen's wartime experiences, as well as childhood sources ("Niko, however happy your childhood may have been, it is certain that you did not get *enough* touch, holding, affection"[43]). Welch repeatedly advocated holding as a cure, and eventually Tinbergen undertook it as a regular practice, doing nightly holding with Elisabeth. He reported back:

> As to our own holding exercise: we find it helpful and do it practically every day for 30–60 minutes. Comments by elderly people: we soon get cramp, stiff necks and painful backs, but we can manage by shifting positions. No personal grievances or confessions float to the surface, but then we have after all lived together for over 50 years and have talked out our emotionally tinted clashes; on some differences we agree to disagree and we can't get worked up about them. But it does help us

to relax and turn our attention away from the outside world and upon each other, which we both find extremely constructive. We often begin to yawn and fall nearly asleep.[44]

While their advocacy of holding therapy remains the most troubling aspect of the Tinbergens' research on autism, it is clear that their adoption of it, far from being the exercise of top-down expertise, was instead closely bound up with their own habits, needs, and vulnerabilities. It was in fact an expression of a ceding of scientific authority late in life, rather than a confirmation of it. Furthermore, this exchange demonstrates how, in the face of Welch's recourse to psychological explanation, Tinbergen emphasizes behavior, maintaining a strict focus on the activity of holding and its concrete results.

HUMAN ETHOLOGY

Tinbergen's commitment to an ethological approach to the diagnosis and treatment of psychological disorders involved him in human and animal comparisons, but not in the extrapolation of observations about animal behavior to claims about human nature. The distinction is crucial. The Tinbergens' research formed part of a broad set of experiments in human ethology: researchers in the natural and social sciences turned to methods designed for the study of nonhuman animals to human behavior. In some, but not all, cases the results of these studies were used to ratify existing cultural arrangements. That was certainly the case for Lorenz, whose 1963 book, *On Aggression*, was filled with claims about the innate human drive for dominance.[45] Tinbergen, by contrast, repeatedly insisted that what the study of humans could gain from ethology was methods rather than conclusions.[46]

To underline this distinction between methodology and ontology in human ethology, consider the case of Desmond Morris. Morris is known as one of the major proponents of sociobiology, but his training in observational ethology runs counter to his best-known work. Morris studied zoology at Oxford and wrote a PhD thesis with Tinbergen on the reproductive behavior of sticklebacks. Across his career, he engaged in two forms of human ethology. Morris is remembered primarily for his popular work of evolutionary biology, *The Naked Ape* (1967), in which he analyzes contemporary male and female roles in light of the hunting and sexual habits of early man. Morris extrapolates from speculative claims about the behavior of early humans to make normative claims about the *character* of that "intensely vocal, acutely exploratory, overcrowded ape"—"modern man."[47] In *Manwatching: A Field Guide to Human Behavior* (1977), Morris pursues a form of human ethology closer to Tinbergen's commitment to observation. Rather than rely on speculative history or assertions about male and female nature, he looks closely at the behavior of *modern* men and women, using photographs to see what is hidden in plain sight. Although these two books might be conflated, their methods are distinct: *The Naked Ape* offers an example of analogical thinking that stabilizes the concept of the human; *Manwatching*, by contrast, models the comparison of gestures to each other, without a concept of man to anchor them. In the later book, Morris avoids making pronouncements about the meaning of man's life on Earth. Instead, he engages in fine observations of considerably lighter matters. Observing everyday acts of communication and interaction, he points to the small elements of behavior that make up an individual's gestural repertoire.[48]

NOTES OF A WATCHQUEEN

Although he did not study with Tinbergen, and was trained instead in the social sciences, Laud Humphreys engaged in his own project of manwatching, borrowing heavily on naturalistic approaches. In *Tearoom Trade: Impersonal Sex in Public Places* (1970), Humphreys made use of small-scale observation in a setting that Tinbergen never anticipated. The subject of an extended public controversy, *Tearoom Trade* is most often taught now as a case study—and an object lesson—in the ethics of human subject research.[49] Employing Eugene Webb's "unobtrusive" or "oddball" measures, Humphreys went undercover. He spent many hours posing as a "watchqueen" in order to describe the activities of men having sex in restrooms in public parks in the 1960s.[50] Positioned near the entrance to the bathroom, Humphreys served as both voyeur and lookout, scanning the environment for potential interlopers, and meanwhile observing the encounters within. The anonymity and impersonality desired by the men who frequent the tearooms is reflected in Humphreys's methodology. He documents these "sexual encounters without involvement" (2) impersonally, with floor plans and "systematic observation sheets." By these means, he carefully maps the world of the tearoom, recording the activities— gestures, glances, and sex acts—that take place there. Humphreys inquires into the purpose and effect of moves in what he calls the "tearoom game" (62). But he does not speculate about the deeper motivation or meaning of tearoom behavior. Like Goffman at a gaming table or Tinbergen in a gull colony, Humphreys is eager to show us how the tearoom works, not what it means.

Recording his observations gathered while acting as a watchqueen, Humphreys models a strictly observational method, suggesting both the benefits and drawbacks of seeing human activity as behavior. But this is not all that Humphreys is up to in *Tearoom Trade*: the book is curiously divided into two parts, the first given over to the anatomy of the tearoom, and the second offering much fuller portraits of the men who spend time there. In this second part, Humphreys gave up his position as observer, pursuing the men beyond the tearoom in order to go behind their visible behavior. The focus of the study shifts from the space of the tearoom to the men themselves, as Humphreys offers biographical and psychological portraits drawn from interviews and surveys. Although the book as a whole scandalized with its frank portrayal of illicit sex, it is this second part that has remained controversial, because of the means that Humphreys used to gather information on the tearoom participants, but also because of the ways he compromised their anonymity. Having seen men in the tearooms, Humphreys tracked them afterward, noting their license plates and looking them up in a police registry. He then got their addresses out of the phone book and interviewed them in their homes using the pretext of an unrelated survey. By presenting a neutral and nonjudgmental account of bathroom sex, *Tearoom Trade* suggests the unexpected utility of observational methods, which, while they may be reductive or even dehumanizing, offer a refreshing departure from psychological speculation and moral censure. But the book also offers a cautionary tale about the temptations of biography. Humphreys proposes to use impersonal methods to treat encounters that the men themselves see as impersonal. But he cannot resist the lure of explanation, even as his efforts draw him into increasingly unsavory and risky behavior.

Before Humphreys pursued this study, he served as a pastor, which is why, he writes, he is not shocked by the activities that he observes. For his work in *Tearoom Trade*, however, he began to "listen to sexual deviants with a scientist's rather than a pastor's ear" (24). The book opens in a discursive, dry register at odds with the explicit erotic material it treats. Humphreys offers what he refers to as an ecological account of the interactions of men in search of "kicks" in anonymous tearoom settings. Humphreys derives this approach from Goffman, drawing explicitly and repeatedly on his work. Humphreys writes: "Erving Goffman's writings on face-to-face interaction have provided me with vocabulary and an approach to conceptualization." Elaborating Goffman's concept of the "interaction membrane," Humphreys details how individuals are drawn into play, how interactions are initiated, what its phases are, and what constitute closing moves. His accounts of these interactions—complete with schematic diagrams detailing the placement and moves of actors—might easily be taken for records of chess matches, were it not for the fact that they are intermittently punctuated by mentions of fellatio and hand play. Tearoom participants are treated, at least for most of the text, as interactants, players in a game that is rule bound and that unfolds in a delimited space and time. There is no mention of the biographies or internal fantasy lives of the actors. What is of concern is their actions, portrayed as moves in a game. Humphreys repeatedly puts the word *private* in scare quotes when describing these sexual encounters in public. People are demoted in this account; what matters is the shared social space and the unfolding events that it allows. This ecological understanding of the space is reflected in the participants' own experience: "I have noted more than once," Humphreys writes, "that these men seem to acquire stronger sentimental attachments to the buildings in which they meet for sex than to the persons with whom they engage in it" (14).

According to Humphreys, there are two important gains in his choice of the tearoom as a subject:

> These facilities constitute a major part of the free sex market for those in the homosexual subculture—and for millions who might never identify with the gay society. For the social scientist, these public toilets provide a means for direct observation of the dynamics of sexual encounters in situ; moreover, they facilitate the gathering of a representative sample of secret deviants, for most of whom association with the deviant subculture is minimal. (21)

This account of the benefits for the social scientist of the tearoom example recapitulates the central division in the book, between naturalistic observation of interaction in the field and, through subsequent study, a portrait of the lives of a "sample of secret deviants." Humphreys gathered data on the "tearoom purlieu" (12) by means of silent observation, filling in biographical details only later. While one might argue that neither Humphreys's research in the tearooms nor his follow-up interviews were consensual, the interviews targeted the person, not the interactant, and were therefore much more invasive.

Humphreys's gathering of biographical data about his subjects without disclosing his identity or research aims is at the heart of the critique of *Tearoom Trade*. At a moment when homosexuality was criminalized, it is clear that Humphreys's research entailed significant risks for his research subjects—risks that they were unable to consent to, not having been informed of the true context of his study. But many of the objections to his work also have to do with his impersonal methods. As Humphreys notes in a retrospective essay, the book was faulted not only for its invasion of privacy, but also for its lack of interest in psychology. Humphreys counters objections to the "'clinical,' 'hip,' or 'dehumanized' nature of [his] tearoom sociology," arguing that the "anonymity and lack of commitment of the tearoom participants forced [him] to write of them in a cool, dispassionate manner" (226). Humphreys's research can be seen as part of a movement after WWII in the human sciences to refuse speculation about psychological motivation and experience on ethical grounds. Ethology, with its focus on the behavior of animals, was one source of inspiration for this work. Goffman, with his strict refusal to plumb the interior depths of his subjects, was another. For this refusal, Goffman, like Humphreys, was criticized for his hip, cold, and inhuman approach to sociology. But while we can now see more clearly the political significance of Humphreys's halting or partial refusal to expose the inner feelings of the men he studied, it has been much harder to see that a similar impulse drove Goffman's work. And yet without Goffman's methodological example, Humphreys's interventions in *Tearoom Trade* would hardly have been possible.

In a 2005 article arguing that thick description has been overvalued and that thin description can also yield rich data and important analytic insights, Wayne H. Brekhus, John F. Galliher, and Jaber F. Gubrium consider Humphreys's naturalistic work in *Tearoom Trade* and praise his detailed account of social practice. They write,

> The hallmark of naturalistic work is the presentation of richly scenic data, not exclusively the frequency, distribution, and patterned relationships evident in research material. *Tearoom Trade* presents Hum-

phreys as a naturalist and takes the reader into the setting in which the action unfolds. His is a "survey" in Mayhew's sense of the term, in which a social landscape is entered into and personally observed for complex patterns of living and distinctive social worlds.[51]

Brekhus, Galliher, and Gubrium highlight the distinction between the first and second half of the book, considering Humphreys's thickening of his accounts of these men through the use of interviews and fuller biographical data. They emphasize the practical value of the descriptive minimalism of the first part of the book: "The thinness of tearoom participants' conduct as compared with their otherwise highly variegated lives ensconced at considerable distance from the park setting, makes their deviant status, not their urban anonymity, a 'fact' blown way out of proportion. Humphreys felt justified in offering the following public policy recommendation: 'In order to alleviate the damaging side effects of covert homosexual activity in tearooms, ease up on it'" (876).

Brekhus, Galliher, and Gubrium draw an ethics out of Humphreys's method. By presenting the participants in the games of sexual exchange as mere players, Humphreys is able to thin out the account of deviance— to effectively void the subjectivity of these men, otherwise overly legible as sexual deviants, homosexuals, closet cases, sex addicts, or—fill in the blank. The point is that once you are caught in the crosshairs of a thick psychological account of the subject, all kinds of extrapolation (psychological, moral) are allowed. This type of speculation and projection is excluded in the natural history of the tearoom, resulting in a different account of subjectivity, a different ethics, and even a different set of policy recommendations. This strategy of voiding psychological content to push back against social control is a key weapon in the queer arsenal. It is of course in tension with Humphreys's own powerful desire to know his subjects intimately, a temptation that *Tearoom Trade* ultimately gives in to. Nonetheless, this portrait of impersonal sex—sex without involvement, even without people—remains indelible. One might argue through recourse to biography that it was Humphreys's later self-identification as a gay man that informed his sympathetic attitude toward the men he observed. But the lesson of *Tearoom Trade* is that the politics is in the method, not the attitude. Humphreys's book shows the promise of ethological method: in its attention to visible behavior and its disinterest in psychology, it emphasizes the interactional and social parameters of sexuality as an observable phenomenon rather than the psychic property of an individual. In such a framework, both sympathy and censure are beside the point.

IN THE HIDE

Perhaps nothing condenses anxieties about the observational practices I've considered in this chapter like the "bird blind," offspring of the hunter's hide. Tinbergen was deeply influenced by a year he spent in Greenland in his twenties, and he reflected throughout his life on the kinship between his own practice of naturalistic observation and the habits of hunters. Crediting a "largely innate, typically masculine love of the hunting range," Tinbergen discusses his attraction to hunting in the wild in "Watching and Wondering":

> Although circumstances have never allowed me to actually be a hunter
> . . . it is in the spending of long days in an uncultivated wild countryside (the wilder the better) and in the outwitting of elusive animals—whether to enjoy their natural beauty, or to see them behave naturally, or to fool them by my experiments—that I have always found my deepest fulfillment. Knowing from personal experience how it feels to have killed, cleanly and without cruelty, one of those extremely alert Arctic seals after a long stalk over the fjord ice, I can testify that the experience of the genuine hunt (as distinct from the English way of fox "hunting" or the massacring of grouse) is indistinguishable from that of watching, unseen, from a well-built hide, the natural behavior of, say, a family of shy hawks, or that of succeeding, after long preparations, in filming an oystercatcher expertly opening a mussel on the low-tide seashore without him being aware of me. (432)

Tinbergen's reflections on hunting are inflected both by masculinism and by primitivist idealization of the lives of native Greenlanders. He also suggests that his observational practices are merely capture by other means: while they are to be distinguished from the organized killing of the fox hunt (the implied parallel is with laboratory biology), they demand the skills of the hunter—wiliness, stealth, singleness of purpose. What is different is the aim of the pursuit, which is aesthetic and scientific rather than practical and lethal.

Helen Macdonald, a trained naturalist and the author of the best-selling memoir *H Is for Hawk*, reflects on the ethics of the hide in a discussion of "covert naturalists." Macdonald emphasizes the asymmetries—of exposure, of knowledge, of instrumentation, and of power—that structure both hunting and natural observation. She writes,

> Hides create a disembodied observer with no consequential presence. They are an architectural attempt to guarantee the epistemological reliability and truth of behavioural data through an assurance that the scientist in no way affects the behaviour of the animals observed. In a related sense, the hide literalises and concretises that ascetic withdrawal from the immediacy of the observed phenomena which is at the heart of the positivist-pragmatic ethos—translating a methodological, cognitive freeing from subjective involvement to a literal freeing from involvement.[52]

We are familiar with this critique of the heroic endurance, neutrality, and disembodiment of the scientist. Yet Tinbergen's experience of being inside a hide is hardly one of disembodiment. Tinbergen's accounts of his time in hides emphasize cold and hunger, damp and cramp. Nor was this an experience of unlimited agency: one had to be put in the hide by someone else, who would then walk away in order to let the animals believe they were alone; one also had to be let out of the hide and, in the meantime, to stay put. Experience in the hide is a defining aspect of ethological practice, giving weight to the idea that this research must take place in the landscape, rather than outside or above it. As the biologist Saúl Nava explained to me, ethologists distinguish their work from experimental biology with the neat formula: "The behaviorist puts the animal in a box to study it, but the ethologist puts himself in a box."[53]

Two drawings from Tinbergen's book *Kleew: The Story of a Gull* lend support to this image of the ethologist (figures 1 and 2). During his time in the POW camp, Tinbergen produced a series of illustrated stories that he sent home to his children; he published two of these stories after the war.[54] According to the blurb for *Kleew*, the book describes how "the seagull Kleew and his mate Klia grow from hatchlings, learn to fly, tolerate curious humans, and eventually build a nest and raise youngsters of their own." In an image of a hide, Tinbergen represents a "curious human" as a box in the landscape, with no sign of the naturalist inside. The gulls play around the hide: one cleaning its feathers on the roof, another tugging with its beak

Figure 1. Sketch from Niko Tinbergen from *Kleew: The Story of a Seagull* (New York: Oxford University Press, 1947), 37. Courtesy of the Estate of Niko Tinbergen and Rowman and Littlefield. Photograph: Royal Danish Library.

at a guy. In a second illustration, Tinbergen offers a view of the ethologist inside, peering out at the landscape. Fixed in place, eyes narrowed, this image suggests the anxiety of long confinement as well as longing for the voluntary confinement of the hide.

Humphreys was also, in his way, a covert naturalist. His techniques for maintaining his cover while pursuing his research aims—for seeing without being seen—made him notorious. It is impossible to defend Humphreys's practices, which violated the privacy of his research subjects and exposed them to the scrutiny of the reading public. Yet I do not think that the story of *Tearoom Trade* is only one of predation. The fact that the hide was once used for hunting does not mean that hunting is the only thing you can use it for; the hide does not make a hunter of every man. The technology that makes possible drones, surveillance cameras, and gun sights is the same technology used in bird-watching and durational cinema.[55] Conducting research on sexual deviance as a secret deviant meant that Humphreys was as much prey as hunter. We can see Tinbergen's sketch as an image of the isolated, disembodied researcher, but it also recalls the watchqueen looking out through the broken window of a public restroom. In this sense, we can read it as an image of the enforced secrecy and the wayward sociality of the closet. In assessing the ethics of the hide, we might recall another

Figure 2. Detail from a sketch from *Kleew: The Story of a Seagull* (New York: Oxford University Press, 1947), 36. Courtesy of the Estate of Niko Tinbergen and Rowman and Littlefield. Photograph: Royal Danish Library.

meaning of the Greek word *ethos*: mimic. Mimicry in the context of camouflage refers to concealment, and to the disappearing act that is the prerogative of the researcher. Humphreys performed this kind of mimicry in his covert observation of sex in the tearoom. But mimicry also refers to the sharing of a behavioral repertoire, and a world. Humphreys was a mimic in this sense too. He was hunting, but not only for knowledge. He was hiding, not only *from* his research subjects but also *with* them. He was watching, but he was also caught up in the choreography of the tearoom.

3 · A Sociological Periplum

Many things in the world have not been named; and many things, even
if they have been named, have never been described.

Susan Sontag, "Notes on 'Camp'"[1]

Does description have a place in queer life? Is it better to try to escape de-
tection? In the face of historical erasure, queer artists and scholars are
curiously divided about whether to fill in the gaps or to refuse representation altogether. There is, on the one hand, a tendency to address historical
gaps through means of assiduous documentation. The collection and the
search for ancestors derive from this impulse to work against historical
absence. On the other hand, given the violent suppressions of historical
memory, as well as the overrepresentation of queer pathology in the historical record, some queers refuse the evidentiary paradigm: they insist
that the history that matters cannot be captured in an archive. Fantastical
stories of impossible lives and artificial paradises are the products of this
impulse. Both responses aim to redress the twinned invisibility and hyper-
visibility of queer lives, but they rely on opposing strategies, one involving the embrace of truth and the other its refusal.[2] Artist and filmmaker
William E. Jones's 2007 film *Tearoom*, screened at the 2008 Whitney Bi-
ennial, offers an example of a queer documentary impulse. In making this
film, Jones lightly edited police surveillance footage of men having sex in a
bathroom in Mansfield, Ohio, during a 1962 crackdown. Jones's repurpos-
ing of found footage used to train police in covert surveillance raises many
of the same ethical issues as Laud Humphreys's *Tearoom Trade*: at the
same time, the afterlife of these images as queer artwork suggests the unpredictable value of documentation.[3] On the other end of this spectrum is
the work of the contemporary media artist Zach Blas, whose facial cages
and masks are designed to frustrate both digital surveillance technology
and demands for LGBT visibility.[4]

More often in queer representation, however, the urge to document and
the urge to disappear, though contradictory, are fused. This fundamental

ambivalence about whether to expose hidden worlds to view is legible, for example, in Michel Foucault's writing on historiography, in which he emphasizes the thrill of coming into contact with "real existences," but at the same time argues, via Nietzsche, that the "will to truth" founders on the "unavoidable sacrifice of the subject of knowledge."[5] Andy Warhol took the art of queer opacity to new heights, and yet he was also devoted to practices of recording and transcription that we associate most readily with surveillance.[6] Or consider Isaac Julien's *Looking for Langston*, the 1989 film that both memorializes Hughes and helps him to escape the fixity of the biopic form. Julien mixes archival footage of the streets of Harlem with silent fantasy sequences set in unreal landscapes. The filmmaker lovingly creates a simulacrum of a Harlem speakeasy populated by Black and inter-racial couples. But, when 1980s skinheads come to raid the bar, the men have disappeared, a spinning turntable, a disco ball, and some lingering smoke the only traces of them.[7] To take a more recent example, Alison Bechdel's *Fun Home: A Family Tragicomic* (2006) demonstrates the impor-tance of an aesthetics of "documentary witness" in substantiating queer truths. Bechdel, through a meticulous process of archival research, per-formance, and copying, reconstructs snapshots, diary entries, maps, book covers, and city landscapes in order to make visible otherwise unbeliev-able stories of transgressive desire, family secrets, and intergenerational trauma.[8] In each of these instances, the desire to document competes with the belief that documentation is a kind of violence, and that the truth of queer life escapes the grids of intelligibility.

Through framing, irony, reflexivity, and what Nicholas de Villiers calls "tactics of opacity," queer artists manage to both employ and remediate practices of documentation and description. The possibilities for remedia-tion in the context of the human sciences seem much less promising, not only because of constrained representational means but also because of damaging histories of objectification, spectacle, and physical and psycho-logical harm in these fields. It is, in fact, in protest against the represen-tation of queer subjects in the medical and social sciences that queer art-ists invent alternative ways of representing gender and sexual deviants. As a result, queer scholars trained in the interpretive humanities have fol-lowed suit, lauding "resistant" and "subversive" representations in litera-ture and the visual arts, and demonizing empirical research for stabiliz-ing and objectifying the lives of queer subjects—without recognizing such research as the source of much of our knowledge about queer life. In the twentieth century, our sense of what went on inside bars, tearooms, porn

theaters, bathhouses, and other quotidian spaces of queer life owes much
to the labors of historians, urban sociologists, social workers, and anthropologists. It is thanks to documentary practices developed in the social sciences—case histories, ethnographies, and statistical surveys—that literary
and artistic forms reflect the texture and makeup of queer social worlds.
In a 1995 piece addressing the disregard for gay and lesbian studies in the
ascendant field of queer theory, Lisa Duggan clarifies the crisis that results from a failure to recognize the contributions of the social sciences:
"There has been a progressive impoverishment of the empirical, historical grounding for textual analyses of various sorts. The impressive expansion of increasingly sophisticated analyses is balanced precariously atop a
stunted archive. (We get yet another article on Gertrude Stein, without any
accompanying expansion of the research base for analyzing the changing
discursive context for her writing at the turn of the century.)"[9]

Gayle Rubin makes a more forceful argument for the value of empirical
research in "Thinking Sex" (1984). For Rubin, it is not only an evidentiary
base that such research provides. Instead, she argues that descriptive research involves another form of politics: rather than the transformation of
existing ways of life, it substantiates queer worlds, particularly in making
space for marginal sexual subjects. Rubin's claim for the value of descriptive scholarship is staked on the controversial terrain of sexology. Rather
than focusing on the pathologizing use of categories in sexology, Rubin
approves this field of knowledge for bringing as yet unknown sexual practices into view. It is through such acts of naming, seen positively as lending
ontological weight to features of experience seen as outlandish or impossible, that she understands sexology to "provide abundant detail, a welcome posture of calm, and a well developed ability to treat sexual variety
as something that exists rather than as something to be exterminated."[10]
For Rubin, sexology and sex research more broadly offered a crucial alternative to attempts to remake sexuality according to feminist principles
in the 1970s. Writing in the moment of the feminist sex wars, Rubin critiques efforts to address sexual and gender practices such as S/M, porn,
and butch/femme, which were understood to be patriarchal. Rubin argues
that gender and sexual minorities are particularly vulnerable to such projects of reform and correction. Contra critiques of empiricism that claim it
stabilizes existing hierarchies and objectifies vulnerable subjects, Rubin
argues that description is crucial in providing discursive space to stigmatized populations, and to recognizing, in her words, the existence of "be-
nign sexual variation" (278).

In this chapter, I follow Rubin's lead in addressing the political value of description in queer writing on sexuality. I address this by revisiting a debate from the early 1990s that was crucial in determining the politics of knowledge in the burgeoning field of queer theory: historian Joan W. Scott's influential reading of a scene in Samuel R. Delany's 1988 memoir *The Motion of Light in Water*. I revisit this debate in an effort to historicize the emergence of queer theory in the context of the history of the disciplines, suggesting that its fate was tied to that of the interpretive humanities. At the end of the 1980s, queer theory represented a timely combination of identity politics and antifoundationalism with a high theory pedigree. Although my own training binds me closely to that moment, I argue that there have been costs: the birth of queer theory during the moment of the linguistic turn has made it difficult for queer scholars to recognize the value of empirical work on sexuality. I suggest that postwar studies of deviance like sexology could and sometimes did reinforce social hierarchies. However, following Rubin, I argue that scholars of deviance also recognized and made discursive space for sexual variety. This effect of deviance research has rarely been noted and its important role in giving rise to sexuality studies has been overlooked.

We can identify a related politics of description in *The Motion of Light in Water* and in Delany's 1999 book *Times Square Red, Times Square Blue*, which recounts the shutting down of New York City porn theaters in the 1980s. Like many of Delany's books, *Times Square Red* mixes genres, combining memoir, anecdotes, urban history, and sociological treatise. While the book might be considered literary in its focus on narrative, its extensive use of personal material, and its impressionism, it also demonstrates Delany's methodological and political inheritance from the tradition of deviance studies. Exploring Delany's use of description, I suggest that he offers a new grounding for queer studies: more open to the historical contributions and methods of the social sciences; corrosive of fixed identities, but attentive to the value of stabilizing marginal worlds. Furthermore, I argue that, by combining empirical and antifoundationalist methods, Delany points toward an expanded definition of the literary.

THE USES OF THE LITERARY

In her 1991 essay "The Evidence of Experience," Scott critiques the use of experience as a foundational category in the exploration of the history of difference. Scott does not target the work of traditional historians. Instead, she considers appeals to experience by historians seeking to recover the voices of those "hidden from history," suggesting that the political urgency of the project of social history drives otherwise progressive scholars to revert to core disciplinary methods.[11] "What is most striking these days," Scott writes, "is the determined embrace, the strident defense, of some reified, transcendent category of explanation by historians who have used insights drawn from the sociology of knowledge, structural linguistics, feminist theory, or cultural anthropology to develop sharp critiques of empiricism."[12] While acts of historical recovery might change the shape of the past or our sense of who counts as a social actor, they do not challenge more fundamental epistemological assumptions. Instead, by remaining "comfortably within the disciplinary framework of history" (776), they shore up existing hierarchies by reifying identity, naturalizing the social order, and reinforcing the reality of unjust social relations. Scott proposes that instead of understanding experience as "evidence for the fact of difference," historians should focus on representations of experience in order to "explor[e] how difference is established, how it operates, how and in what ways it constitutes subjects who see and act in the world" (777).

To explore the relationship between experience, identity, and difference, Scott turns to a moment of first-person witnessing in *The Motion of Light in Water: Sex and Science Fiction Writing in the East Village* (1988), a memoir by the Black, gay science-fiction writer Samuel R. Delany. In a much-cited scene, Delany describes his response to entering the Saint Mark's Baths in New York City for the first time. In the pre-Stonewall era, Delany narrates his discovery of a world of queer male intimacy in painstaking detail.[13] "In the gym-sized room," Delany writes, "were sixteen rows of beds, four to a rank, or sixty-four altogether. I couldn't see any of the beds themselves, though, because there were three times that many people (maybe a hundred-twenty) in the room. Perhaps a dozen of them were standing. The rest were an undulating mass of naked, male bodies, spread wall to wall. My first response was a kind of heart-thudding astonishment, very close to fear."[14] The scene reminds Delany of another moment when he witnessed a police raid of the trucks parked on the West Side of Manhattan. Then too, he was taken aback by "the sheer number of men who suddenly began to appear . . . here and there from between the vans" (174). Both scenes bring home to Delany "a fact that flew in the face of that whole 50s image" (174) of homosexuality. He writes,

The myth said that we, as isolated perverts, were only beings of desire, manifestations of the subject (yes, gone awry, turned from its true object, but, for all that, even more purely subjective). But what this experience said was that there was a population—not of individual homosexuals, some of whom now and then encountered, or that those encounters could be human and fulfilling in their way—not of hundreds, not of thousands, but rather of millions of gay men, and that history had, actively and already, created for us whole galleries of institutions, good and bad, to accommodate our sex. (174)

The Motion of Light in Water addresses itself to the gap between the myth of homosexuality, characterized by isolation, perversion, and pathology, and a visceral experience of homosexuality as irreducibly social, erotic, and collective. Scott's tour-de-force reading of Delany also focuses on this gap, highlighting the difficulty of distinguishing between discourse and experience by reading this scene twice—first as an affirmation of the autonomy and authenticity of experience, and finally, at the end of the essay, as a questioning of the very category of experience.

"The Evidence of Experience" opens with a reading that foregrounds Delany's investment in visibility and transparency. For Delany, as for an old-fashioned empiricist, seeing is believing. Scott points out how important the good lighting inside the baths is to him; at one point, he reports breathlessly, "you could see what was going on throughout the dorm" (173). In this account, Delany is a naive realist: his foregrounding of the senses as a source of knowledge and his emphasis on the self-evident fact of gay community link him to the social historians that Scott critiques. In the end, however, this reading only presents a foil for Scott's characterization of Delany in nearly opposite terms. After a series of detailed arguments with professional historians, Scott returns to *The Motion of Light in Water*, recasting Delany's account of the scene in the baths as an exemplary questioning of experience as the ground of identity. In this second reading, Scott emphasizes the warping effects of corporeal and affective intensity in Delany's account, the wavering of solid reality suggested by the book's title. Furthermore, she sees Delany as invested not in "the discovery of truth (conceived as the reflection of a prediscursive reality)" but rather "the substitution of one interpretation for another." She continues, "Delany presents this substitution as a conversion experience, a clarifying moment, after which he sees (that is, understands) differently. But there is all the difference between subjective perceptual clarity and transparent vision; one does not follow from the other even if the subjective state is metaphorically presented as a visual experience" (794).

Scott's reading exploits an ambiguity at the heart of the concept of empiricism: on the one hand, empiricism is linked to the Baconian tradition of experiment and verification; on the other, since it relies entirely on experience, empiricism threatens to expose positive knowledge as partial and contingent, based entirely on the senses.[15] The turn in Scott's essay, and her rereading of Delany in terms of what we might call radical empiricism, is bound up with a highly self-conscious turn to "the literary" as a way to address the problems of traditional history. According to Scott, literary critics model how to respond to representations of experience *as representations* rather than as "social or natural facts" (791). The literary "way of reading" does not "assume a direct correspondence between words and things, nor confine itself to single meanings, nor aim for the resolution of contradiction." For this reason, borrowing from the field can open "new possibilities for analyzing discursive productions of social and political reality as complex, contradictory processes" (793–94).[16] As Scott writes, "Reading for 'the literary' does not seem at all inappropriate for those whose discipline is devoted to the study of change" (386).

In a striking moment, Scott hands the reins of her argument to the literary critic Karen Swann, citing Swann's extended close reading of this scene from Delany that she had performed in a response to an earlier version of Scott's essay. In her reading, Swann emphasizes the "properties of the medium through which the visible appears"—"the dim blue light, whose distorting, refracting qualities produce a wavering of the visible"—and argues that "in this version of the story . . . political consciousness and power originate, not in a presumably unmediated experience of presumably real gay identities, but out of an apprehension of the moving, differencing properties of the representational medium—the motion of light in water" (Swann, cited in Scott, 794). Swann splits the difference between an antirealist claim about the impossible ground of experience and identity ("presumably unmediated experience," "presumably real gay identities") and a more positive claim about the ambiguity and complexity of sensory experience (evident in her attention to the "dim blue light" and "the wavering of the visible," and in her final citation of the beautiful title phrase "the motion of light in water").

Like many challenges to empiricism in the social sciences, "The Evidence of Experience" turns to "the literary" as a weapon against the regime of the fact. Scott's essay can be understood as part of the turn in the social sciences, from the 1970s onward, to methods and frameworks drawn from the study of language and literature. During this period, sometimes known as the linguistic turn, scholars in anthropology, history, and sociology turned to accounts of the complexity and instability of meaning generated in literary studies in order to challenge the positivism of their disciplines.[17] However, despite its place of privilege, "the literary" in "The Evidence of Experience" is an odd compound, made up of structuralist and poststructuralist insights about the nature of language; claims about the practice of textual interpretation; and more general reflections on poetic discourse. While at times literature is aligned with an epistemological *skepticism* that would undermine the ground of experience, at other times it is associated with the *ambiguity* of experience as an embodied, subjective phenomenon. That is to say, sometimes "the literary" indicates an antifoundationalism developed in poststructuralist literary theory, and at other times it indicates the complexity of affect, consciousness, sensation, and perception that have been seen as the special purview of literature in modernity. In both cases, literature offers a challenge to empiricism—but, on the one hand, by rendering the complexity of experience visible and, on the other, by casting it into radical doubt.

Emphasizing the literary qualities of *The Motion of Light in Water* brings out the complexity and ambiguity that Scott overlooked in her first, flattening reading of the scene in the baths. But if this more nuanced account of Delany's text corrects, it also distorts, since it fails to account for Delany's commitments to the empiricism that "The Evidence of Experience" polemicizes against. These commitments are in tension with other aspects of Delany's aesthetic production, for instance, with his own antifoundationalism, nurtured by deep reading in poststructuralism. In this sense, we can understand Delany as a product of the moment of the linguistic turn: in his Nevèrÿon series, for instance, he combines an anthropological approach to the origins of culture with a persistent attention to the instability of language and representation. Delany's empiricism is also in tension with his identity as a writer of science fiction and fantasy. However, in his reflections about science fiction, Delany emphasizes its realist, and even antiliterary, qualities.[18] He notes that science fiction has avoided the priority of the subject that is common in literary fiction, crediting its incubation in a wide universe of discourse. In "The Semiology of Silence," he writes, "SF, developing in the statistically much wider field of para-literature (comic books, pornography, film and television scripts, advertising copy, instructions on the back of the box, street signs, popular song lyrics, business letters, journalism—in short, the graphic flood from which most of the texts each of us encounters over any day come), has to some extent been able to escape this tyranny."[19] In his view, science fiction "has a very literal quality to it that, even though we would be hard put to call it referential, is nevertheless quite the opposite of metaphor."[20]

If Delany's commitment to the literal aspects of language is evident in his writings on science fiction, his commitments to social history and to empirical methods of observation and description are evident in *The Motion of Light in Water*. Delany's account of the baths emphasizes uncertainty and fallibility—the motion of light in water. But it also emphasizes the solidity and the visibility of that world. Despite the fantastic coloring of his invocation of millions of gay men, Delany's aim is realist and empiricist: the sight of "massed bodies" coming together in the well-lighted dorm serves as an affirmation of the "galleries of institutions" of gay life and gay sex. As Kane Race argues in a reading of this passage, Delany's experience in the baths is "not merely a matter of representation," but it rather "involves physical structures and technical procedures—the room, the light bulb, the moving bodies, the diary form in which the memory is recorded: the distinct practices and conditions of perception that make up all discourse, knowledge, and imagination."[21] The assimilation of Delany's fiction to a version of "the literary" that is opposed to the empirical fails to reckon with his expansive definition of the literary and with his contributions as a social historian. Scott argues that a focus on the literary turns away from the task of "capturing the reality of the objects seen," but it is just this task that concerns Delany. Despite the haziness of his impressions, a documentary impulse is evident in Delany's mustering of detail and in his fascination with the sheer existence of this world. As he argues in a different context, "The social marginality of the situation, and the extreme behavioral range in that margin—for the breadth of human experience generally remaining outside one sub-language or another is far greater than what, from time to time, over-spills into the centers of articulation—militates for a social interpretation."[22]

Scott's concern is that naive empiricism will stabilize marginal identities and therefore strengthen existing social hierarchies, but Delany's aim in this passage is to bolster a marginal and largely unknown world by describing it. Although he frequently polemicizes against false reifications of racial and sexual identity, Delany insists on the need to acknowledge the existence of the hidden world of the baths by bringing it into discourse. Such an impulse can be hard to make sense of within the field of queer studies, which emerged during the height of the linguistic turn, and aligned itself with a politics of disruption rather than one of stabilization. In fact, through Scott's reading, Delany became an important avatar of disruption and destabilization, with "The Evidence of Experience" appearing in the now-canonical collection *The Lesbian and Gay Studies Reader* (1993). Queer readings of "The Evidence of Experience" tend to agree with Scott about Delany's antirealism, simply arguing that she does not go far enough or appreciate Delany's own resistance to a naive notion of experience. Critics fault her for her association of Delany with "unreconstructed narratives of experience, fixed identity, and 'the visual.'"[23]

In this framework, Delany looks like a hero of antifoundationalist queer theory. However, his methodological, epistemological, and political commitments suggest another genealogy for his work: empirical research on sexual deviance conducted in the social sciences in the US after World War II. Studies of marginal sexual worlds undertaken by anthropologists, sociologists, psychologists, and historians are divided in this period from the present by many gaps, both of tone and substance. Deviance research is empirical in its methods; realist (though qualifiedly so) in its epistemology; and its politics depend on the stabilization rather than the destabilization of homosexuality as a socially recognizable form of existence. Scholars of deviance did not feel or did not record feeling the fear or gratitude that Delany describes on seeing evidence of marginal worlds. Perhaps most significantly, social scientists maintained a stance of expertise and professionalism in the face of the small worlds they studied. By contrast, Delany's relation to them is marked by waves of identification and desire. Partisanship hardly covers this attitude, which is not merely one of sympathy or understanding but which aims instead to put marginal subjects center stage without apology, and thus to revalue difference itself. Delany's intense affective response to his encounter with these hidden worlds did not derail his efforts to document them, however. He shares this documentary impulse with the much more sober sociologists of deviance. In the framework of queer studies, this scholarship can look deeply conservative, and queer scholars in the humanities have cited it only rarely, and in the mode of critique. However, Delany's way of looking at, and even loving, otherness owes a great deal to these earlier explorers of unknown worlds.[24]

THE SINGLE, EMPIRICAL EXAMPLE

Delany first visited Saint Mark's Baths in 1963. It was an important year in the history of deviance studies, marked by the publication of both Erving Goffman's *Stigma* and Howard Becker's *Outsiders*.[25] These texts, while not focused on homosexuality, were crucial to the development of an interactionist and microsociological account of deviance. The afterlife of this tradition is evident in Delany's *Times Square Red, Times Square Blue* (1999), which, despite its first-person voice and narrative elaboration, relies heavily on observation and relatively thin forms of description. A generic experiment, the book is made up of two parts: "Times Square Blue" contains personal recollections of sex and sociability inside the theaters; "... Three, Two, One, Contact: Times Square Red" offers an analysis of the sociological and economic conditions of that world, and of the economic redevelopment of the area and policing of public sex in New York City. Unlike Laud Humphreys, Delany never takes up the position of the expert or outsider in relation to the world of the porn theaters: he offers a highly self-reflexive form of auto-ethnography that avoids many of the worst pitfalls of *Tearoom Trade*. The book is told in Delany's own voice—from a position he identifies elsewhere as Black, gay, and male[26]—and he does not conceal but rather foregrounds his desire. It would be impossible to call Delany's methods impersonal, since he is fascinated by the personal stories of the men he meets. If these sexual encounters are casual, they are hardly anonymous. In the course of the book, Delany offers detailed sketches of the men he met in the theaters, describing their appearance, their conversations, and the everyday activities (for instance, getting a meal or visiting Delany's aged mother) he shared with them.

In *Tearoom Trade*, Humphreys addresses the difficulties of pursuing research in contexts where talk is excluded. He writes, "A sociologist without verbal communication is like a doctor without a stethoscope" (36). By contrast, *Times Square Red* is a very chatty book. Many of the book's pleasures consist in the desultory conversations that Delany strikes up with people in the theaters and in the streets of Times Square. Still, because of the subject matter, there are moments when Delany finds himself, like Humphreys, working without a stethoscope. The fact that sex can be a nonverbal exchange elicits a reflection about the challenges and potentials of observational methods in one of Delany's lectures that precedes *Times Square Red*, "Aversion/Perversion/Diversion."[27] In response to a befuddled friend's question about shoe fetishism, Delany reflects, "As I thought about it, it occurred to me that, in similar environments, I'd actually observed many hours of fetishistic behavior by any number of men over the years, though most of those involved work shoes or engineers' boots in specifically S&M contexts—so, therefore, I knew something quite real about that behavior. But, at the same time, I'd spent perhaps less than a single hour talking about that behavior with any or all of the men involved—including Mike. That meant there was a great deal I *didn't* know" (17).

Times Square Red, Times Square Blue is linked to the tradition of deviance studies by its use of observational methods, description, and by its commitment to the practice of documenting marginal sexual worlds. For Delany, as for deviance studies scholars concerned with the ordinariness of marginalized sexual communities, the fact that such worlds are marginal does not imply that they are extreme or anomic. Delany writes, "Public sex situations are not Dionysian and uncontrolled but are rather some of the most highly socialized and conventionalized behavior human beings can take part in" (158). The public sexual encounters that Delany describes inside the porn theater—masturbation, blow jobs, hand jobs, self-exposure, voyeurism, but also group scenes and sex with minors and disabled people—are treated as undramatic, even banal. They are interspersed with encounters that would count as banal in anyone's book, for instance, Delany reading the newspaper or running out to buy ginger ale and sandwiches. Many scholars have attested to the ordinariness in Delany's rendering of sex practices deemed perverse or extreme. As Guy Davidson argues in relation to the S/M scenes in Delany's novel *The Mad Man*, "For all their outrageousness, the sexual practices of [the novel] are not presented under the sign of transgression. On the contrary, Delany takes care to draw our attention to the 'rules' that guide particular encounters." The context, Davidson argues, is one of "civility, rather than being an untrammeled expression of mutual lust."[28] The men portrayed in Delany's accounts of sexual life follow rules, not merely because they are civil beings, but, more fundamentally, because they are social beings.

While Scott emphasizes Delany's undermining of traditional forms of empiricism, other critics have acknowledged the documentary impulse in his work. GerShun Avilez emphasizes Delany's attention to the materiality and dynamics of social space. In an argument that anticipates my own, Avilez suggests that Delany seeks to reconfigure both social and narrative space through his writing. According to Avilez, attending to queer space in Delany's work can make "legible the social work done by literary culture" and can make clear "the value of non-literary methodologies to literary studies."[29] In her book *Signs and Cities: Black Literary Postmodernism*, Madhu Dubey points out the empirical and antiempirical aspects of Delany's work. Dubey acknowledges Delany's deep reading in poststructuralist theory but frames his work as urban history, suggesting that he is concerned above all with economic conditions, social spaces, institutions, and bodily practices. She writes: "Delany styles himself a deconstructionist as well as a 'die-hard, card-carrying materialist.'"[30] At the beginning of "Aversion/Perversion/Diversion," Delany addresses the audience, saying, "I shall assume that you have invited me here as a storyteller." In the rest of the lecture, he obliges, telling stories about drunkenly sleeping with a female student, his liaison with Mike the shoe fetishist, and his own erotic taste for the hands of nail-biters. He emphasizes the utopian potential contained within the kernel of the single anecdote: "In other places I have written that the single, empirical example—and that is all the particular orders of narrative I indulge here can give—is the place from which to start further, operationalized investigation. It is not the place to decide one has found a general fact. And I mean it—here, too. Certainly I would like to see such operationalized study begun. And my utopian hope is that in such stories as these such study might begin. That is why I've told so many of the tales I have."[31]

By combining single, empirical instances collected over decades with structural analysis and critique, *Times Square Red, Times Square Blue* embodies the "operationalized study" that Delany called for in his 1991 lecture. In the author's preface, Delany compares the text to a periplum, a term he takes from Ezra Pound ("Periplum, not as land looks on a map / But as sea bord seen by men sailing" [*Cantos* 82–84]). He explains that "periploi were detailed descriptions of the coastlines of the mainland and the various islands, which, when coupled with a bit of common sense about directions and travel times, allowed early navigators to ascertain where, after a storm, they might have ended up, once a coast came into view." Delany continues:

The dual pieces here present a sociological and diachronic periplum. They are two attempts by a single navigator to describe what the temporal coastland and the lay of the land looked like and felt like and the thoughts he had while observing them. From the most peremptory landings, these pieces register impressions and ideas as they occurred to this navigator, somewhat storm-tossed over thirty-odd years, who

finally sought something no less necessary to his appetitive life than
fresh food and fresh water.[32]

Like the sailors discussed by Pound, Delany gathers details gleaned from
firsthand observation and transforms them—with the help of "a bit of
common sense"—into a representational form usable by others. Delany
frames *Times Square Red* as an empirical text, invested in the arts of observation and description. However, by invoking the periplum, he suggests
that it belongs to a longer history of empiricism, one that includes both
the science of cartography but also more unsystematic practices of observation and description.

As in *The Motion of Light in Water*, Delany suggests that putting marginal worlds into discourse is urgent, comparable to the securing of food
and water for storm-tossed sailors. In the framework of Scott's critique of
the use of experience as evidence, or of queer theory's resistance to empiricism, it would be hard to see the value of this sociological periplum.
The documentation of uncharted territories of public sex does not fit into
an account of the political as driven by disruption and destabilization. But
if the point is to stabilize and lend reality to these marginal worlds—or, as
Rubin writes, "to treat sexual variety as something that exists rather than
as something to be exterminated"—then the value of this empirical and
practical genre is clear. As is so often the case for Delany, the empirical
impulse in his work is divided between the mining of personal experience
and a commitment to more systematic, objective forms of study. Delany's
engagement with the category of experience exploits the term's full range
of meanings, as both the ground of empiricism and its disruption. Experience is the evidence of the senses that forms the basis of modern regimes
of objectivity; at the same time, experience is appetitive and visceral, and
thus can never serve as fully reliable evidence. In confronting uncounted
and unaccountable worlds, Delany depends on practices of description
that are necessarily incomplete and contingent—he makes peremptory
landings, spurred by desire rather than the will to knowledge. But the ambition is to construct a usable map out of fragmentary impressions.

ROUGH EMPIRICISM

Times Square Red includes extended analyses of the political economy of
development in New York City, and in these sections Delany works in the
mode of structural critique and macrosociology. However, Delany's ap-

proach is more consistently tuned to the microsociological sphere of situations, scenes, and interactions, and the book is filled with examples of a rough, improvisatory, local empiricism. Consider, for instance, Delany's reflections on the question of the representational politics of the heterosexual porn films playing in the theaters. Delany argues that, despite their formulaic quality, the expanding audience for porn in the postwar period "improved our vision of sex all over the country, making it friendlier, more relaxed, and more playful" (78). However, the patent sexism of the films offers a more significant challenge, one that Delany meets by counting up images of women in local theaters. Noting that straight male fantasy is not for women per se but rather for women occupying determinate social and vocational roles (secretaries, nurses, waitresses, etc.), he writes,

> Once, when WAP (Women Against Pornography) was leading its tours through the areas in the early eighties, I did an informal tabulation of six random commercial porn films in the Forty-second Street Area and six random legit movies playing around the corner in the same area during the same week. I counted the number of major female characters portrayed as having a profession in each: the six legit films racked up seven (one had three, one had zero). The six porn films racked up eleven. On the same films I took tabs on how many friendships between women were represented, lesbian or otherwise, in the plot. The six legit films came out with zero; the six porn films came out with nine. Also: How many of each ended up with the women getting what they wanted? Five for the porn. Two for the legit. (79)

Delany is not averse to counting, and his quick survey of the neighborhood screens recalls methods of content analysis routinely used in sociological studies of media. Embracing the value of description as method, Delany suggests that the sheer presence of women with jobs appearing on screen counterbalances the sexism of the films.[33]

Such informal tabulations appear throughout *Times Square Red, Times Square Blue*, as Delany builds up his "vernacular periplum" (58) of the area in part by counting. But the main thing that Delany counts is sexual encounters. Counting is a rhetorical convention that is common in narratives of public sex, but Delany avoids the practice of reducing tricks to numbers that characterizes both the genre of the stud file as well as some literary representations.[34] Delany regularly provides names as well as characteristic sexual proclivities, bits of conversation, and biographical and physical detail when recalling men he met in the theaters. Instead of the numerical series, Delany favors the list or catalog, a form that falls between statistical reduction and full characterization. This predilection for listing recalls both Sedgwick's discussion of Tomkins and the methods Kinsey employed to complete his monumental studies of male and female sexualities. Kinsey relied on statistical reduction in his use of computer punch cards to compile and tabulate instances of sexual deviation. But he also relied heavily on interviews, attempting to collect as many life stories as possible. Both in his drive for accumulation and in his eye for stray detail, we see the imprint of Kinsey's work as a naturalist and collector, whose methods can hardly be described in terms of reduction, statistical or otherwise.[35]

Delany's travels through Times Square betray a similar investment in accumulation and taxonomy. Reflecting on his long history in the area, Delany relies on the categories that were most salient in the context of deviance studies—occupations. He writes,

> In the Forty-second Street area's sex theaters specifically, since I started frequenting them in the summer of 1975, I've met playwrights, carpenters, opera singers, telephone repair men, stockbrokers, guys on welfare, guys with trust funds, guys on crutches, on walkers, in wheelchairs, teachers, warehouse workers, male nurses, fancy chefs, guys who worked at Dunkin Donuts, guys who gave out flyers on street corners, guys who drove garbage trucks, and guys who washed windows on the Empire State Building. (15)

In this homosexualized version of a Richard Scarry Busytown, Delany makes the point, elaborated at greater length and more explicitly later in the book, that the theaters are a space of interclass contact. He also uses the technique of listing to suggest that these spaces are marked by a friendly, democratic openness to variety. Number—in the sense of lots of men sharing the space—is crucial in scrambling traditional hierarchies and in reducing the burden of expectation on any one encounter or relation.

Listing also makes possible a kind of characterization that is neither brutally reductive (as in the stereotype) nor full, deep, and rich (as in novelistic characterization): fueled by erotic desire and nonconsuming curiosity about the people he meets, it is a form of typification. A standard operating procedure of deviance studies—which analyzed the doings not of men and women, but of ex-cons and drug addicts, prostitutes and delinquents—typification has been seen as reductive and reinforcing of social hierarchies. But in Delany's view, the proliferation of human types is salutary both socially and sexually. It makes it more likely that you will be able to find your type, but also, he suggests, it makes it possible to "ease up" on the requirements for personhood and intimacy. Extrapolating from Jane Jacobs's work on public space in *The Death and Life of Great American Cities*, Delany writes, "If every sexual encounter involves bringing someone back to your house, the general sexual activity in a city becomes anxiety-filled, class-bound, and choosy. This is precisely why public rest rooms, peep shows, sex movies, bars with grope rooms, and parks with enough greenery are necessary for a relaxed and friendly sexual atmosphere in a democratic metropolis" (127). Delany draws what might seem a counterintuitive link between depersonalization and ethical treatment of the other.

Number—in the sense of frequency—is important to Delany as a democratizing and pleasantly dehumanizing force. Delany makes this argument repeatedly throughout *Times Square Red*, extolling the "humane and functional" aspect of public sexual encounters—in the face of the fact that those adjectives are often understood to be contradictory. The close relation between number, sexual satisfaction, and a thinned-out sense of personhood is clear in a passage about sexual variety:

There are as many different styles, intensities, and timbres to sex as there are people. The variety of nuance and attitude blends into the variety of techniques and actions employed, which finally segues, as seamlessly, into the variety of sexual objects the range of humankind desires. Certainly one of the necessary places where socializing and sexualizing actually touch for, dare I call it, health or just contentment: We do a little better when we sexualize our own manner of having sex—learn to find our own way of having sex sexy. Call it a healthy narcissism, if you like. This alone allows us to relax with our own sexuality. Paradoxically, this also allows us to vary it and accommodate it, as far as we wish, to other people. I don't see how this can be accomplished without a statistically significant variety of partners and a fair amount of communication with them, at that, about what their sexual reactions to us are. (However supportive, the response of a single partner just cannot do that. This is a quintessentially *social* process, involving a social response.) (45-46)

Delany offers a glimpse of utopia here, suggesting that the process of collecting enough single, empirical examples will contribute to the flourishing of democratic values such as variety, flexibility, and recognition. Recognition has its limits, however. Although he goes on to cite Jacques Lacan in the following sentence ("One desires the desire of the other"), the perspective Delany articulates is not psychoanalytic as much as it is descriptive, behaviorist, and functional. The subject of this healthy narcissism shows no signs of having an unconscious; rather, we get to know him (as he is known in the theaters) through his actions and behaviors.

Delany shares with Laud Humphreys an ecological view of sexual encounters in public. If Delany emphasizes the salutary qualities of biodiversity, and Humphreys the enabling function of environmental parameters, they both see sexuality as produced and sustained by institutions. Like many scholars of sexual deviance, they emphasize the determining power of social spaces and deemphasize individual motives and desires. As in *Tearoom Trade*, Delany's focus on the rules of the game requires some diminishment of the players, the reduction of whole people to types, or to a few typifying details. The personal, narrative, and literary qualities of *Times Square Red* set it apart from Humphreys's more scholarly and detached sociological study. But both books depend on quantification, reduction, and objectification, suggesting that these processes can be useful and gratifying in situations of both sexuality and study.[36]

One way to describe the "personal" nature of *Times Square Red* is that Delany so often puts himself in the frame. However, in contrast to the passage in *The Motion of Light in Water* that Scott analyzes, Delany tells us less about how he feels than about what he sees, what he does, and what he likes to do. In one passage, Delany discusses the penis size of a few men he met in the theaters, adding: "On a scale of small, medium, and large I fall directly on the borderline between the latter two" (44). Such glimpses also occur in *Tearoom Trade*, as in the odd flash we get of Humphreys ("I zipped pants and moved in front of left window" [35]) in the "Description of Action" section of a "Systematic Observation Sheet" he reproduces in the text. While Humphreys emphasizes the impersonality of the encounters he witnesses in the tearooms, Delany's more expansive account relies on similar methods of objectification and self-objectification. Furthermore, Humphreys and Delany can both be seen to be working in the ethological tradition pursued by Tinbergen and, in his own way, Goffman. All of them pursue some version of participant observation, risking bodily involvement as they record what they see from within rather than outside a given situation.[37]

At the end of the author's preface to *Times Square Red*, Delany returns to the metaphor of the periplum, expressing his utopian aspirations for the reception of the book:

> I hope these two extended essays function as early steps (though by no means are they the first) in thinking through the problem of where people, male and female, gay and straight, old and young, working class and middle class, Asian and Hispanic, black and other, rural and urban, tourist and indigene, transient and permanent, with their bodily, material, sexual and emotional needs, might discover (and even work to set up) varied and welcoming harbors for landing on our richly variegated urban shore. (xx)

Delany's celebration of democratic inclusion relies on a view of knowledge production that allies it with the empirical and practical genre of the periplum. It is difficult to reconcile Delany's vision with the antifoundationalism and antiempiricism of queer studies, which puts its faith in disruption rather than description. Despite Delany's stature in the field, queer scholars have failed to grapple with the impulse behind his documentation of marginal worlds. Scott's challenge to experience as evidence was part of a successful movement to show the limits of identity politics by making a link between realist epistemology, empirical methods, and the reinforcement of existing social hierarchies.[38] Yet facts are not necessarily the enemy of progressive politics. As in postwar research on sexual deviance, the description of the world can lead to its transformation.

Critiques of the stabilizing force of description tend to center populations that have long had a place in discourse, and whose hold on tools of representation, including description, is likened to hegemony. However, description means something quite different for those whose place in the social world remains marginal: in such contexts, gaining a foothold in representation is crucial, an act of survival. Description has yet other uses. It is clear that finely drawn, exhaustive portraits of the social world are useful in creating the desire for social change. By meticulously showing how the world is, scholars and artists can also effectively point to what is wrong with it. Furthermore, they can attest to how it is put together and how it works—works very well for some, and against the interest of others.

This diagramming of the operations of the social world would be one definition of Left scholarship, which aims to map the world's problems so that
it is possible to make sense of them and ultimately to take them on. However, this crucial role for scholarship in supporting the work of activism has
been obscured by a view that conflates scholarship with activism, and sees
description's role as inevitably ideological.

THE HUMAN WORLD

At the end of *Times Square Red*, Delany discusses his consternation at a
panel in response to a 1998 OutWrite Conference of Lesbian and Gay
Writers in Boston. Describing the "elaborate indirection" of the participants' reflections—reflections that led away from the panel's key questions ("Why is there homophobia?" and "What makes us gay?") toward
"great philosophical conundrums"—Delany asserts his preference for socially and materially grounded analysis (184). Reflecting on the relation
between metaphysics, discourse, and social reality, he writes:

> It is language (and/as social habit) that cuts up the world into the ele-
> ments, objects, and categories we so glibly call reality—a reality that in-
> cludes the varieties of desire; a reality where what is real *is* what must be
> dealt with, which is one with the political; the world *is* what it is cut up
> into—all else is metaphysics. That is all that is meant by that troubling
> poststructuralist assertion that the world is constituted of and by lan-
> guage and nothing more that we have any direct access to. (192)

Demonstrating his chops as a poststructuralist, Delany concedes that
reality is mediated by and can only be accessed through language.

Delany immediately qualifies this statement, however. Affirming his
commitments as a materialist, he issues a warning about the limits of the
claim for universal mediation by language. He writes,

> The problem with this assertion is that one of the easiest things to
> understand about it is that if language/social habit makes/produces/
> sediments anything, it makes/produces/sediments the meaning of
> words . . . I am not convinced that this is an important observation tell-
> ing us something truly important about ontology or epistemology. It
> may just be an empty tautology that can be set aside and paid no more
> attention to. Personally, I think the decision as to whether it is or is not

interesting is to be found *in* ontology and epistemology themselves—rather than in theory. That is to say, if the observation emboldens us to explore the world, cut it up in new and different ways, and learn what new and useful relationships can result, then the observation is of use and interest; but it is not interesting to the extent that it leads only to materially unattended theoretical restatements of itself. (192–93)

Delany's commitment to the linguistic constitution of the world; his attention to themes of memory, embodiment, desire, and experience; and his use of an intermittently lyrical first-person voice may distract us from the sociological nature of his work—evident not only in his analyses of political economy and institutions, but in descriptions of sexual worlds as well. What is especially clear is Delany's impatience with doctrine. Understanding that the world is mediated by language is nothing on its own. It is only of interest to the extent that it helps us to remake the world. Other insights might do as well or better, in which case this idea—easy to understand, hard to enact—should be abandoned, replaced with something more effective.

With his skepticism about antifoundationalism and his investment in concrete spaces and practices, Delany is an awkward fit with the version of the literary that emerged during the linguistic turn. His literary qualities cannot be separated from his commitment to exploring and cutting up the world—processes that depend on concrete practices of observation and description. Delany's expansion of the definition of the literary is echoed in Dubey's reflections in *Signs and Cities* on how her engagement with Black postmodernist texts disrupted her assumptions about the superiority of literature as a means of explaining social life. She writes: "But the recognition that all knowledge is textual need not provoke a disheartened retreat from any effort to know and understand the world. I am convinced that it is necessary to posit some notion of the real in order to make any claims about social life, while remaining fully aware that because human knowledge of reality is always discursively mediated, it is also always fallible and revisable" (13).

In the 1970s and 1980s, literary studies played a crucial role in disrupting the scientism of the social sciences, and in moving empirical disciplines toward antifoundationalism and textual interpretation. These were heady times for the field: for once, literary critics could finish historians' sentences, and the words of a Black, gay sci-fi writer could transform the methods of a notoriously conservative academic discipline. It is clear in "The Evidence of Experience" that one of the key uses of literature for

Scott is as a tool to move her discipline. After extolling the virtues of a literary approach to representations of experience, she suggests that the field of history has been limited by the fact that it "has typically constructed itself in opposition to literature" (793). But the identification of "the literary" with the realm of uncertainty, ambiguity, and the "differencing" properties of representation resulted in an impoverished account of literature—a shift of focus to differencing made it difficult to account for existing differences. What social scientists borrowed from literary studies was less a determinate methodology than an idea of "the literary" meant to be deployed within and against the social sciences.

In pointing to the selectivity of Scott's reading of Delany, my aim is not to argue that poststructuralism went too far, nor do I hope to "return" to a sober epistemological realism. Such solutions, even if they were possible, would reinforce the split between the disciplines by granting a spurious substance to both the "realist" and "antirealist" positions in this debate.[39] Instead, I am interested in the consequences of the historical deployment of literature and "the literary" as a lever to move the social sciences. The rise of literary studies as *the* antifoundationalist discipline resulted in an elevation of its status but also a limiting of its purview. Literary studies, and the form of queer thought that was closely associated with it, thus became a powerful form of critique on the condition that it give up its claims to produce positive knowledge or to account for what John Guillory calls the "human world."[40] As poststructuralist insights have become more widespread and their market value has declined, it is not clear if this was a good deal for literary studies or for queer theory. What, in the end, did these fields have to offer the social sciences besides a correction?

BY WHAT LIGHT?

At the end of *Minima Moralia*, Adorno writes, "The only philosophy which can be reasonably practiced in the face of despair is the attempt to contemplate all things as they would present themselves from the standpoint of redemption. Knowledge has no light but that shed on the world by redemption: all else is reconstruction, mere technique. Perspectives must be fashioned that displace and estrange the world, reveal it to be, with its rifts and crevices, as indigent and distorted as it will appear one day in the messianic light."[41] This is the strongest version of the argument against the method of description, which in *this* light appears as mere technique. This statement, written under the pressure of catastrophe and as a reflection on "damaged life," suggests that to describe the world as it is means redoubling its violence, and blocking the possibility of utopia. This understanding of the limits of description and call for the nonidentical as the basis for thought informs important recent queer work, for instance, José Esteban Muñoz's passionate insistence that "this world is not enough" and his call to strive "in the face of the here and now" "to think and feel a *then and there*," a queer utopia.[42]

But Adorno adds to this call to set the world beside itself, to produce perspectives that reveal the "rifts and crevices" of the world, the following caveat: "To gain such perspectives without velleity or violence, entirely from felt contact with its objects—this alone is the task of thought" (247). For Adorno this kind of thinking is both necessary and impossible, "because it presupposes a standpoint removed, even though by a hair's breadth, from the scope of existence, whereas we well know that any possible knowledge must not only be first wrested from what is, if it shall hold good, but is also marked, for this very reason, by the same distortion and indigence which it seeks to escape" (247). In imagining a descriptive politics of stigma against the more familiar background of a politics of queer performativity, I want to underline this double aspect of thought. According to Adorno, thought must situate itself both within the existent and beyond it; it must be developed "wholly by one's contact with objects" at the same time as it strives to set the world beside itself. Muñoz's utopian thought of the "not yet here" meets this criterion. Although Muñoz is passionately resistant to queer pragmatism, by which he means accommodation to what exists, his insistence on the possibility of a transformed future is at the same time a melancholic engagement with the *here* and the *now*.

By sketching a history of relations between deviance studies and queer theory, I have attempted to show that queer studies' preference for setting the world beside itself is not only a matter of politics. It is also a matter of disciplinary training. In the splitting up of thought in the structure of the disciplines, the humanities have taken up the work of setting the world beside itself—leaving description to empirical disciplines therefore deemed to be both realist in their epistemology and conservative in their politics. On this side of the divide, we have taken up errancy as an epistemological program, as a commitment to thought as exposure and destabilization. We have left the study of errancy as an event in the phenomenal world to others. But while this choice to abdicate the empirical to the sciences and the social sciences might extend our imaginative reach, it radically diminishes our feel for the world as it is.

4 · Doing Being Deviant

The tattoos I have on me ally me with the herd, the toughs, the lower-class, the criminal—and I like it not only sexually but because that world spits in the face of the one which has contained me thus far.

Samuel Steward[1]

The study of norms and deviance is central to the intellectual genealogy of queer studies. A significant aspect of what Gayle Rubin has described as the "obscured" history of the field, research on deviance and social problems in the social sciences, shaped queer studies' commitment to subcultures, to nonnormativity, and to a constructionist view of sexuality. Yet there is no doubt that classic deviance studies scholarship throws up some obstacles to understanding and enjoyment for the contemporary queer critic. Detailed, detached analyses of the folkways of the homosexual can strike an odd note in a moment when queers are doing it for themselves. The dated language, stance of neutrality, and frequent appeals to common sense in postwar research on sexuality suggest a perspective on norms and their violation alien to the explicitly political field of queer studies. These tonal differences have made it difficult to see the connections between deviance studies and queer studies and to see what this older knowledge formation has to contribute to the contemporary study of sexuality and gender. Yet the field of queer studies—with its emphasis on marginality, nonconformity, and miscellaneous forms of difference (what Edward Sagarin referred to in his 1971 collection as the "other minorities"[2])—is unthinkable without the contributions of postwar research on social problems, including homosexuality. In its embrace of a politics of stigma and its reliance on a general category of social marginality, queer theory borrowed its account of difference from deviance studies.

As is well known, *queer* sidesteps traditional identity categories such as gay, lesbian, and bisexual in favor of a more general category of social marginality. Less recognized are the similarities between *queer* and the categories developed in postwar empirical research in the social sciences: the underdog, the alien, the outsider, and the deviant. The image of the social outsider became key to the stigma-centric, solidarity politics of queer studies. In addition, scholars in deviance studies articulated several of the concepts that have been central to the study of sexuality since the rise of queer theory: social construction; stigma as dynamic and relational (see, for instance, Schur's claim that "it takes two to deviance"[3]); a dramaturgical account of the self and behavior; power as central to group and individual identity; and the contingency of personal and social life. Through textured, in-depth studies of the social lives of hustlers, con men, prostitutes, alcoholics, and juvenile delinquents, these researchers developed a dynamic, detailed account of the constitution and maintenance of social norms, as well as the consequences of conformity and nonconformity.

How to explain the lack of attention to the history of deviance studies among queer scholars? Apart from the widespread tendency to write off earlier modes of scholarship as dated, profound shifts in the professoriate and in styles of criticism from the 1960s to the 1990s partly explain this misrecognition. While social problem researchers in the postwar period saw themselves as experts on social deviance, they were cautious about identifying with the communities that they studied. Queer theory by contrast was defined from the start as undertaken by and for queer people: explicitly political, against expertise, and highly critical of the ideology of objectivity.

In 1993, Eve Kosofsky Sedgwick wrote, "A hypothesis worth making explicit: that there are important senses in which queer can only signify *when attached to the first person.* A possible corollary: what it takes—all it takes—to make the description 'queer' a true one is the impulsion *to* use it in the first person."[4] As a colloquial term of abuse, *queer* might have come straight from the pages of classic deviance studies, but queer theorists and activists did not adopt *queer* as an ethnographic term. Instead, they embraced it, in Judith Butler's account, as "a site of collective contestation," dynamized by ongoing transformation or *queering* "in the direction of urgent and expanding political purposes."[5] In the frame of deviance studies, *queer* did not suggest a militant stance against social norms; it alluded to everyday taxonomies and to the marginal social position of homosexuals. The objectifying of social norms, deviant behaviors, and the lives of social outsiders in classic deviance scholarship clashes with the transformative imperative of queer studies, which saw deviance as a rallying cry rather than an object of study. While deviance studies focused on the description and analysis of social norms, queer scholars saw themselves as participating in their subversion.

While this shift might be understood as straightforward narrative of progress toward politicization, such a frame depends on a definition of politics that is both historically contingent and strongly marked by disciplinary rivalry between the humanities and social sciences. The stabilization of homosexuality as an object of sociological knowledge in the 1960s and 1970s was a significant achievement for social scientists with profound political consequences. Social science research in the postwar period defined homosexuality as a social phenomenon, a structured and meaningful set of practices and organized communities. By shifting the frame from individual pathology to social organization, these researchers built a portrait of the homosexual community as ordinary and rule bound. This account of sexual practices and communities was crucial in suggesting that, despite the taboo associated with it, homosexuality was subject to the same methods of observation, measurement, and description as other sociological phenomena. From the perspective of social science researchers, the decoupling of homosexuality from medical pathology was an unmixed triumph, the founding moment of modern sexuality studies. However, from the perspective of queer critique, treating sexuality as a sociological phenomenon posed as many problems as treating it as a medical or psychological phenomenon. The critique of empiricism in queer studies meant that critics in the field tended to emphasize the role of the disciplines in the production and surveillance of sexual and gender minorities. Ongoing conflicts between humanists and social scientists turn on the question of whether the empirical study of sexuality should be understood as social recognition or as epistemological violence.

These divergent perspectives on the value of empirical research inflect contemporary discussions about norms and normativity. Scholars of deviance studied homosexuality alongside prostitution, delinquency, addiction, disability, and other forms of social marginality; while such a grouping might be seen as pathologizing, these researchers aimed to normalize homosexuality along with a range of nonconforming behaviors. Questioning the division between the normal and the deviant, they showed nonconforming sexual behavior to be socially patterned. This meaning of normal—as perceptible, meaningful, structured, and present—was opposed not to the politically subversive but to understandings of deviance as random, illegible, meaningless, and sick. *Normal* in this positive sense did not survive into queer theory or the broader, more diverse field that grew out of it, queer studies. Instead, from the early 1990s on, queer was defined as, in Michael Warner's phrase, "against the regimes of the normal"[6]: while the closest analog to normal for deviance studies might be social, normal became identified in queer theory with the forces of normalization or hegemony (including the forces of academic hegemony). By contrast, the concept of deviance thrived—but rather than being a descriptive term it became prescriptive. Queer theorists embraced deviance not as an inevitable counterpart to conforming behavior and an integral aspect of the social world but rather as a challenge to the stability and coherence of that world.

The shift from a descriptive to a prescriptive view of the world might be understood—and indeed has been understood by queer scholars—as a process of politicization. But to say that scholars of deviance studied norms rather than setting themselves against them is not the same thing as saying that their work was apolitical. To cast such differences as primarily political is to misunderstand both the historical context of postwar research on sexuality and to treat a contentious view of empirical research as inherently conservative as if it were a matter of fact. While queer studies has understood itself alternately as interdisciplinary and as antidisciplinary, frequent dismissals of social science methodologies and epistemologies undermine such claims—and show up the radicalism of the queer break with academic norms as a familiar form of disciplinary rivalry. Queer antinormativity has taken as its explicit targets heterosexuality, the family, and gender binarism; however, it is directed as much against the protocols and epistemology of the social sciences as it is against prevailing social norms.

DESCRIBING DEVIANCE

By understanding deviance as a departure from the social world rather than a part of it, queer theory profoundly challenged representational and epistemological regimes of sexuality. Yet such shifts have not transformed the material conditions of academic scholarship or the power relations between professional academics and the marginal subjects they study. In returning to the history of postwar studies of sexuality, I hope to have demonstrated the value of a descriptive view of sexual practices and sexual communities. While practices of objectification have been dismissed within queer studies, these methods are useful in capturing the experience of gender and sexual minorities in a moment of rapid social transformation and in an academic context in which the social referent of *queer* can be quite elusive. Postwar scholars of sexuality also demonstrate an impressive capacity to objectify the position of scholars themselves—a capacity that has often been absent in queer scholarship, despite the value that the field places on self-reflexivity. Although deviance studies may strike many as dated or conservative, its capacity to objectify sexual practices and communities—and the position of the scholars who study them—makes it a useful model for contemporary queer criticism.

Although postwar scholars of sexuality saw social deviance as integral to social life, they did not see it as fixed or permanent; instead, they defined deviance as a relation, the product of social interaction. In their publications from the late 1960s, John H. Gagnon and William Simon developed a relational account of sexual deviance that emphasized the dynamic between norms and deviance. In their introduction to *Sexual Deviance* (1967), they focus on the social life of deviance, framing it as neither essential ("There is no form of behavior, sexual or nonsexual, that is intrinsically deviant or deviant because of the behavior it involves") nor exceptional ("Deviance exists in social systems as a necessary complement to conformity").[7] Their "inclusive" view of social problems emphasized the variability and inevitability of deviance:

> Deviance, then, may be considered one of the facts of social life. While the "why," the "what," and the "how" of its definition and the response of those so defined may vary from society to society, or from community to community in more complex societies, or even from one period in the history of a single community to another period, the probability of the occurrence of deviance is great, for to speak of norms is to anticipate their violation. (2)

Deviance, far from being a radical break with the social world (or in any sense antisocial), is in this view as integral as conformity to the constitution and reproduction of the social world.[8]

Several of the essays collected in *Sexual Deviance* emphasize the ordinariness of homosexuality and its proximity to other modes of social life. In their headnote to Evelyn Hooker's foundational article "The Homosexual Community," Simon and Gagnon explain that Hooker's attention to the ordinariness of homosexual life brought out its complexity. They explain that the homosexual community

> provides many of the same things that other communities provide for their members. It is a training ground for learning values and behav-

ior, a milieu in which persons already trained may live every day, and a source of social support and information for its members. Seen in this framework, homosexuality loses much of its exotic flavor and can be viewed as a life career composed of many contingencies and crises of identity and personal choice. Once again, as in the case of the prostitute, we move away from a simple category toward the complexity of experience and life as it is lived.[9]

Hooker wrote her ethnography of gay bars in a social context in which homosexuals were not considered a community but rather a "mere aggregate of persons" (171). In order to frame homosexuality as a "fact of social life" and not merely an attribute of disturbed persons, Hooker describes patterns of behavior and settlement that demonstrate its community character. She defines community as a group of people "engaging in common activities, sharing common interests, and having a feeling of sociopsychological unity" (171). She points out that neither residential settlement nor commercial activity in the city among homosexuals are random, and goes on to elaborate on the features of the gay "life or 'scene'" (172). Hooker's attention is directed toward bars as key institutions of this scene, where men can meet to gossip, exchange information, and cruise.

The fact that the bars function as rule-bound sites with a shared set of behaviors and expectations is crucial for Hooker. Her description of the activity of cruising is highly detailed, suggesting both how conventional these community norms are and how much time Hooker put into observing them. She defines bars as sexual markets—"places where agreements are made for the potential exchange of sexual services, for sex without obligation or commitment" (175)—and goes on to elaborate the means by which such agreements are made:

> If one watches very carefully, and knows what to watch for in a "gay" bar, one observes that some individuals are apparently communicating with each other without exchanging words, but simply by exchanging glances—but not the kind of quick glance which ordinarily occurs between men. It is said by homosexuals that if another catches and holds the glance, one need know nothing more about him to know that he is one of them. The psychological structure of that meeting of glances is a complex one, involving mutual recognition of social, but not personal, identity, sexual intent, and agreement ... Occasionally, we may see a glance catch and hold another glance. Later, as if in an accidental

meeting, the two holders-of-a-glance may be seen in a brief conversation followed by their leaving together. Or, the conversation may be
omitted. Casually and unobtrusively, they may arrive at the door at the
same time, and leave. If we followed them, we would discover that they
were strangers, who by their exchange of glances had agreed to a sexual
exchange. (175-76)

Hooker retrospectively defines this activity as cruising, describing a highly
structured system of communication that depends on shared norms and
expectations among patrons. Gay men's sexual lives had previously been
seen as an example of "primary narcissism" or some other disturbance
of their "psychodynamic structure" (176). Hooker argues that the "system effects of the community"—that is, social conditions and prevailing
norms—have been undervalued in relation to individual needs and desires.

While Hooker emphasizes the ordinariness of homosexuality, her
tracking of the smallest details of cruising rituals casts the activities of the
men in a mysterious light. The researcher is detached, alert to the smallest gestures and signs, decoding behavior inexplicable to the untrained
eye. The scene recalls Hooker's citation of the "commonplace ... analogy"
of the "tip of the iceberg" (172), referring to the submerged and invisible
world of gay life, known only to initiates. Identifying herself as an outsider
whose primary involvement is her "research role" (169), Hooker becomes
an expert through close, sustained observation. The similarities between
observation and more interventionist forms of watching are striking: like
a naturalist, the social scientist looks very carefully; like a private detec-
tive, policeman, reformer, stalker, or jealous lover, she imagines following
this newly formed couple to the site of their private encounter. This desire
to get a look at the whole iceberg, even those parts that are purposefully
guarded from view, has given social scientific studies of homosexuality a
bad name among queer critics. However, one might argue that Hooker's
observational style is a method that fits the optical and erotic arrangements of the bar space. Furthermore, it is through the process of objectification that Hooker comes to see the activities of men looking for sex as
patterned, meaningful community behavior. Through such sustained acts
of looking—looking for patterns instead of looking at people—Hooker redefines the homosexual community as "a 'deviant community'" instead of
a "'community of deviants'" (184).

Understanding deviance as social meant seeing it as a function of relations between persons (and their concretization in norms) rather than as a trait inherent in persons. As is evident in Hooker's emphasis on her research role in "The Homosexual Community," this account of the relational aspects of deviance included consideration of the relation between the deviant and the scholar. Even the earliest work on social problems demonstrates an understanding of stigma as a relational concept. Willard Waller's 1936 article "Social Problems and the Mores" opens with a reflection on the role of the researcher's values in determining what counts as a social problem:

> The term social problem indicates not merely an observed phenomenon but the state of mind of the observer as well. Value judgments define certain conditions of human life and certain kinds of behavior as social problems; there can be no social problem without a value judgment. When our attitude toward a phenomenon is involved in our concept of it, logical difficulties arise which can only be avoided by shifting to an inclusive point of view which enables us to study both the thing and our attitude toward it.[10]

If theories of social pathology frame deviance as an objective fact or state of affairs or as characterizing a particular kind of person, deviance studies has always understood deviance and stigma as products of social interaction, making the problems of observation and judgment central. During the 1960s and 1970s, the collective contestation of social norms became increasingly central to definitions of deviance and social problems. Yet deviance studies scholars remained committed to the objective study rather than the wholesale transformation of social problems, avoiding the appearance of bias in scholarship that, despite tectonic shifts during the period, remained committed to principles of science. One result of this embrace of objectivity was that the relation between scholars and their objects of study was itself held up to scrutiny as one of the most important sites for the production of deviance.

An influential discussion of the ethics of deviance research is Howard Becker's 1967 essay "Whose Side Are We On?" in which he wrestles with "the problem of taking sides as it arises in the study of deviance" (239).[11] The essay begins with a reflection on the question of values: in their study of contemporary social problems, sociologists are "caught in a crossfire" since some people "urge them to be neutral and do research that is technically correct and value free" and others "tell them their work is shallow and useless if it does not express a deep commitment to a value position" (239). Becker suggests that the dilemma is a false once, since value- or bias-free scholarship is impossible. He argues that sociologists, like other people, "cannot avoid taking sides, for reasons firmly based in social structure" (239). Scholars of deviance tend to take sides with "underdogs" against those responsible for their care and punishment: "the forces of approved and official morality" or "the official and professional authori-ties in charge of some important institution," including "professors and administrators, principals and teachers" (240). In taking the part of sub-ordinates against superordinates and granting credence to their point of view, deviance studies scholars incur the charge of bias since their attitude contravenes the *"hierarchy of credibility"* (241, emphasis in original)—the order that grants a sense of truth and reality to the views of "those at the top" (241). The top in this context is defined not as raw economic or juridi-cal power but as the moral authority of those in charge. Their defensive-ness can be regarded as a function of their responsibility, Becker writes:

> They have been entrusted with the care and operation of one or another of our important institutions: schools, hospitals, law enforcement, or whatever. They are the ones who by virtue of their official position and the authority that goes with it, are in a position to "do something" when things are not what they should be, are the ones who will be held to ac-count if they fail to "do something," or if what they do is, for whatever reason, inadequate. (242)

Becker addresses what he calls "the apolitical case," a situation in which "conflict and tension exist in the hierarchy, but conflict has not be-come openly political"—there is no organized opposition, and no one pro-poses a reorganization of the social structure (students switch places with teachers, inmates switch places with their jailors, patients switch places with their doctors, etc.) (240–41). In the "political case," open conflict has broken out, which simplifies the question of bias; although the sociologist may come under attack from any and all involved parties, he will not be in the position of upsetting the accepted moral hierarchy, of going against the point of view of both "responsible officials and the man in the street" (243). During the era of the new social movements, homosexuality (along with many other forms of difference) was redefined as an example of the "political case." It was during this time that, in Becker's words, "judg-ments of who has a right to define the nature of reality" that had been "taken for granted" became "matters of argument" (244). The key shift was from seeing homosexuals as sick or as moral outcasts to seeing them as members of a persecuted minority. This shift, often associated with the decline of deviance studies, marks the transition to early lesbian and gay studies and the openly partisan stance that characterized it.[12]

The emergence of queer studies in the early 1990s was an extension of this trajectory, as the field defined itself as an explicitly political enterprise. But the field's framing of its goals as *against rather than for* marks a crucial difference. Departing from the homophile commitments of lesbian and gay studies, queer scholars defined the field as a form of "antihomophobic inquiry" more committed to contesting normativity than to forwarding the specific interests of lesbians and gays.[13] While queer studies scholars embraced an openly partisan stance that was the product of the redefinition of homosexuality as a political rather than a moral issue, they remained committed to the conflict over morality and the hierarchy of credibility that was characteristic of apolitical struggle—or homosexuality in the era of deviance. Rather than shift definitively into the realm of the political, then, queer studies embraced the stance of open conflict in order to invert the traditional moral hierarchies of deviance. The "against-ness" of queer studies can be understood as a mixture of Becker's apolitical and political cases, but one that can fail to acknowledge the distance queer scholars have climbed up the hierarchy of credibility.

Becker offers a pragmatic assessment of the position and allegiances of the professional scholar, and suggests that, though bias is inevitable, we need to continue to affirm disciplinary norms of rigor and falsifiability. He writes,

> Given all our techniques of theoretical and technical control, how can we be sure that we will apply them across the board as they need to be applied? . . . We can, for a start, try to avoid sentimentality. We are sentimental when we refuse, for whatever reason, to investigate some matter that should be properly regarded as problematic. We are sentimental, especially, when our reason is that we would prefer not to know what is going on, if to know would be to violate some sympathy whose existence we may not even be aware of. Whatever side we are on, we must use our techniques impartially enough that a belief to which we are especially sympathetic could be proved untrue. We must always inspect our work carefully enough to know whether our techniques and theories are open enough to allow that possibility. (246)

One may take exception to Becker's refusal of sentimentality and sympathy as linked to error and falsehood, although he goes on to argue that the incorporation rather than the exclusion of one's own perspective is the best way to deal with inevitable bias. He advocates the use of impartial methods as the only means of access to the object as something other than a reflection of our own values. In the framework of queer theory, such stabilizing methods—with their suggestion of a neutral or unbiased view—have been seen as a form of violence. However, we might also understand these methods as implying respect for our objects, since their aim is to keep open the possibility that one might be surprised or proven wrong.

BUSINESS AS USUAL

Among the many experiments—intellectual, methodological, stylistic, and political—of early queer theory, one of the most significant was the attempt to bring the energy and ethos of radical activism into the academy. In his introduction to *Fear of a Queer Planet*, Michael Warner describes queer theory's refusal of existing norms of scholarship as a resistance to "normal business in the academy" (xxvi). This business included traditional methods as well as styles of self-presentation (propriety, seriousness, and objectivity). "Being interested in queer theory," Warner writes, "is a way to mess up the desexualized spaces of the academy, exude some rut, reimagine the publics from and for which intellectuals write, dress, and perform" (xxvi). Queer theory opened new spaces in the university for different personnel, behavior, and methodology. The fact that these scholars wanted to change the rules of the academic game was a function not only of theoretical avant-gardism, but also of the activist and antiacademic orientation of many of the players. While early attacks on queer theory called out its elitism, what is most striking in retrospect about this moment is the paradoxical rise to academic prestige of a mode of scholarship deeply critical of institutions, professionalism, and traditional methods. For some observers, this outsider stance was merely bad faith, a disavowal of institutional and other forms of privilege. However, the success of queer theory was never guaranteed; it was always a work in progress, an unanticipated and in many ways an unwanted gift. The stunning success of queer theory can in part be explained by this constitutive ambivalence and a remarkable ability to combine insider cachet with outsider attitude.

Queer theory did break with academic business as usual in many ways, but its rejection of the social sciences is not one of them. Instead, this rejection is consistent with the pattern of territorial disputes between the social sciences and the humanities. The refusal of the legacy of deviance studies is not only a radicalization of the role of the critic; it also replays a familiar rejection of social scientific methods by critics trained almost exclusively in the humanities (literary studies, philosophy, classics, art history, critical theory, and cultural studies). The antifoundationalist, explicitly political interventions of queer thinkers transformed traditional humanistic inquiry, but also extended it. A negative consensus about the protocols, epistemology, and ethics of the social sciences marked this moment, evident in widespread critiques of description, objectivity, neutrality, and expertise. The investment in scholarly protocols of neutrality and distance among even radical sociologists does not translate well into the frame of queer inquiry, where it reads as quietism, conservatism, or collusion with state violence.

The disciplinary allegiances of queer theory are evident in attacks on what was understood as the methodological normativity of the social sciences. Warner, with Lauren Berlant, discussed the field's resistance to method in their 1995 *PMLA* essay "What Does Queer Theory Teach Us about X?" Berlant and Warner suggest that *queer* resists the ideology of utility entailed in offering "a general description of the world."[14] They write:

> The question of x might be more ordinary in disciplines that have long histories of affiliation with the state. Sociology, psychology, anthropology, and political science, for example, have earned much of their funding and expert authority by encouraging questions of utility. Queer theory has flourished in the disciplines where expert service to the state has been least familiar and where theory has consequently meant unsettlement rather than systematization. This failure to systematize the world in queer theory does not mean a commitment to irrelevance; it means resistance to being an apparatus for falsely translating systematic and random violences into normal states, administrative problems, or minor constituencies. (348)

While queer theory turns its attention to the traditional objects of social problem research, it questions the normative frameworks that make these forms of behavior, persons, and communities legible to researchers, reformers, and political strategists. By refusing closure and capture in relation to her objects, the queer theorist is able to do justice to x.

In *Fear of a Queer Planet*, Warner's resistance to social scientific proto-cols extends to a critique of the concept of the social realm. Arguing that "queer politics opposes society itself" (xxvii), he writes,

> The social realm . . . is a cultural form interwoven with the political form of the administrative state and with the normalizing methodolo-gies of modern social knowledge. Can we not hear in the resonances of queer protest an objection to the normalization of behavior in this broad sense, and thus to the cultural phenomenon of societialization? If queers, incessantly told to alter their "behavior," can be understood as protesting not just the normal behavior of the social but the idea of normal behavior, they will bring skepticism to the methodologies founded on that idea. (xxvii)

Chief among the methodologies founded on the idea of normal behavior is the sociological study of deviance, and yet Warner's account of a queer front against the regimes of the normal is unthinkable apart from the his-tory of deviance studies. However, there is a key disagreement at the level of methodology, since the study of sexuality as an objective phenomenon is fundamental to sociology and anathema to queer theory. Social prob-lem research sought to account for both normal and deviant behavior as aspects of the social. While scholars of deviance might be on the side of so-cial outsiders, they did not negate the normal and the deviant as categories integral to social life, nor did they contest the existence of the social order.

The dismissal of sociological studies of deviance by queer humanities scholars is the result of a misreading of the concept of deviance as it was developed in the postwar period as well as a persistent refusal of the em-pirical premises and methodological protocols of the social sciences. We might trace this disagreement to the concept of objectification, which in a social science frame refers to the consideration of homosexuality as an as-pect of social life (rather than an individual pathology) but in the humani-ties suggests turning it into a thing, divorcing it from living processes, and rendering its stigmatization permanent and fixed. The humanities view of social scientific objectification fails to recognize the dynamism and com-plexity of deviance and stigma in sociological work from the period. But it also fails to recognize the important role of objectification in cultivating self-reflexivity; the scientific protocols of observation and description em-ployed by postwar social scientists often positioned the researcher as an object of study.

In *Language and Symbolic Power*, Pierre Bourdieu offers a critical account of objectification but also emphasizes the need to objectify objectification. He writes,

> But to objectify objectification means, above all, objectifying the field of production of the objectified representations of the social world, and in particular of the legislative taxonomies, in short, the field of cultural or ideological production, a game in which the social scientist is himself involved, as are all those who debate the nature of social classes.[15]

In Bourdieu's view, one cannot be against objectification, one can only objectify it, attempting to provide an account of the social field in which scholarship is undertaken. While deviance studies scholars might identify as social outsiders or align themselves with them, they continued to argue for the importance of objective, empirical methods and the distinctness of the research role in their work. Queer theory was a revolt against scholarly expertise in the name of deviance, yet it resonated in many ways with academic norms. Queer academics might be activists, organic intellectuals, radical experimenters in their personal, professional, and political lives. But they are also superordinates in the context of the university: professional knowledge workers, teachers, and administrators.

SYMPATHY FOR THE DEVIL

In their article "Social Deviance and Political Marginality," Irving Louis Horowitz and Martin Liebowitz discuss the erosion of the distinction between "personal deviance and political dissent" in the campus protest movements of the 1960s.[16] They note the affinities between the New Left and marginal social groups, and the embrace of a politics of rebellion against norms of propriety and social participation. In contrast to the Old Left with its stance of working-class solidarity and its habits of respectability, the new social radicals take up a politics of everyday life that pushes them toward the fringes of society. They write,

> If there is a hero, it is the alienated man who understands what is wrong and seeks escape. Often, escape takes the form of social deviance, which is considered no worse than the forms of behavior which are traditionally defined as normative. The traditional hero has been supplanted by the anti-hero who wins and attains heroic proportions by

not getting involved in the political process. This anti-hero is defined by what he is against as much as by what he is for; he is for a world of his own, free from outside constraints, in which he is free to experiment and experience. (289)

Horowitz and Liebowitz address the convergence between the culture of Left protest and the margins of society, considering the unlikely alliance between the antiwar movement and the Hell's Angels, or the identification among student activists with forms of social marginality (homosexuality, mental illness, and addiction) in order to escape the draft. Horowitz and Liebowitz's account of the student movement as "a celebration of deviance itself as the ultimate response to orthodox politics" (289) resonates with dismissals of both student protest and queer studies as engaging in a narcissistic and indulgent politics of personal liberation. Yet the importance of struggles over the definition of norms and deviance have been crucial in queer activism, since those subject to social stigma and inferiorization are drawn to contest, as Edwin M. Schur notes, the "oppressive conditions governing their everyday experience" (195).

Horowitz and Liebowitz's account of the New Left resonates with Herbert Marcuse's account of Orpheus and Narcissus in *Eros and Civilization*, and with a recently ascendant ethics of refusal, self-divestiture, and impossibility in queer studies. Marcuse contrasts the image of Prometheus, which he associates with the modern performance principle, with that of Orpheus and Narcissus, who are identified with the realm of the underworld, the aesthetic, and death. He writes,

> In contrast to the images of the Promethean culture-heroes, those of the Orphic and Narcissistic world are essentially unreal and unrealistic. They designate an "impossible" attitude and existence. The deeds of the culture-heroes also are "impossible," in that they are miraculous, incredible, superhuman. However, their objective and their "meaning" are not alien to the reality; on the contrary, they are useful. They promote and strengthen this reality; they do not explode it. But the Orphic-Narcissistic images do explode it; they do not convey a "mode of living"; they are committed to the underworld and to death.[17]

Marcuse's account of the Orphic-Narcissistic realm offers an image of what Horowitz and Liebowitz understand as the fusion of revolt and deviance. While Marcuse invokes the mythological realm of the underworld, his description of an impossible, death-bound existence that inverts moral hierarchies draws on the image repertoire of a sociological underworld—the dwelling place of exiles and outcasts.

Marcuse associates the Orphic-Narcissistic revolt with homosexuality and with a more general revolt against sexual norms: "The classical tradition associates Orpheus with the introduction of homosexuality. Like Narcissus, he rejects the normal Eros, not for an ascetic ideal, but for a fuller Eros. Like Narcissus, he protests against the repressive order of procreative sexuality. The Orphic and Narcissistic Eros is to the end the negation of this order—the Great Refusal" (171). The importance of homosexuality in Marcuse's allegory of the New Left is crucial, for homosexuality offers a fusion of protest and deviance, revolution and refusal. Queer studies took up this mantle of Orphic-Narcissistic revolt, and remains invested in the idea of an impossible—because absolute—withdrawal from the social.

Today, queer studies—prestigious but unevenly institutionalized—still signals radical protest against the profession and against norms of scholarship. In their influential 2004 essay "The University and the Undercommons" (and in the 2013 book that followed from it), Fred Moten and Stefano Harney rely on such an understanding of queer (as well as concepts borrowed from Black studies, feminism, ethnic studies, and anticolonial thought). They call for betrayal, refusal, theft, and marronage as modes of resisting the iron grip of the academy, pointing to an uncharted and collective space they call the undercommons. "To enter this space," they write, "is to inhabit the ruptural and enraptured disclosure of the commons that fugitive enlightenment enacts, the criminal, matricidal, queer, in the cistern, on the stroll of the stolen life, the life stolen by enlightenment and stolen back, where the commons give refuge, where the refuge gives commons."[18] Moten and Harney speculate about whether the "thought of the outside" (105) is possible inside the university, and suggest that if there is an outside it is along the margins and at the bottom. Yet their imagination of that outside is indebted to the inside—in particular to the conception of deviance produced within sociology. Their account of the undercommons reads like a rap sheet, a list of the traditional topics of deviance studies: theft, homosexuality, prostitution, incarceration.

Moten and Harney do not describe the undercommons, but rather ask their readers to join it, to participate in active revolt against professional and disciplinary protocols. To offer an objective account of the social position of radical academics would be to further business as usual in the academy; dwelling in the undercommons requires giving up on the usual protocols of description. Moten and Harney argue against the traditional role of the "critical academic" (105), which they see as just another turn of the professional screw, since work that opposes the academy objects to certain features of its operation but accepts its basic structure. They argue that "to be a critical academic in the university is to be against the university, and to be against the university is always to recognize it and to be recognized by it, and to institute the negligence of the internal outside, that unassimilated underground, a negligence of it that is precisely, we must insist, the basis of the professions" (105). In contrast to the figure of the critical academic, they forward the image of the "subversive intellectual" who is "in but not of" the academy (101). Without dismissing the galvanizing effect of such a call to the undercommons, it is important to consider the limits of the refusal of objectification as a strategy. To be unlocatable, to be nowhere, to be in permanent revolt—Moten and Harney describe the path that queer inquiry laid out for itself. Objectification—recognition, description, critique—can be a way to reinforce the status quo, but it is also a way of acknowledging one's institutional position and the real differences between inside and outside. Even the most subversive intellectuals in the academy are "on the stroll" in a metaphorical but not a material sense. The fate of those who came "under false pretenses, with bad documents, out of love" (101), if they survive, is to become "superordinates" in Becker's sense. One may disidentify utterly with this position of power, and cultivate an intellectual and political life that refuses its dictates. But to refuse its reality does not liberate anyone, least of all subordinates for whom the facts of hierarchy remain all too clear.

Whose side are we on? Can we hold on to the critical and polemical energy of queer studies as well as its radical experiments in style and thought while acknowledging our implication in systems of power, management, and control? Will a more explicit avowal of disciplinary affiliations and methods snuff out the utopian energies of a field that sees itself as a radical outsider in the university? To date, both the political and the methodological antinormativity of queer studies have made it difficult to address our implication in the violence of knowledge production, pedagogy, and a profoundly uneven social landscape. Such violence is inevitable, and critical histories of the disciplines—and the production of knowledge about social deviance—are essential. However, undertaking such work will not allow escape into a radically different relation to our objects. To imagine a social world in which those relations are transformed—in what Moten and Harney refer to as the "prophetic organization" (102)—may be crucial for the achievement of social justice, but to deny our own implication in existing structures is also a form of violence. Deviance studies is a crucial context for thinking through the politics of queer knowledge production because of its objectification of deviance and of the position of scholars in the field. This thorough objectification offers an important provocation to queer scholars who see their work as protest and as a violation of social norms.

QUEER METHOD

Over the past several years, queer scholars have addressed the history of the field and its disciplinary allegiances under the rubric "queer method." The publication of Kath Browne and Catherine J. Nash's edited volume *Queer Methods and Methodologies: Intersecting Queer Theories and Social Science Research* (2010) called attention to the "method" deficit in the field. Echoing Lisa Duggan's concerns about the hypertrophy of theory built upon a "stunted archive," Browne and Nash argued that the highly developed theory in the field was not matched by a similar commitment to method. They write, "queer researchers are in good company with other scholars drawing on poststructuralist and postmodernist approaches such as some feminist, anti-racist, and postcolonial scholars, in consciously seeking to articulate their ontologies and epistemologies but who are seemingly less inclined to consider the implications of these approaches to methodologies and methods."[19] Browne and Nash understand the critique of traditional methods as central to queer studies, and situate it in relation to other fields that regularly struggle with the problem of impossible or ephemeral evidence. But they argue that the field has failed to develop beyond the moment of critique, to develop full self-consciousness about its epistemology and its relation to disciplinary, institutional, and material structures. As often as disciplinary boundaries are crossed and re-crossed in queer studies, focusing the question of method—turning from "what" to "how"—tends to make visible more fundamental disagreements in epistemology and practice. If scholars in the social sciences have never forgotten (have never been able to forget) the existence of such differences, some humanities scholars have begun to engage them more robustly in recent years.

What has driven the turn toward queer method? The institutionalization of queer studies, incomplete as it is, has made the field's antidisciplinary stance harder to countenance. In addition, the decline of high theory or linguistic preoccupations across disciplines has put pressure on the field of queer studies to address its disciplinary identity—and the traditional sidelining of the social sciences—more urgently. Recent work has taken up these difficult questions, emphasizing pedagogy and academic labor, the material history of archives and funding structures: with the shift from theory to practice, there has been a renewed awareness of the working conditions that make intellectual production possible. Scholars have engaged fields of inquiry that had been little valued in queer studies, such as philology, biology, and sexology, and they have taken up outré tools such as taxonomy and quantification in the service of progressive aims. The shifting ground of queer critique has led scholars to reflect at length on questions of epistemology and ethics. For instance, in a 2011 article, anthropologist Margot Weiss considers the ambivalence of empiricism in queer theory, noting how scholars in the field value abstraction at the same time that they emphasize the significance of knowledge from below. Contrasting the "conceptual simplicity of our theoretical categories" with the complexity of community knowledge produced by the core disciplinary methods of ethnography and participant observation, Weiss also resists the call for "more data" to enrich the field. Instead, she argues that theory and data are forever entangled, and suggests that we see the (impossible) longing for grounded theory as a spur to pay "more attention to the production of all knowledge."[20]

My engagement with questions of method began in 2012 when I invited several scholars to come and talk about their training and working methods in a PhD class in queer studies. When I asked a direct question—"What is your method?"—several demurred, or responded simply, in the negative, "I have no method." It was out of a desire for a fuller avowal of the disciplinary and institutional frameworks of queer studies, as well as recognition of the field's ongoing innovations in method, that several of the students in this seminar planned the 2013 "Queer Method" conference at Penn.[21] Recently, two significant publications have continued these engagements: a 2018 book, *Other, Please Specify: Queer Methods in Sociology*, and another from 2019 (based on a 2016 special issue of *WSQ*), *Imagining Queer Methods*.[22] As the editors of these volumes point out, the very idea of "queer method" evokes a classic odd couple, uptight *methods* attempting to impose order on the slovenly *queer*. As Jane Ward writes in her contribution to *Imagining Queer Methods*, "to pair the terms 'queer' and 'methodology'—the former defined by its celebrated failure to adhere to stable classificatory systems or be contained by disciplinary boundaries, and the latter typically defined by orderly, discipline-specific, and easily reproducible techniques—produces something of an exciting contradiction, a productive oxymoron."[23]

Conflict is an inevitable but perhaps not a regrettable consequence of plumbing this oxymoron. Avowing her commitment to "confronting frictions, disciplinary and otherwise," Valerie Traub takes a hard look at the incomplete exchanges, misconnections, and open disagreements that often characterize attempts to communicate across disciplines. She writes, "An emphasis on method, I suggest, helps us appreciate that protocols that would lubricate interactions are still in the process of being worked out. Not only does such a practice entail valuing the thorny issue, the dilemma, the impasse, but it also enjoins a willingness to unpack incommensurate idioms and resist the impulse to either assume sameness in the room or strive for premature unity. Rather, the naïve question, which denaturalizes what is taken for granted within disciplinary knowledge, can provide a key tactic for managing collaborations—whether with one's own interdisciplinary self or one's disciplinary others."[24] In its most utopian and anti-institutional forms, queer theory appeared to take such difficulties in stride, smoothing the way for collaboration among scholars with radically different training by means of shared political and intellectual goals. The impact of such exchanges has been profound, changing the landscape of work across disciplines. But as the dreams of a common queer project have faded, scholars like Traub have drawn attention to tensions internal to the field that were never resolved. Pointing to the difficulty of reconciling one's own disparate epistemological commitments as well as the more obvious ones that divide scholars in different disciplines, Traub makes clear the hard work that is necessary to forge a truly interdisciplinary community of queer scholars. This attempt requires a grappling both with the history and the current institutional configuration of the field, a task that is impossible unless we are to undertake its thorough objectification. In this context, the lingering traces of the idea that queer studies happens somewhere outside or in opposition to the academy is a major obstacle to thought.

Recognizing queer studies' debt to sociological studies of deviance, as well as its commitments to humanistic methods, can help push back against narratives of heroic antinormativity. It can also help us to objectify our own situation as scholars. Such a call for objectification will not appeal to critics trained to refuse it at all cost. However, while the critique of objectification addresses important forms of epistemological and material violence in the history of the disciplines, it can also serve as a romantic disavowal of our position as scholars. Objectification may be a blunt instrument, but it is necessary if we are to account for our objects and our own relations to them. In our role as professional knowledge workers, we not only do battle with dominant social norms, but we also study them, and profit from instances of their transgression, extracting knowledge from the situation of marginal subjects. Extreme self-reflexivity and deep questioning of the prerogatives that allow scholars to speak about others were crucial to the development of queer inquiry, in revolt against objectification in the study of homosexuality. While we might avoid some of the more direct violence of aversion therapy or nonconsensual studies of homosexuality through such approaches, the conditions of inequality—epistemological and social—that frame research on homosexuality still apply, even when we study our "own" communities. If we are *in*, we are also *of*. This situation may be mitigated but not overcome through extreme self-reflexivity; to deny its reality is to perpetrate a different form of violence.

THE TROUBLE WITH ORDINARY

To focus on the ordinary aspects of deviance is an uncertain prospect in a moment of widespread normalization. However, the field of queer studies has been riven almost from the beginning by gendered debates about the relationship between antinormativity and the ordinary. Biddy Martin's critique of queer theory was grounded in an embrace of the ordinariness of existence. In 1993, she wrote: "Radical anti-normativity throws out a lot of babies with a lot of bathwater . . . Implicit in these constructions of queerness, I fear, is the lure of an existence without limit, without bodies or psyches, and certainly without mothers . . . An enormous fear of ordinariness or normalcy results in superficial accounts of the complex imbrication of sexuality with other aspects of social and psychic life, and in far too little attention to the dilemmas of the average people we also are."[25] In a recent account of the everyday intimacies between women in Jamaica Kincaid's fiction, Keja L. Valens argues that her work "pluralizes the normal" rather than opposing it. In a reading of the way that the normal "repeats with a difference" in *At the Bottom of the River*, Valens argues that Kincaid's attention to the "range of things that can be normal demonstrates the pervasiveness of the normal as much as it shows its mutability."[26]

Intimacies between women have a privileged place in the elaboration of the concept of a queer ordinary, a fact that Sharon Marcus addresses directly in her account of the importance of female same-sex intimacies in

Victorian England, *Between Women*. Marcus argues against queer studies' tendency to focus on prohibited behavior and suggests that women have appeared in such accounts "only to the extent that they illustrate the reach of medical discourses of difference" (14). Marcus writes, "The focus on secrecy, shame, oppression, and transgression in queer studies has led theorists, historians, and literary critics alike to downplay or refuse the equally powerful ways that same-sex bonds have been acknowledged by the bourgeois public sphere" (13). It is through a reading of ordinary relations between women that Marcus develops the method of "just reading"—or seeing what is explicitly represented in literature and the historical record rather than what is absent, hidden, or repressed. Marcus refers to this tendency to look for homosexuality in the shadows as the "deviance paradigm" and credits Foucault as its author (266–67n31). However, the deviance paradigm, as I have argued, has a longer lineage, in which homosexuality, although illicit, appears out in the open, along with other visible forms of difference. The view of sexuality as hidden and transgressive might therefore be better named the antinormativity rather than the deviance paradigm of homosexuality.

With the legalization of same-sex marriage, the question of antinormativity moved center stage in queer studies. By bringing down a powerful material and symbolic barrier to citizenship for LGBT people, the 2015 Supreme Court decision *Obergefell v. Hodges* struck a blow for freedom. But it also struck a blow against the image of queers as proud exiles, outcasts from fundamental structures of social and biological reproduction. Being included in such structures raises questions about the definition of queer people as gender and sexual outsiders. Outsiders to what? While some queer activists and critics have maintained a fierce opposition to marriage and the family, others have sought change within it, hoping that we might discover new ways of inhabiting traditional forms. The loosening of gender roles, the extension of networks of care, the opening of the couple, the remaking of generations: these are some of the changes that queerness promises to bring to the institution of marriage. Yet this institution has proven remarkably durable and flexible, able to incorporate but also to neutralize many kinds of difference. Is it possible to desire access to marriage and the family and still challenge key structures of gender and sexual oppression? How—if at all—has the expansion of marriage rights affected the patriarchal and racist legacies of this institution? If LGBT people are no longer defined by the illegitimacy of their kinship relations, or are no longer routinely denied basic legal and civic protections, on what basis are they to forge solidarity with society's outsiders? In short, what does queer politics look like in the era of gay marriage?

While at an earlier moment simply being in a same-sex couple might seem like a form of resistance, it is now often understood as a form of capitulation. This situation has led some to harden the lines between resistance and assimilation, suggesting that it is possible to maintain a bright line between radicals and conformists. Such a response fails to reckon with both the general and the specific forms of complicity that characterize all of our lives. The complexity of this new landscape has led some others to reassess the vanguardism of queer politics. In 2015, Robyn Wiegman and Elizabeth A. Wilson edited a special issue of the feminist journal *differences* called "Queer Theory without Antinormativity" that questioned the centrality of antinormativity in queer studies—and its equation with politics tout court.[27] Wiegman and Wilson do not focus on marriage; nonetheless, their questioning of the stance or ethos of queer radicalism is informed by a situation of growing legal recognition and civic inclusion. Although queer scholars continue to critique the assimilative logic of the mainstream LGBT movement, it is no longer clear where to locate these enemies, or how to distinguish their lives and desires from our own. For many activists and scholars today, holding to a position both outside and against "the normal"—against queer family and queer domesticity—risks division not only from "mainstream politics" but also from queer community itself.[28] To address these shifting realities, many artists and writers have challenged the idea that there is a fatal contradiction between queer radicalism and the quotidian realities of queer lives.[29] However, given the origins of queer in revolt and negativity, it is unclear whether the achievement of the queer ordinary is desirable, or even possible.

DOING BEING ORDINARY

In his 1970 lecture, "Doing 'Being Ordinary,'" Harvey Sacks considers the work it takes to transform potentially overwhelming or disconcerting experience into unexceptional and banal accounts. Influenced by the tradition of interactionist sociology that tracked the complexities of everyday experience, Sacks emphasizes the fact that "you live in a world much more finely organized than you imagine" (215). To see the labor that goes into the work of sustaining social organization requires a shift in perspective: "an initial shift," Sacks writes, "is not to think of an 'ordinary person' as some person, but as somebody having as their job, as their constant preoccupation, doing 'being ordinary.' It's not that somebody *is* ordinary, it's perhaps that that's what their business is. And it does take work, as any other business does."[30] Sacks distinguishes between the ordinary and the natural, suggesting that there are not ordinary and extraordinary kinds of people. Instead, ordinariness is a job, something that everyone has to work at. Recalling the emphasis on the everyday quality of homosexuality, Sacks suggests that even extreme or illegitimate experience is readily routinized: "When you have an affair, take drugs, commit a crime, etc., you find that it's been the usual experience that others who've done it have had" (219).

Sacks does not suggest that there is no extraordinary experience, or that rupture with ordinary ways of life is impossible; instead, he argues that ordinariness is a widespread and unacknowledged form of labor. Not everyone has access to that achievement: he points to the example of the inmate engaged in the unusual activity of examining every crack in the wall of his cell. Some refuse it: "if one were to pick up the notebooks of poets, writers, novelists," Sacks writes, "you're likely to find elaborated studies of small real objects"—but this is because the job of novelists is to "make distinctive observations about the world," not to be ordinary (217). Like his peers, Sacks's aim is to disturb the calm surface of life, and make visible its component parts, the tensions that must be overcome to maintain the illusion of naturalness. His view of ordinariness as an achievement complicates any easy distinction between the normative and the antinormative. It is clear that behavior deemed antinormative or even antisocial must be smoothed by social norms even to be perceptible as such. In his account, taking drugs, having affairs, and committing crimes must become ordinary experiences to be experienced at all.

Sacks's perspective, and the framework of microsociological studies of interaction that gave rise to it, is important in a moment when we are confronted with the ordinariness, even the banality of many forms of queer life. The faith in transgression and its radical potential to negate society is deeply challenged by widening social support for LGBT life. This new acceptance coexists with ongoing violence and discrimination, a state of contradiction that we are familiar with in many realms of life. Sacks provides a crucial reminder of the imbrication of queer life with social life more generally. But he also puts a key tenet of queer scholarship to the test, suggesting that it is the job of the scholar to draw attention to the cracks in the surface of everyday reality. Since the publication of *Gender Trouble*, scholars in the field have sought to expose the hidden work supporting gender and sexual normativity, believing that such an exposure would make space for new forms of practice and embodiment. The fact that Sacks and his contemporaries saw such work as subtending all elements of social life makes clear the challenge of this work, a challenge that has today mostly been forgotten. How the corrosive force of that insight can be mobilized and to what end is unclear in a moment when the lines between ordinary and extraordinary, legitimate and illegitimate, insider and outsider are shifting. Exploring this history of queer studies confronts us with the fact that the wholesale refusal of normativity does not offer us a viable way forward. Instead, we must make our way with the scholarly tools we have forged, which are, for better or for worse, well suited to analyzing the work that goes into producing reality. We have as our guides in this those scholars from the postwar period, who turned their attention to the business of doing being ordinary, and doing being deviant.

Afterword

THE POLITICS OF STIGMA

A certain fragility has been discovered in the very bedrock of existence—even, and perhaps above all, in those aspects of it that are most
familiar, most solid and most intimately related to our bodies and to our
everyday behavior.

Michel Foucault, "Two Lectures"[1]

The decision to call this book *Underdogs* is a provocation: the phrase suggests a form of subordination that is permanent rather than temporary; it
implies that some groups are, by their nature, fated to marginality. This
view of social inequality, so prominent in the era of deviance studies,
was challenged by the civil rights movement, student protests, and other
mass mobilizations associated with the 1960s. But it is also the case that
the version of marginality and resistance inscribed in deviance studies
scholarship helped to create the conditions for these movements. In particular it helped to cement a vision of shared marginality that was essential to coalition-building and, eventually, to the upsurge of critical identity studies in the university. For queer studies especially, deviance studies
was crucial: the contingent, miscellaneous, and provisional account of
identity that undergirds the field was an inheritance of deviance studies,
along with the image of a far-flung collection of outsiders and rebels in
revolt against social norms. Although this model of stigma-centric, coalitional politics was transformed in campus protests, liberation movements,
and in the activist ferment of the AIDS crisis, the deviance paradigm continues to underwrite a queer political imaginary even today.

The title *Underdogs* also points to one of my long-standing preoccupations: Does queer thought require a utopian horizon? In his "Theses on the
Philosophy of History," Walter Benjamin offers a caution about the kind
of politics that fixes its hopes on the image of "liberated grandchildren":
instead, through his concept of "dialectics at a standstill," he argues for
a politics that would interrupt the empty time of progress and seek lib-

eration in the image of "enslaved ancestors."[2] Nonetheless, while Benjamin cautioned against images of the future, he embraced a notion of the present as "shot through with chips of Messianic time," that is to say, inflected in every moment by the possibility of liberation. But this openness to the future is very different—and in fact excludes—determinate images of transformation. What would politics look like if it turned its back on the future, and admitted no images of a redeemed world? Is it possible to devote oneself entirely to the shame and stigma suffered by one's ancestors and one's contemporaries without betraying one's grandchildren?

In *Feeling Backward* I sought to refuse, insofar as possible, false consciousness as an interpretive framework. This framework was used to diagnose the political "backwardness" of early twentieth-century queer subjects and to make the present a consolation for the suffering of the past. In that book, I focused on literary texts that were so saturated with ideology that they could not be taken up without major revision or reframing in the present—they had become an embarrassment. My question in *Feeling Backward* was how to pay those texts what, to my mind, we owed them: gratitude for their efforts to represent lives that were rejected, and a reappraisal since, in our own time, they had become statically identified with a past we'd left behind. Doing justice to these texts, I felt, meant stepping back from the project of critique—to think alongside them and their struggles, rather than to judge them by the standards of the present. So often, contemporary readings judged these texts and authors to be internally homophobic. Who isn't? And where is the place outside of ideology from which we could decide?

In *Underdogs*, I have pursued the problem of critique and utopia as a question of method. In particular, I have attempted to see how far one might push Gayle Rubin's claim about a politics of description. When Rubin argues in "Thinking Sex" that the descriptive research of sexologists provides "a better grounding for a radical politics of sexuality" than the prescriptive scholarship of feminist critics, she suggests that the social world does not need to be remade, but rather stabilized, particularly in its weakest points. To lend stablility, coherence, and visibility to the world is generally understood not as radical but as conservative, which, in the sense of aiming to preserve what is of value, it is. Particularly in traditions of Left thought, description is associated with reification, rear-guardism, and the reinforcement of social hierarchy. But description is an essential, even an unavoidable, aspect of all scholarly practice. In the context of queer theory, it has served a crucial if unrecognized role both in making space for marginal worlds and in cataloging injustice.

Erving Goffman offers a painstaking description of the visible world and its operations, focusing on what can be accounted for through observation alone. I was originally drawn to Goffman precisely because of his reductive, flattening account of social injury; he captured so much of what interested me in the history of homosexuality, but *from the outside*—with very little attention to interiority or experience. And yet, on balance, little seemed to be missing from these enormously detailed accounts. Furthermore, Goffman's presentation of the effects of the collective denigration of social outsiders was stark. Identity, for Goffman, is *spoiled* by the violence, ignorance, and condescension that "normals" routinely exhibit toward the stigmatized. To say it is otherwise is to soft-pedal the routine and pervasive nature of this violence. In describing strips of behavior, he drew on the observational social and natural sciences, fields such as ethology and kinesics that are less interested in motivation than in behavior and pattern. Perhaps most distressing in Goffman's work is the fact that the people he describes lack insides, interior depths where one could locate the wellsprings of resistance. He does not lend agency or humanity to those who appear to lack it, those whom brutalizing conditions have left with only the most minimal resources. Goffman forgoes the role of the witness or judge in his work, and with it the gratifications of rescue or moral condemnation. Instead, he inhabits the scenes he describes in the somewhat unsavory role of the bystander. His question is not "What is to be done?" but instead "What is it that's going on here?"

It is not only Goffman's method that makes him a challenging figure for the field of queer studies; his explicit and repeated rejection of politics is also at odds with the activist orientation of the field. Refusing to redeem spoiled identity has the virtue of fully acknowledging the experience of stigma rather than anticipating its transformation, or wishing it away. What it risks, however, is not being a politics at all; it risks giving up entirely on the project of transformation. In pushing back against the premature transformation of shame, one might fail to transform it at all. Goffman's stance of performative detachment is a provoking example for scholars today. Although he disavowed politics, and insisted that his job was to describe the world and not to change it, his work did in fact have considerable effects. This is in part due to his large readership, the result of his disarming style and of the broader audience for sociology in the postwar period. But it is also, I would argue, an effect of his observational gifts: Goffman described the world so vividly and with such precision that he did not need to argue that it should be changed. The stories of mental patients stripped of everything in the asylum; of homeless people engaged in diversionary activity to keep the police at bay; of homosexuals playing endless games of information management, ever on their guard; of wheelchair users cracking self-deprecating jokes to ease the tension produced by their presence: these scenes spoke, and still speak, for themselves.

Furthermore, by paying attention to the minutiae of everyday interactions, Goffman brought to life a microscopic world that was not fixed and stable but in flux and vulnerable: as, in Bourdieu's words, a "discoverer of the infinitely small," Goffman perceived infinitesimal cracks in the foundation of social life. If this perception did not lead Goffman to advocate for change, neither did it lead him into false claims about the efficacy of his scholarship. Goffman was there to observe the glitches in the appearance of social life, not to create them. The fact that his account of these glitches was, ultimately, effective makes it clear that describing the world is not the same as endorsing it. Description, like polemic, can have a conservative cast. But it can also serve as a protest against the conditions it meticulously maps. It is impossible to determine in advance what kind of scholarship will lead to social transformation. However, to dismiss representations that do not provide a vision of a transformed future rules out many valuable accounts of the world as it is. It is also to center moral imagination and political conviction as the key aspects of academic ethos. These are important elements of academic thought, but so are responsiveness and fidelity to fact.

The animus that Goffman inspires may in fact be based on recognition. Charges of quietism are leveled against cultural critics for a reason: the effects of our scholarship and teaching are uncertain at best. Goffman does not solve this problem, and he does not make us feel any better about it. He simply identifies it as *our* problem—and aggravates it to the point that it frustrates our evasions. Like the manic he describes in "The Insanity of Place," Goffman "reminds us what our everything is, and then reminds us that this everything is not very much."[3]

* * *

Weighing the potential for a politics of shared stigma has become excruciating in the contemporary political moment, when the fate of gender and sexual outsiders is less clear than ever. Are we still underdogs? Will we be? On what grounds do we identify with the marginalized and the excluded? And if those points of identification fade, as we might hope that they will, what will become of the queer vision of a collectivity of the shamed, the marginalized, and the stigmatized?

Today the system of sexual stratification is in flux: many forms of gender and sexual nonnormativity have become acceptable; at the same time, gay and lesbian identity can be wielded with increasing success against other marginalized groups. New civic inclusions and a gay and lesbian platform of patriotism, prosperity, and pride have made it difficult to see how queer sexuality and stigma are linked. The changing status of gay life around the world has meant a singular focus on the politics of sexuality can be used to further racial, ethnic, religious, and national domination: one might point to the linking of secularism, anti-immigrant sentiment, and antihomophobia in many contexts; the embrace of LGBT rights by the Israeli state as an example of what has been called "pinkwashing"; or of the fact that multinational corporations such as Lockheed Martin and Goldman Sachs have been leaders in providing full benefits to gay, lesbian, and transgender employees. Many scholars have responded to this situation by turning their attention away from sexuality altogether, focusing instead on other sites of power in modernity.[4]

Such developments suggest that queers in the twenty-first century have outlived their underdog status. With the legalization of gay marriage in the US in 2015, the most obvious barrier to citizenship and civic belonging has fallen. Integration into marriage and the family seems to complete the slow march toward assimilation, and comes on the heels of inclusion in government, the economy, the media, and the military. These inclusions are of course most effective for those who already have a viable claim to citizenship: they make less difference to the unemployed and the undocumented, to those who are homeless or incarcerated. Poverty and race bar so many Americans from full access to health, employment, housing, and safety: the freedoms granted to LGBT people are granted unequally in a profoundly unequal society.

The granting of these rights is provisional, both in the sense that they can be withdrawn as the political climate shifts, but also in the sense that they require a form of queerness that is purged of its association with other stigmatized categories. It is White, prosperous LGBT couples who are valued members of the nation, and can therefore contemplate full inclusion as a possibility. Indeed, to gain recognition queers must purge themselves of associations with the underworld itself, destroying their ties to that imaginary landscape populated by racialized and perverse others. This is the key operation of homonormativity, which makes civic inclusion contingent on the refusal of stigma—the stigma of gender and sexual deviance that remains tied to other, indelible forms of stigma.

This selective granting of admission to the central precincts of culture has left some in doubt about the ongoing salience of queer stigma. Has homosexuality been so revalued as to make it no longer the grounds for social exclusion? In "Thinking Sex," Rubin took a position on this question, affirming that sex was a "vector of oppression" alongside other more familiar vectors. She wrote:

> The system of sexual oppression cuts across other modes of social in-equality, sorting out individuals and groups according to its own in-trinsic dynamics. It is not reducible to, or understandable in terms of, class, race, ethnicity, or gender. Wealth, white skin, male gender, and ethnic privileges can mitigate the effects of sexual stratification. A rich, white male pervert will generally be less affected than a poor, black, female pervert. But even the most privileged are not immune to sexual oppression.[5]

Writing in 1984, Rubin sought to bring sex oppression—we might call it homophobia, although she intended it more broadly—into focus as a distinct and consequential form of oppression. She brought attention to the specific effects of sexual oppression. While pointing to its entanglement with "class, race, ethnicity, and gender," she still insisted that it might work to oppress a "rich, white, male pervert." It is this last claim that has become controversial in the present, as so many barriers have fallen to rich, White gays and lesbians, putting into doubt to what extent sexual stratification remains in effect as an independently operating system of oppression.

Rubin's essay, written almost forty years ago, is foundational for the field of queer theory and still speaks with force to our current situation. And yet, in a moment when White gay men are often seen as profiting from their dominant position in racial and gender systems of stratification, her assertion that this "rich, white, male pervert" is oppressed is contentious. It instructive to recall the context of Rubin's article. Her point in forwarding the figure of the rich, White, male pervert was heuristic. Rubin was attempting to show the analytic separability of sexual oppression from other vectors of oppression in order to make a claim for the significance of homophobia as a distinct and recognizable social force. She made a materialist and structural argument for the existence of homophobia as a sorting mechanism with powerful legal and economic effects. We are less inclined now to single out sexual oppression from other forms of oppression, but there is no need to do so since Rubin made sexual oppression perceptible and knowable. Her aim was to make homophobia evident, and to give it weight in social analysis. The fact that it is less weighty in the lives of some gays and lesbians does not undermine Rubin's original point. Despite the well-founded critiques of race and class privilege in queer studies, Rubin's claim that homophobia exists and has material effects still stands.

* * *

The remarkable gains of some LGBT people in US law and social life put pressure on the idea of queer coalition, and have further exposed fractures in the field of queer studies. Kadji Amin points to the fractures that have emerged in the expansion of the field's racial, temporal, and geographical boundaries, noting that different geopolitical conditions expose the limits of antinormativity as a political strategy. In a framework that goes beyond the late twentieth-century US, it is no long possible to think that power operates as the imposition of a single norm. What looks like heteronormativity in a queer frame may constitute resistance in other contexts; conversely, the antinormativity celebrated in queer studies may have damaging effects for poor people and in communities of color. While Amin is drawing on examples in the history of migration and forced labor, it is also clear that that there is no single norm against which queerness can be judged in the present. Queer studies scholarship, accustomed to defining itself against every dominant value, has been called out repeatedly for what Hiram Pérez identifies as its "racial unconsciousness shaped by nation, empire, and the dispositions of global capitalism."[6] In fighting a war against normativity, queer scholars have often left Whiteness intact. But, Pérez asks, "What can be more normative to modernity than whiteness?" (1).

In contrast to Rubin, who argues for the persistence of sexual stigma for "a rich, white male pervert," Pérez argues that Whiteness insulates those who possess it from the stigma of queerness. The difference in their positions can be explained by the gap in publication dates: when Rubin wrote, law and custom made rich, White male perverts more vulnerable to sexual oppression than today. The difference also represents a change in the field of queer studies, which has increasingly refused to isolate sexual stigma, assuming a background of race and class privilege. Much of this work has taken place under the rubric of queer-of-color critique, and has turned its attention to the interconnections between the major systems of oppression, seeing sexual stigma as inseparable from class and race stigma. At a time when White queers are able to escape the historical associations of deviance, Black and Latino sexuality is still marked by links to perversion, criminality, and disordered kinship.

The challenge to White queer studies concerns this failure to address the imbrication of race and sexuality. But it also responds to the queer belief in the ability to work across or athwart difference, to forge coalition in spite of disagreement. This is at the heart of queer politics, a key reason why activists refused to pursue gay and lesbian rights in order to work toward a broader and more inclusive community. That queer strategy has disappointed, revealing that it was guided by identitarian investments all along, and erasing or fetishizing difference in the name of inclusion. Despite these failures, the idea that a politics might be founded on shared stigma and a widespread antagonism to normativity remains vital, central to continuing investments in the possibility of queer politics.

Eve Sedgwick gave voice to this idea of identification through stigma across difference in her 2008 preface to *Epistemology of the Closet*. She describes the complex reasons why she chose to write a book in gay and lesbian theory without identifying as such. Explaining her reluctance to place herself in the binary system of heterosexuality and homosexuality, Sedgwick then conjures the specter of homophobic violence, pointing to the "simpler matter of solidarity."[7] She explains:

> Growing up in a Jewish family after World War II, I had been sensitive enough to stigma that my child mind was deeply penetrated by any story about it. Especially pondered was one story in which, the morning after Nazi occupation in 1940, all the citizens of Denmark appeared in public wearing yellow stars. While the story is not exactly true, it remains an excitingly elegant index of the force of minimal, in fact nonverbal, performative utterance. Other such powerfully minimal or negative acts, associated with the resistance to McCarthyism and later with the civil rights movement, were also presences as I was growing up, and I'm

sure that musing on them ripened me for later thinking about closet
dynamics. (xvii)

As she explains, Sedgwick spent her career fielding critiques about her
treatment of male homosexuality as someone who, although she refused
the label of straight woman, was visibly not a gay man. These critiques
began with her publication of *Between Men* in 1985 (which led to "attacks
by gay scholars" [xvii]) and, in 2008, she is still defending her decision.

It is clear from Sedgwick's reflections that identification across difference is fundamental to queer thought, and that it has always been controversial. Solidarity, though hardly simple, is at the origin of the field.
The vision of a queer community of outsiders is driven by Sedgwick's
complex identification with gayness, and as a gay man. This act of cross-
identification was unsettling for many gay, lesbian, and feminist scholars,
who articulated fears of appropriation and also anger and disbelief that
queer studies would be the province of straight academics. But the scandal
of queer's reach across difference has only grown since Sedgwick was at-
tacked at conferences and in print. Debates surrounding Sedgwick's identification across gender and sexuality, explosive at the time, seem almost
quaint in the context of more thoroughgoing critiques of queer imperial-
ism. Sedgwick provides fodder for those critiques here, explaining that
her experience of Jewishness as a child informed her interest not only in
"closet dynamics" but also in civil rights protest. But she also rearticulates
the guiding principle of queer politics: that the experience of stigma awak-
ens you to its wider effects and that mass assumption of stigma—as in the
Danish example—is an effective political strategy.

Sara Ahmed has addressed this moment in Sedgwick's writing. As
Ahmed points out, Sedgwick's proximity to stigma was crucial to her articulation of queerness. She assesses the political promise of Sedgwick's
claim that her upbringing made her "sensitive enough" to stigma to be
alert to its operations in other contexts. Ahmed writes,

Is there a promise as well as hope in Eve's "sensitive enough": a promise
that an experience of a proximity to one kind of stigma can create a sensitivity to other kinds? I have for my own reasons been rather suspicious
of this kind of promise. I grew up in Australia, where the desire for recovery from the violence of the colonial past is often a form of covering
over. I am well aware of how whiteness can be performed *as* sensitivity

to stigma. Sensitive white people can be scary; sensitive whiteness can
be whiteness that wants proximity to the very scenes of its undoing,
where the un-doing is at once a re-doing. ("Sensitivity to Stigma")

In response to Sedgwick's account of her childhood and the way it called
her attention to the operations of stigma, Ahmed counters with a description of her own childhood in White Australia. Her story is not about becoming sensitive enough, but about bearing the sensitivity of others.
Rather than seeing sensitivity to other people's stigma as a merely personal quality heightened by the shadow of the war and genocide, Ahmed
identifies this trait with Whiteness itself. In the context of Australia's colonial history, Ahmed identifies a White desire to be proximate to stigma,
to challenge Whiteness while retaining its privileges. It is because of this
double intention—to interrogate Whiteness and to consolidate its epistemological and material advantage—that Ahmed writes that "sensitive
white people can be scary." Ultimately, Ahmed does not find Sedgwick's
sensitivity scary, although others have. Sedgwick did not conceal that sensitivity or her desire to be present on the scene of other people's stigma.
But more than her forthrightness, Ahmed points to Sedgwick's openness
to risk, the fact that she did more than show up at the scene of stigma. It
was her willingness to change places with others—what Ahmed sees as her
talent for vicarious relations—that set Sedgwick's sensitivity apart. Ahmed
focuses on a moment described in Sedgwick's preface when a student and
friend gave her his sign to carry at a protest. For Ahmed, this moment demonstrates Sedgwick's gift for vicarious feeling and her willingness to take
on stigma that is not her own. Having raised doubts about White appropriation of a racist and colonial history, Ahmed ends by calling sensitivity
to stigma "a queer methodology."

     If sensitivity to stigma is a queer methodology, it is one that is inherited
in large part from Sedgwick. That sensitivity was personal, the effect of
Sedgwick's attunement to language, her penchant for identification across
difference, and her willingness to take on stigma that was not her own.
But this sensitivity was also produced in a particular historical moment.
Sedgwick describes coming of age in the shadow of European genocide,
trained into attention to a scene that happened elsewhere but was not
wholly other. That disposition set the pattern for Sedgwick's witnessing
of the struggle for civil liberties and racial justice in the US. What she describes is a sensitivity tuned up by an imaginative encounter with an exis-

tential threat, which she then turned to other scenes of violence and resistance: anti-Communist purges, the civil rights movement, AIDS activism. As Sedgwick tells it, her early fixation on the Holocaust layed the groundwork for her sensitivity to these other struggles, and in this she was joined by many American liberals after the war. The Holocaust played a crucial role in the career of postwar sociologists as well, many of whom had grown up in Jewish families and whose work on the dangers of American conformity and fear and hatred of the other clearly bears the traces of this era.

Goffman's concept of stigma is also a product of this moment. The use of visual signs of stigma to mark categories of disqualified persons functions as a kind of gloss on the organizing principles of genocide. And Goffman's concern with the minute and the quotidian can be understood in this context as a kind of vigilance, an attempt to respond to the eruption of state-sponsored mass murder out of civil society. Goffman never claimed to be sensitive to stigma, and he has been castigated over the past several decades for his lack of empathy. His violence toward his subjects has been seen as more overt, less a matter of vicarious feelings or appropriation than Sedgwick's. Although he also appeared on the scene of other people's stigma, Goffman kept his distance. But in his attention to "minimal or negative acts," to minute forms of nonverbal communication, and to the cracks in the foundation of everyday life, Goffman did exhibit a kind of sensitivity—what we might simply call attention. One would never be tempted to discuss Goffman in terms of vicarious feeling, or a willingness to carry the signs of others. But in his attention to the details of stigmatization across identity categories, we see his close links to queer studies.

The fact that the field of queer studies is so clearly marked by this moment in the 1950s will only cement the case against it. It underscores aspects of the field that have come under serious attack in recent years. Tracing queer methodology to the microanalytic studies of social interaction and deviance at midcentury clarifies its focus on individuals rather than structures; its links to a White liberalism that is distinctly American; and its false universalism, evident in the ease with which forms of stigma can be substituted for each other. Addressing these connections also makes it clear that queer sensitivity to stigma is not only a personal trait, but a professional inheritance. Acknowledging this inheritance underlines how deep the challenges facing queer politics are. Yet despite these challenges, the queer dream persists that, in Ahmed's words, the "experience of a proximity to one kind of stigma can create a sensitivity to other kinds." It is hard to let go of this dream, because it contains the knotted histories of other people's stigma, and our own. But we also refuse to let it go because of the promise that sensitivity will give way to solidarity. The concept of stigma has so far failed to create a truly collective movement, but the experience of stigma keeps this dream alive.

Acknowledgments

This was not the book I expected to write, and I finished it under circumstances I could not have anticipated. My interest in the history of queer studies led me to a deep engagement with the work of the brilliant sociologist and critic Erving Goffman. I kept going, heading deep into the history of postwar social science, where I came face to face with both my ignorance and spurs to unfamiliar thought. I regret the ignorance, but not the series of intellectual surprises that made this book possible.

I couldn't have undertaken this trip alone. First thanks go to Mara Mills, who gave me the confidence to venture into unfamiliar territory. She was a superb guide to the history of biology and to broader questions of method. Her depth of knowledge and keen insight about so many questions that concern me here made her an essential interlocutor.

I was also lucky to be able to work closely with Gayle Rubin early in this project, and her influence is legible throughout. Seeing her collection of classic works of Chicago school sociology alongside twentieth-century lesbian literary classics was a key moment for me and in many ways set the itinerary for my research. Her work on the history of the social sciences and their influence on queer thought is foundational to my argument. I was also deeply influenced during the book's composition by conversations with Cindy Patton. Being privy to Cindy's remarkable mind was an education in itself. Thanks to her for helping me to clarify the stakes of the project.

My first editor at the University of Chicago Press, Douglas Mitchell, was an early supporter of the book and an inspiration to look deeper into the archives of twentieth-century social science. Doug's intimate knowledge of most of the central players in the book, and his enthusiasm for their work, gave me an inkling of the kind of reader that I might hope for. Profound thanks to Alan Thomas for taking over as my editor. I am grateful to him and to everyone else at the Press who helped to bring this one across the finish line. Thanks also to my anonymous readers: I am indebted to them for their brilliant, sympathetic, and tough readings.

I learned from many more readers along the way. I am grateful to audiences from various disciplines, especially to the sociologists and anthropologists who took the time to engage with me. I also want to thank the granting agencies that gave me time to work, including the Stanford Humanities Center, Princeton University's Stanley Kelley Jr. Visiting Professorship, the Margaret Bundy Scott Professorship at Williams College, the Howard Foundation at Brown University, the Wolf Humanities Center at the University of Pennsylvania, and the R. Jean Brownlee Associate Professorship at the University of Pennsylvania. I am also grateful to the English department at Penn, which has provided steady and humane support throughout my time there. During the writing of this book, the kindness and good sense of Jed Esty and Paul Saint-Amour were a mainstay.

I would also like to thank the librarians and archivists who supported my work on this project. The Special Collections and the Digital Media Archive at the University of Chicago were extremely helpful to me early on—special thanks to Kathleen Feeney and Joe Toth. I was able to find many resources in the University of Pennsylvania Archives, where I was aided by the excellent advice of Katherine Pourshariati. I consulted the Nikolaas Tinbergen collection at the Bodleian Library at the University of Oxford, where I received key and timely assistance from Helen Gilio. As the pandemic closed libraries around the world, making research a challenge, Helle Brünnich Pedersen at the Photographic Division of the Royal Danish Library went out of her way to provide extraordinary, last-minute help by providing high-resolution digital images. I am grateful to Nikolaas Tinbergen's family for taking an interest in the project and granting me permission to reproduce his drawings, and also to Rowan & Littlefield who holds the copyright for Tinbergen's *Kleew*.

The opportunity to work with Penn's outstanding graduate students over the years has fed my thinking: the students who took the seminar "Queer Method" in fall 2012, and went on to organize and run a conference of the same name in 2013, saw this project in its infancy. The Wolf Humanities Center sponsored the "Year of Sex" at Penn, which brought together a number of scholars across fields who inspired me and expanded my thinking. I am also thankful for the time I had at Cornell University's

School of Criticism and Theory, which provided an ideal community to discuss this work as it was nearing completion. Among colleagues and friends, particular thanks to Kadji Amin, Lauren Berlant, Stephen Best, Beth Blum, Pearl Brilmyer, Matt Brim, Eduardo Cadava, Margot Canaday, Patricia Clough, Ann Cvetkovich, Henning Engelke, Matthew Engelke, Jeffrey Escoffier, Roderick Ferguson, Jonathan Flatley, Diana Fuss, Bernard Geoghegan, Lochlann Jain, David James, Liza Johnson, Patty Keller, Regina Kunzel, Joan Lubin, Gage McWeeny, Joanne Meyerowitz, Durba Mitra, Stephen Muecke, Alondra Nelson, Tavia Nyong'o, Kathy Peiss, Carrie Rentschler, David Russell, Barbara Savage, Kristen Schilt, Mark Seltzer, Rachel Sherman, Michael Trask, Hent de Vries, Judith Walkowitz, Michael Warner, Seth Watter, Robyn Wiegman, and Elizabeth Wilson for their conversation, suggestions, and ideas. The intellectual camaraderie of my New York–based writing group buoyed me considerably during the research and writing process.

As it happened, finishing this book required novel forms of support, and lots of it. Yujiao (Cecily) Chen began research on this project early on and always seemed to understand what was at stake, often before I did. In the final push toward completion, as I was dealing with major vision loss and other medical challenges, Cecily's dedication and intelligence were crucial. It was a sustaining joy to work closely with her throughout the dark fall of 2019, and I literally could not have finished the book without her editorial help.

The love and generosity of friends, family, students, and colleagues sustained me during the writing of this book, and well beyond. For all that you have done for me, but mostly for the intense pleasure of your company, I thank Laura Amelio, Becky Arnold, Nancy Bentley, Deborah Cohen, James English, Rita Felski, Sharon Hayes, Maibritt Henkel, Peregrin Henkel, Perry Hewitt, Emaline Kelso, Juliet Kelso, David Kurnick, Meghan Love, Sharon Marcus, Ricardo Montez, Robert Mudd, Brooke O'Harra, Josephine Park, Bethany Schneider, Kate Thomas, and Patty White. And to Tina Lupton—for the book, for love, for life.

Notes

PREFACE

1. While we may regard that form of recognition with some suspicion from a future in which inclusion in the human is aligned with domination and false universalism, it was a crucial turning point in the past, and is inextricably bound up with later histories of liberation. I take one path through the history of midcentury social science, evaluating its effects in the study of sexuality. It is beyond my ability or intention to survey the effects of the study of the other marginal groups that sociologists, anthropologists, psychologists, and communications researchers studied during this period. I hope that the tensions, contradictions, and surprises in the history of sexuality studies might lead other researchers to reconsider this archive.

INTRODUCTION

1. Eve Kosofsky Sedgwick, "Queer Performativity: Henry James's *The Art of the Novel*," GLQ 1, no. 1 (1993): 1–16, 4.
2. *GLQ* was founded by Carolyn Dinshaw and David Halperin, as *A Journal of Lesbian and Gay Studies*. It immediately became the premier journal in queer *theory* (in contrast to existing journals such as the *Journal of the History of Homosexuality* and *Sexualities*); it has continued to define the field even as its disciplinary and methodological range has widened.
3. Sedgwick made many of her most brilliant theoretical interventions via agonistic engagements with other critics. She acknowledges these debts and addresses the mix of excitement and frustration that marks her relation to a few key texts (including *Gender Trouble*) in the introduction to *Touching Feeling*, in which "Queer Performativity" was republished, *Touching Feeling: Affect, Pedagogy, Performativity* (Durham, NC: Duke University Press, 2002), 2. We might also take Sedgwick's meditation on the meaning of "beside" in this introduction as a commentary on her relations with close peers in the founding generation of queer studies. The interest of "beside," she observes, "does not . . . depend on a fantasy of metonymically egalitarian or even pacific relations, as any child knows who's shared a bed

with siblings. Beside comprises a wide range of desiring, identifying, representing, repelling, paralleling, differentiating, rivaling, leaning, twisting, mimicking, withdrawing, attracting, aggressing, warping, and other relations," 8. I addressed the mixture of aggressive and reparative impulses in Sedgwick's criticism in "Truth and Consequences: On Paranoid Reading and Reparative Reading," *Criticism* 52, no. 2 (Spring 2010): 235–41.

4. Judith Butler, *Gender Trouble: Feminism and the Subversion of Identity* (New York: Routledge, 1999 [1990]), 190.

5. Sedgwick, *Epistemology of the Closet* (Berkeley: University of California Press, 1990), 48.

6. Sedgwick, "Paranoid Reading and Reparative Reading, or, You're So Paranoid, You Probably Think This Essay Is about You," *Touching Feeling: Affect, Pedagogy, Performativity*, 130, 138–43.

7. For a somewhat different assessment of the significance of this transition in Sedgwick's thought—which has nonetheless been influential in my own thinking—see Robyn Wiegman's account of Sedgwick's work on affect and reparation in the 1990s in her essay "The Times We're In." Wiegman emphasizes the continuity between Sedgwick's early and late work, the close connections between Sedgwick's and Butler's thought, and, more generally, the need for a more thorough historicization of the field of queer studies. Regarding her reading of reparative impulses at a moment earlier than is generally acknowledged, Wiegman writes: "This makes the centrality of Judith Butler's work for Sedgwick's anatomy of paranoid reading especially important, as it highlights Sedgwick's awareness of their divergent critical instincts before their dual billing as 'founders' of queer theory was firm. It also alerts us to the coexistence of paranoid and reparative critical practices as part of the queer theoretical project from the outset, making it important to address not only how these distinctions are currently cast, but the poverty of any intellectual history of the field that writes them either as antithetical or sequential." Robyn Wiegman, "The Times We're In: Queer Feminist Criticism and the Reparative 'Turn,'" *Feminist Theory* 15, no. 1 (2014): 4–25, 12.

8. Queer and "gender-dissonant" childhood has become an important topic in queer studies (and beyond) in the intervening years, thanks in part to Sedgwick's influence both in this essay and in "How to Bring Your Kids Up Gay," in *Tendencies* (Durham, NC: Duke University Press, 1993). See also *Curiouser: On the Queerness of Children*, ed. Steven Bruhm and Natasha Hurley (Minneapolis: University of Minnesota Press, 2004); "Child," ed. Sarah Chinn and Anna Mae Duane, *WSQ* 43, nos. 1–2 (Spring/Summer 2015); "The Child Now," ed. Julian Gill-Peterson, Rebekah Sheldon, and Katherin Bond Stockton, special issue, *GLQ* 22, no. 4 (2016). For an early and forceful critique of the place of childhood and in particular teen suicide in Sedgwick's work and in queer theory more broadly, see Angus Gordon, "Turning Back: Adolescence, Narrative, and Queer Theory," *GLQ* 5, no. 1 (1999): 1–24. Sedgwick has been critiqued many times for her perceived distance from the gay and lesbian community, and has addressed this point at length in print. My point is not to renew this critique but rather to historicize the etiolation of identity and community in Sedgwick's work in relation to a broader argument about disciplinary conflict in the rise of queer theory.

9. There is more to be said about proximity and the periperformative in Sedgwick: queerness often appears to be close to, or in the neighborhood of, gay and lesbian identity.

10. Sedgwick and Frank, "Shame in the Cybernetic Fold: Reading Silvan Tomkins," *Critical Inquiry* 21, no. 2 (Winter 1995): 496–522. This essay was republished as the introduction to the edition of Tomkins's work that Sedgwick published with Frank: *Shame and Its Sisters*, ed. Sedgwick and Frank (Durham, NC: Duke University Press, 1995). It appears again as an essay in Sedgwick, *Touching Feeling*. Citations in this chapter are from the version in *Touching Feeling*.

11. Sedgwick and Frank do not use the phrases "sublimely alien" or "a different place to begin" to describe their relation to Tomkins, but instead to describe Tomkins's relation to his own historical and disciplinary moment. Nonetheless, I find these phrases useful in accounting for the sense of intellectual freshness that Tomkins imparts. "Sublimely alien," they write, "we found this psychology, to the developmental presumption/prescription of a core self; sublimely resistant, we might have added, to such presumption—except that the sublimity lies in an exemplary cartographic distance, not in a dialectical struggle. Even rarer in U.S. psychology of the cold war period is the plain absence, not only of homophobia, but of any hint of a heterosexist teleology. This mostly silent and utterly scrupulous disentanglement is the more compelling for the range and heterogeneity of Tomkins's disciplinary sources: ethology, social psychology, psychoanalysis, and so on are each structured around foundationally heterosexist assumptions, and each differently so. Again, however, Tomkins's achievement seems to result not from a concertedly anti-homophobic project (nor from any marked gay interest, for that matter) but rather from, almost simply, finding a different place to begin" (99).

12. I discuss these genealogical links at greater length in chapter 1.

13. The concept of "appreciative" studies of deviance appears in David Matza, *Becoming Deviant* (Englewood Cliffs, NJ: Prentice-Hall, 1969). For a retrospective account of this field, particularly as it related to studies of sexuality, see Carol A. B. Warren, "Sex and Gender in the 1970s," *Quantitative Sociology* 26, no. 4 (Winter 2003): 499–513.

14. Rubin, "Blood under the Bridge," *GLQ* 17, no. 1 (2010): 15–48, 18.

15. Rubin, "Studying Sexual Subcultures: Excavating the Ethnography of Gay Communities in Urban North America," in *Out in Theory: The Emergence of Gay and Lesbian Anthropology*, ed. Ellen Lewin and William L. Leap (Urbana: University of Illinois Press, 2002), 17–67, 53–54.

16. Rubin has called attention most persistently to the neglect of empirical work on sexuality in the postwar period. The key essay is "Studying Sexual Subcultures: Excavating the Ethnography of Gay Communities in Urban North America." She also cites the influence of figures such as Jeffrey Weeks, Mary McIntosh, and Kenneth Plummer in her much-cited 1994 interview with Judith Butler ("Sexual Traffic"), noting "how quickly people forget even recent history" (295). Both pieces appear in Gayle S. Rubin, *Deviations: A Gayle Rubin Reader* (Durham, NC: Duke University Press, 2011). In addition to Rubin's reflections, a range of other scholars have attempted to return attention to this scholarship: John D'Emilio, Jeffrey Escoffier, Arlene Stein, Jeffrey Weeks, Plummer, John H. Gagnon, William Simon, Kath

Weston, Steven Epstein, Peter M. Nardi, and Beth E. Schneider. In a reflection on
the legacy of Mary McIntosh's 1968 essay "The Homosexual Role," Weeks writes,
"It is frustrating for those of us who have been toiling in this particular vineyard
since the turn of the 1960s and 1970s to have our early efforts in understanding
sexuality in general, and homosexuality in particular, refracted back to us through
post-Foucauldian abstractions . . . and then taken up as if the ideas are freshly
minted." Jeffrey Weeks, "The 'Homosexual Role' after 30 Years: An Appreciation
of the Work of Mary McIntosh," *Sexualities* 1, no. 2 (1998): 131–52, 132.

17. That image has wavered in recent years, as historians have questioned the extent
of the security state's influence on intellectual life and critics have identified more
creative and dynamic aspects of knowledge production in the period. For classic texts tracing the effects of American foreign policy and anticommunism in the
rise of area studies, modernization theory, behaviorist psychology, game theory,
and related fields, see the 1995 special issue of *Radical History Review*, "The Cold
War and Expert Knowledge: New Essays on the History of the National Security
State," ed. Michael A. Bernstein and Allen Hunter, no. 63 (Fall 1995); Chomsky
et al, *The Cold War and the University: Toward an Intellectual History of the Postwar Years* (New York: New Press, 1997); and *Universities and Empire: Money and
Politics in the Social Sciences during the Cold War*, ed. Christopher Simpson (New
York: New Press, 1999). In a shift visible in the collection *Cold War Social Science*
(2012), some critics and historians have suggested that the characterization of all
social science produced in the period as Cold War social science is too sweeping.
See *Cold War Social Science: Knowledge Production, Liberal Democracy, and Human
Nature*, ed. Mark Solovey and Hamilton Cravens (New York: Palgrave Macmillan, 2012). In a 2007 essay "The Human Sciences in Cold War America," Joel Isaac
takes exception to reductive accounts of Cold War research. He acknowledges the
temptation: "In the case of the Cold War it seems impossible to ignore the social
determination of the 'scientific' study of humanity. This was a time when scholars
shuttled back and forth between governmental and academic positions, carried
out research on military contracts, collected corporate consultancies, and faced
the threat of McCarthyite censure. It is hard to imagine a better proving ground of
the theory that ideas—even ostensibly abstract ideas—are inextricably historical."
Isaac, "The Human Sciences in Cold War America," *Historical Journal* 50, no. 3:
725–46. Isaac joins other critics, such as David Engerman, who argue that, if we follow the money, we should follow it all the way, because many projects in the period
were "far more interesting than a deduction from the resource of funding might
suggest" (99). In a point that resonates with my work on deviance studies, Engerman argues that "the social scientists of the 1950s should not be examined solely
through the lenses of the late 1960s" (100). David Engerman, "Social Science in
the Cold War," *Isis* 101 no. 2 (2010): 393–400. For a revaluation of the knowledge
emerging from the Cold War, see Jamie Cohen-Cole's account of cognitive science
as an alternative to behaviorism, Cohen-Cole, *The Open Mind: Cold War Politics
and the Sciences of Human Nature* (Chicago: University of Chicago Press, 2016).

18. The passage as a whole testifies to Sedgwick's acute awareness of the gendered
implications of her choice of affect and of shame specifically as an object of study:
"Readers who have paid attention to the recent, meteoric rise of shame to its pres-

ent housewife-megastar status in the firmament of self-help and popular psychology—along with that of its ingenue sidekick, the Inner Child—may be feeling a bit uneasy at this point . . . Surely then I can hardly appeal to *Toxic Shame, Healing the Shame That Binds You*, or *Guilt Is the Teacher, Love Is the Lesson*, can I, for my very methodology? Am I really going to talk about Henry James's inner child? My sense of the force of the affect shame is clearly very different from what is to be found in the self-help literature, but there it is: Henry James and the inner child it must be" (6).

19. For a strong statement of the sex panic thesis, see Gayle Rubin, "Thinking Sex: Notes toward a Radical Theory of the Politics of Sexuality," in *Pleasure and Danger: Exploring Female Sexuality*, ed. Carole S. Vance (Boston: Routledge and Kegan Paul, 1984): 157–210. Also see Jennifer Terry, *An American Obsession: Science, Medicine, and Homosexuality in Modern Society* (Chicago: University of Chicago Press, 1999).

20. I take the phrase "totally administered society" from Herbert Marcuse, *One-Dimensional Man* (New York: Beacon Press, 1964).

21. The culture of the 1950s figured more directly in some criticism of the period. See for example D. A. Miller, "Anal Rope," *Representations* 32 (Fall 1990): 114–33, and "Visual Pleasure in 1959," *October* 81 (Summer 1997): 34–58. Also see Lee Edelman, *Homographesis* (New York, Routledge, 1994). Although published later, the Hitchcockian strains of Edelman's *No Future* attest to the imprint of the American midcentury in queer thought. Edelman, *No Future: Queer Theory and the Death Drive* (Durham, NC: Duke University Press, 2004). For a revisionist reading of the link between the Cold War and queer theory, see David Greven, *Intimate Violence: Hitchcock, Sex, and Queer Theory* (New York: Oxford University Press, 2017). For other important work on homosexuality and Cold War America, see Robert J. Corber, *In the Name of National Security: Hitchcock, Homophobia, and the Political Construction of Gender in Postwar America* (Durham, NC: Duke University Press, 1993), *Homosexuality in Cold War America: Resistance and the Crisis of Masculinity* (Durham, NC: Duke University Press, 1997), and *Cold War Femme: Lesbianism, National Identity, and Hollywood Cinema* (Durham, NC: Duke University Press, 2011); David K. Johnson, *The Lavender Scare: The Cold War Persecution of Gays and Lesbians in the Federal Government* (Chicago: University of Chicago Press, 2007); Deborah Nelson, *Pursuing Privacy in Cold War America* (New York: Columbia University Press, 2001); Joseph Litvak, *The Un-Americans: Jews, The Blacklist, and Stoolpigeon Culture* (Durham, NC: Duke University Press, 2009), and Trask, *Camp Sites* (2013); Eric Cervini, *The Deviant's War: The Homosexual v. the United States of America* (New York: Farrar, Straus, Giroux, 2020). For a different genealogy of homophobia in the period, one that situates this moment in a longer twentieth-century history, see Margot Canaday, *The Straight State: Sexuality and Citizenship in Twentieth-Century America* (Princeton, NJ: Princeton University Press, 2011).

22. The term *sleaze* comes up repeatedly in Sedgwick's dialogue with Michael Moon about John Waters and Divine, which I discuss below.

23. Joanne Meyerowitz affirms this account of the postwar sexual culture of the US in a 2014 article. Attempting to reconcile the popular "containment thesis" view of Cold War crusades against homosexuals and other deviants with views that emphasize the challenges to sexual norms both in official discourse and vernacular

sexual cultures after WWII, Meyerowitz offers an account of the 1950s that avoids both forms of simplification. Instead, she emphasizes "the buzz of political conflict that animated the sexual discourse of past decades—and continues to animate it today." Joanne Meyerowitz, "The Liberal 1950s? Reinterpreting Postwar American Sexual," in *Gender and the Long Postwar: Reconsiderations of the United States and the Two Germanys, 1945–1989*, ed. Karen Hagemann and Sonya Michel (Baltimore, MD: Johns Hopkins University Press and Woodrow Wilson Center Press, 2014), 297–319, 311.

24. On "antihomophobic and feminist inquiry," see Sedgwick, *Between Men: English Literature and Male Homosocial Desire* (New York: Columbia University Press, 1985); on some distinctions between them, see Sedgwick, *Epistemology of the Closet*. The fact of Tomkins's distance from queer culture may not be entirely arbitrary. As in the case of Sedgwick's account of shyness, there is a suggestion that finding distance from homophobic forms of thought may require taking distance from homosexuality. It is true that a more explicit thematization of homosexuality tends to result in more collusion with homophobic forms of representation: this is as true of putatively homophilic texts as it is of homophobic ones. Nonetheless, the insistent generalization of "queer" runs the risk of losing the referent of sexuality altogether.

25. This description also links Tomkins's taxonomies to Sedgwick's account of the "rich, unsystematic resources of nonce taxonomy" in *Epistemology*, 23.

26. Several scholars have now discussed Sedgwick's and Tomkins's critique of Ann Cvetkovich in "Shame in the Cybernetic Fold," including Cvetkovich herself (in *Depression: A Public Feeling* [Durham, NC: Duke University Press, 2012]). But the critique of theory, despite its impersonality, has the rhetorical energy of an ad hominem attack.

27. Most postwar histories of radical sociology begin around 1968. See, for example, Rhonda F. Levine, ed., *Enriching the Sociological Imagination: How Radical Sociology Changed the Discipline* (New York, Paradigm, 2005). For a critical genealogy of the opposition between "mainstream sociology" and radical sociology, see Craig Calhoun and Jonathan VanAntwerpen, "Orthodoxy, Heterodoxy, and Hierarchy: 'Mainstream' Sociology and Its Challengers," in *Sociology in America: A History*, ed. Calhoun (Chicago: University of Chicago Press, 2007), 367–410. For an argument that Black sociology significantly predates and preempts radical (Marxist) sociology, see Dennis Forsythe, "Radical Sociology and Blacks," in *The Death of White Sociology: Essays on Race and Culture*, ed. Joyce A. Ladner (Baltimore, MD: Black Classic Press, 1998 [1973]): 213–33. An expanded history of political sociology in the US in the first half of the twentieth century would perhaps begin with W. E. B. DuBois's *The Philadelphia Negro* (1899) and include the work of many Chicago school sociologists, and could conclude with St. Clair Drake and Horace R. Cayton Jr.'s *Black Metropolis: A Study of Negro Life in a Northern City* (1945). See *The Philadelphia Negro: A Social Study* (New York: Oxford University Press, 2017) and *Black Metropolis: A Study of Negro Life in a Northern City* (Chicago: University of Chicago Press, 2015).

28. A great deal of recent scholarship has attempted to assess both the research methodology and the ideological effects of the work of the Institute for Sex Re-

search. See, for instance, Donna J. Drucker, *The Classification of Sex: Alfred Kinsey and the Organization of Knowledge* (Pittsburgh: University of Pittsburgh Press, 2014), Stefan Bargheer, "Taxonomic Morality: Alfred C. Kinsey and the Natural History of Survey Research," Sarah Igo, *The Averaged American: Surveys, Citizens, and the Making of a Mass Public* (Cambridge, MA: Harvard University Press, 2007), Escoffier's *American Homo*, Miriam G. Reumann, *American Sexual Character: Sex, Gender, and National Identity in the Kinsey Reports* (Berkeley: University of California Press, 2005), and Joan Lubin, "'Tired of Cruising? Try *Numbers*!': Pulp Sexology and the Literature of Quantity," forthcoming, *Post45*.

29. See Ben Zimmer's discussion of this usage in the play *Dead End* by Stanley Kingsley (as well as his discussion of the Shelley Winters quote that follows) in his essay "A Far Fetched Etymology," published on the website *Visual Thesaurus* (https://www.visualthesaurus.com/cm/wordroutes/a-far-fetched-etymology-that-seems-a-little-cockamamie/). For an account that illuminates the extreme stigma attached to the practice of tattooing at midcentury, see Justin Spring's biography of the writer Samuel Steward. Justin Spring, *Secret Historian: The Life and Times of Samuel Steward, Professor, Tattoo Artist, and Sexual Renegade* (New York: Farrar, Straus, and Giroux, 2010).

30. Herbert Mitgang, "Portrait of a Mild Winters," *New York Times*, April 29, 1956.

31. "Homer's Phobia," *The Simpsons*, season 8, episode 15, February 16, 1997. Written by Ron Hauge; directed by Mike B. Anderson.

32. In this book, I use the term "queer theory" to refer to the antidisciplinary and generally poststructuralist, anti-identitarian scholarship produced in the early 1990s and "queer studies" to refer to the broader interdisciplinary field of study that grew out of it and that is more widely institutionalized (and in some measure integrated with LGBT studies). I use "queer inquiry" or "queer critique" to refer to queer thought more generally, in a way that is meant to be inclusive of both of these forms of scholarship.

33. In referring to the "deviance paradigm," I am citing Sharon Marcus's critical account of the cultural centrality of female same-sex intimacies in Victorian England, *Between Women*. Marcus argues against what she calls the "deviance paradigm of homosexuality" for its failure to account for socially approved bonds between women. I discuss Marcus's critique in greater detailed in chapter 4. Sharon Marcus, *Between Women: Friendship, Desire, and Marriage in Victorian England* (Princeton, NJ: Princeton University Press, 2007), 31.

34. Kadji Amin, *Disturbing Attachments: Genet, Modern Pederasty, and Queer History* (Durham, NC: Duke University Press, 2017), 17.

35. A more recent example demonstrates the enduring appeal of the deviance studies paradigm: immense popular interest in the figure of Samuel Steward, a.k.a. Phil Andros, university teacher turned tattoo artist and pornographer. His diaries and life story attest to the overlapping worlds of sexual and social marginality at midcentury, offering a template for their later conjunction in the political and intellectual context of queer thought. Justin Spring's 2011 biography of Steward was one of the best-selling LGBT books of the last decade. Justin Spring, *Secret Historian: The Life and Times of Samuel Steward, Professor, Tattoo Artist, and Sexual Renegade* (New York: Farrar, Straus and Giroux, 2011).

36. Kevin Mumford shows how these connections were concretized and lived in urban vice districts, which constituted gathering places for society's most marginal members. See *Interzones: Black/White Sex Districts in Chicago and New York in the Early Twentieth Century* (New York: Columbia University Press, 1997).

37. It is clear that a longer and more geographically diverse history of the deviance paradigm than the one I offer here is a crucial piece. See, for instance, Durba Mitra's work on research on female sexual deviance as the foundation for the rise of social scientific knowledge in modern India (*Indian Sex Life: Sexuality and the Colonial Origins of Modern Social Thought* [Princeton, NJ: Princeton University Press, 2020]).

38. Laud Humphreys, *Tearoom Trade: Impersonal Sex in Public Places* (New Brunswick, NJ: AldineTransaction, 1970), 21.

39. Howard Becker, *Outsiders: Studies in the Sociology of Deviance* (New York: Free Press, 1963), 1.

40. Erving Goffman, *Stigma: On the Management of Spoiled Identity* (Englewood, NJ: Prentice Hall, 1963), 2–3.

41. Alvin W. Gouldner, *The Coming Crisis of Western Sociology* (New York: Basic Books, 1970), 379.

42. See Gouldner, "The Sociologist as Partisan: Sociology and the Welfare State," *American Sociologist* 3, no. 2 (May 1968): 103–16, 105. This contrast between an erect and flaccid style was the subject of a satirical poster about Gouldner that was posted at Washington University, presumably by Laud Humphreys, which led to Gouldner's notorious physical attack on Humphreys. For an account of the attack, see "Sociology Professor Accused of Beating Student," *New York Times*, June 9, 1968. For a broader discussion of the incident that includes a reproduction of the poster, see John F. Galliher, Wayne H. Brekhus, and David P. Keys, *Laud Humphreys: Prophet of Homosexuality and Sociology* (Madison: University of Wisconsin Press, 2004), 19–22 and 191 (appendix C).

43. Ian Taylor's review of *The Coming Crisis* begins: "In American intellectual life, Alvin Gouldner is to sociology as Norman Mailer is to the novel." Ian Taylor, review, *British Journal of Criminology* 11, no. 3 (July 1, 1971): 299–301, 299. Gouldner's son, Richard Lee Deaton, repeats the comparison in a discussion of his father as an "intellectual street fighter" in the preface to James J. Chriss, *Confronting Gouldner: Sociology and Political Activism* (Leiden: Brill, 2015), vii–xxxiii, xx.

44. Michel Foucault, "Nietzsche, Genealogy, History," in *Language, Counter-Memory, Practice: Selected Essays and Interviews*, ed. D. F. Bouchard (Ithaca, NY: Cornell University Press, 1977), 139–140.

45. The quote is from Halperin, *Saint Foucault*, 19. More broadly, Halperin offers a useful analysis of attacks on Foucault's politics, suggesting that it was straight-identified Left academics who were the most exercised by Foucault's attention to the microphysics of power. The charge of quietism is from Edward Said's review of *The History of Sexuality*; "self-indulgent radical chic" is a phrase of Richard Rorty's. See David Halperin, *Saint Foucault: Towards a Gay Hagiography* (New York: Oxford University Press, 1995), especially 21–24.

46. For the canonical midcentury discussion of the double bind, see Gregory Bateson et al., "Towards a Theory of Schizophrenia," *Behavioral Science* 1 (1956): 251–64.

47. On the burden of representation, see Kobena Mercer, "Black Art and the Burden of Representation," in *Third Text* 4, no. 10 (1990): 61–78. See also John Tagg, *The Burden of Representation: Essays on Photographies and Histories* (Minneapolis: University of Minnesota Press, 1993).

48. See Becker, "Whose Side Are We On?," *Social Problems* 14 (1967): 239–47, and Gouldner's critique in "The Sociologist as Partisan." While we can understand many of these alignments as strategic identifications across class and racial lines by white liberal academics, researchers also studied forms of marginality that affected them intimately. See my discussion of Humphreys's study of "secret deviants" in *Tearoom Trade* in chapter 3.

49. For a stark assessment, see Colin Sumner, *The Sociology of Deviance: An Obituary* (New York: Continuum, 1994). Sumner claims that the field of deviance studies died in 1975. For an empirical challenge to this claim, see J. Mitchell Miller, Richard A. Wright, and David Dannels, "Is Deviance 'Dead'? The Decline of a Sociological Research Specialization," *American Sociologist* 32, no. 3 (Fall 2001): 43–59.

50. Alexander Liazos, "The Poverty of the Sociology of Deviance: Nuts, Sluts, and Preverts," *Social Problems* 20, no. 1 (Summer 1972): 103–20, 104. Regarding the unconventional spelling of *perverts*, Liazos explains in a note: "The subtitle of this paper came from two sources. a) A Yale undergraduate once told me that the deviance course was known among Yale students as 'nuts and sluts.' b) A former colleague of mine at Quinnipiac College, John Bancroft, often told me that the deviance course was 'all about those preverts'" (103).

51. As Kitsuse notes, many of the deviants of the 1960s had become by the 1970s "active and visible practitioners of the arts of social problems." Published as John I. Kitsuse, "Coming Out All Over: Deviants and the Politics of Social Problems," *Social Problems* 28, no. 1 (October 1980): 1–13, 3.

52. "Coming Out All Over" is notable for its reliance on the detailed list or catalog, so familiar from the history of deviance studies, in accounting for the activities of the "new deviants." The essay's ironic charge derives from the retention of this rhetorical form to account for a wholly new set of activities—while nonetheless still suggesting that ethnographically rich accounts of deviants' everyday activities might have a place: "Given our sociological conceptions of the effects of societal reactions on deviants, who would have thought that prostitutes would lobby the halls of legislative bodies to denounce 'your tired old ethics'; or that mental patients would organize to demand discharge from institutions that provide only custody but not treatment; or that paraplegics would be able to leave the mark of their political clout on so many street corners across the nation; or that marijuana would be openly used at 'puff-in' demonstrations on the steps of government buildings; or that American Nazis would parade down the streets of the predominantly Jewish community of Skokie, Illinois; or that the chief of police of San Francisco would sponsor a program of recruiting gay men and women for positions on the force?" (2).

53. The discussion of the relation between queer studies and deviance studies is more robust in the UK, where the relevance of queer studies to the field of criminology is an important topic. See Matthew Ball, *Criminology and Queer Theory: Dangerous Bedfellows* (London: Springer, 2017), as well as a lecture series at the Open Univer-

sity: http://www.bbk.ac.uk/events-calendar/criminology-seminar-series-tbc
-professor-jo-phoenix-open-university. The robustness of these links can be
understood as a result of the close connections between deviance studies, subcul-
ture studies, and criminology in the 1960s in the UK, whereas in the US deviance
studies did not have a "cultural wing."

54. Lynne Huffer surveyed this territory in *Mad for Foucault*, arguing that a richer account of sexuality and social exclusion can be derived from Foucault's early work
on madness than from *The History of Sexuality*. Lynne Huffer, *Mad for Foucault:
Rethinking the Foundations of Queer Theory* (New York: Columbia University Press,
2009).

55. Steven Epstein, "Thinking Sex Ethnographically," in "Rethinking Sex," ed.
Heather Love, special issue, *GLQ* 17, no. 1, (2010): 85–88, 86.

56. Rubin makes this connection in a retrospective essay on "Thinking Sex" when she
notes the "protoqueerness" of the essay and its commitment to coalitional politics.
Gayle Rubin, "Blood under the Bridge: Reflections on 'Thinking Sex,'" in *GLQ* 17,
no. 1 (2010): 15–48, 20–23, 40.

57. Chad Heap, "The City as Sexual Laboratory: The Queer Heritage of the Chicago
School," *Qualitative Sociology* 26, no. 4 (Winter 2003): 457–87.

58. Michael Warner, "Introduction," *Fear of a Queer Planet: Queer Politics and Social
Theory* (Minneapolis: University of Minnesota Press, 1993), xxvi.

59. Cathy J. Cohen, "Punks, Bulldaggers, and Welfare Queens: The Radical Potential
of Queer Politics?," *GLQ* 3, no. 4 (1997): 437–65, 438.

60. Roderick A. Ferguson, *Aberrations in Black: Toward a Queer of Color Critique* (Minneapolis: University of Minnesota Press, 2004).

61. The figure of Divine, named by John Waters after a character in *Our Lady of the
Flowers*, suggests again Genet's significance in proliferating images of deviance
across the late twentieth century.

62. Sedgwick (written with Michael Moon), "Divinity: A Dossier, a Performance Piece,
a Little-Understood Emotion," in *Tendencies* (Durham, NC: Duke University Press,
1993), 215–51, 250.

63. Jeffrey Escoffier, *American Homo* (Berkeley: University of California Press, 1998),
103. Escoffier makes this point in an essay, "Inside the Ivory Closet: The Challenge
Facing Lesbian and Gay Studies," which was first published in *OUT/LOOK* in 1990.
Escoffier attempts to map the institutional and historical conditions determining the production of scholarly knowledge about sexuality, arguing that uneven
institutionalization of the field has had profound effects on its research agenda.
Humanities scholars in sexuality studies have on the whole fared better in the
academy than those working in the social sciences. The resentment that is audible
in many critiques of queer theory is not only a matter of disciplinary and intellectual differences, although it is that; it is also a response to real material differences.
Critical responses to Escoffier's piece in queer theory did not engage the sociological framing of his argument; factors such as relative institutional privilege are not
readily incorporated into queer theoretical discussions that are primarily conceptual and discursive. As Lisa Duggan points out in her careful account of responses
to Escoffier's essay ("The Discipline Problem"), the objectifying force of Escoffier's
argument was largely ignored; Eve Kosofsky Sedgwick, as Duggan notes, simply

branded his thinking "anti-intellectual." Sedgwick cited in Lisa Duggan, "The Discipline Problem," in *Sex Wars: Sexual Dissent and Political Culture*, ed. Duggan and Nan D. Hunter (New York: Routledge, 1995), 200.

64. The work of an empirical psychologist like Tomkins constitutes an exception. However, in Sedgwick's corralling of Tomkins for the burgeoning field of queer affect studies, he appears to focus on practice (affect as doing) and collective life (all affects are relational).

65. Barbara Johnson, *The Critical Difference: Essays in the Contemporary Rhetoric of Reading* (Baltimore, MD: Johns Hopkins University Press, 1985), 13.

66. Sedgwick, *Between Men: English Literature and Male Homosocial Desire* (New York: Columbia University Press, 1985), 10.

67. Gayle Rubin, "Thinking Sex: Notes for a Radical Theory of the Politics of Sexuality," in *Pleasure and Danger: Exploring Female Sexuality*, ed. Carole S. Vance (Boston: Routledge & Kegan Paul, 1984): 267–319, 284. Whether early sexologists were involved in sheltering precarious existences or in bringing them into being is at issue. Foucault gives us the tools to think critically about this process, to consider the emergence of the homosexual as species as part of what he calls the "implantation of perversions." But also, through his concept of "'reverse' discourse," he asked us to think about this moment as the origin of our own political life.

68. The question of what counts as doxa is itself deeply ideological, and no two readers will have the same account of the norms of the discipline. Nonetheless, my aim is to invoke a shared sense of the constraints—always enabling too—of contemporary queer thought. This is an argument that can of course only stand on the persuasive value of the evidence presented.

69. I discuss my motivation for this research and its relation to my training and previous work at greater length in Love, "Safe," *American Literary History* 25, no. 1 (Spring 2013): 164–75.

70. Goffman, *Frame Analysis: An Essay on the Organization of Experience* (Cambridge, MA: Harvard University Press, 1974), 10.

71. Goffman's fine-grained attention to nonverbal communication and to gesture make his work significant in the rise of visual methods in the social sciences in the late twentieth century. His links to visual anthropology are clearest in his book *Gender Advertisements*, most of which was originally published in the journal *Studies in the Anthropology of Visual Communication* 3, no. 2 (1976).

72. The title of the essay is also "Spoiled Identity." Love, "'Spoiled Identity': Stephen Gordon's Loneliness and the Difficulties of Queer History," *GLQ* 7, no. 4 (2001): 487–519.

CHAPTER ONE

1. Goffman, *The Presentation of Self in Everyday Life* (New York: Doubleday, 1959), 17.

2. Steven Epstein, "A Queer Encounter: Sociology and the Study of Sexuality," *Sociological Theory* 12, no. 2 (July 1994): 188–202, 188. This essay was reprinted in Steven Seidman, ed., *Queer Theory/Sociology* (Oxford: Blackwell, 1996), 145–67.

3. On the relations between Foucault and Goffman, see Ian Hacking, "Between Michel Foucault and Erving Goffman: Between Discourse in the Abstract and

Face-to-Face Interaction," *Economy and Society* 33, no. 3 (2011): 277–302. Hacking
argues that Goffman's and Foucault's methods are "complementary," Goffman
providing the interactional texture to Foucault's systematic thinking. He writes,
"Foucault's research was 'top-down,' directed at entire 'systems of thought'—to
refer to the title of the chair he chose for himself at the Collège de France. Goffman's research was 'bottom-up'—always concerned with individuals in specific
locations entering into or declining social relations with other people" (277–78).
This distinction is less salient in the case of Foucault's *The History of Sexuality*,
vol. 1. While the book addresses the regime of modern sexuality as an abstract
system of thought, it is also concerned with its instantiation in face-to-face interaction. Where Hacking sees complementarity, others see continuity, even equiva-
lence. In a slash-and-burn piece on contemporary sexuality studies, Camille Paglia
argues that Goffman's influence was forgotten (or suppressed) by Foucault. In a
highly polemical denunciation of the field as narrow and jargon filled, Paglia refers
to Goffman as "the great Canadian-American sociologist whose work in such pioneering books as *The Presentation of Self in Everyday Life* (1959) was one of Foucault's primary and deviously unacknowledged sources." Camille Paglia, "Scholars in Bondage: Dogma Dominates Studies of Kink," *Chronicle of Higher Education:
The Chronicle Review*, May 20, 2013.

4. Goffman's influence in performance studies is well established because of the
canonical status of *The Presentation of Self in Everyday Life*, but also because of the
influence of postwar social science in the formation of the field. As Jon McKenzie
writes in an account of the origins of performances studies, the field's intellectual
roots "can be found in the 1940s and 1950s, at a moment when theorists in the
social sciences—linguistics, anthropology, and sociology—began to employ theater
as a model for studying uses of language, ritual, and everyday interactions." Jon
McKenzie, "Performance Studies," in *The Johns Hopkins Guide to Literary Theory*
(Baltimore, MD: Johns Hopkins University Press, 2005). The 1976 collection *Ritual,
Play and Performance*, edited by Richard Schechner and Mady Schuman, offers a
useful map of a now somewhat obscured disciplinary formation: it includes studies
of theater (by Schechner and Victor Turner) alongside work by Goffman as well
as other social scientists on everyday life and social ritual; it also includes work
by natural scientists, especially in the field of animal ethology (I discuss the influence of this body of work at greater length in chapter 2). For Goffman's influence in
studies of race, see Kenji Yoshino, *Covering: The Hidden Assault on Our Civil Rights*
(New York: Random House, 2006), and Imogen Tylor, *Stigma: The Machinery of
Inequality* (London: ZED Books, 2020), and several essays in Chris Bruckert and
Stacey Hannem, *"Stigma" Revisited: Implications of the Mark* (Ottawa: University
of Ottaway Press, 2012); in fat studies, see Amy Erdman Farell, *Fat Shame: Stigma
and the Fat Body in American Culture* (New York: New York University Press, 2011).
Because of Goffman's lack of attention to interior experience, his influence in affect studies is harder to see. But Goffman profoundly influenced the foundational
scholarship of Arlie Russell Hochschild, especially her *The Managed Heart* and *The
Commercialization of Intimate Life*. For some reflections on Goffman's reception in
disability studies, see "Forum Introduction: Reflections on the Fiftieth Anniversary of Erving Goffman's *Stigma*," ed. Jeffrey A. Brune and Rosemarie Garland-
Thomson, *Disability Studies Quarterly* (2014).

5. Didier Eribon, *Insult and the Making of the Gay Self*, trans. Michael Lucey (Durham, NC: Duke University Press, 2004 [1999]).

6. The optimism of Goffman vis-à-vis Foucault is mitigated by the fact that the freedom of Goffman's actors is, in Nunokawa's account, the freedom to fail. Regarding Goffman's attention to inept or improper performances, Nunokawa writes, "These farcical or tragic repetitions of more ordinary presentations of the self are enacted without the glorious costumes of political purpose: the actors who perform them are queer in the old-fashioned sense of one whose earnest efforts to imitate normality have been baffled, rather than in the renovated one of the rebellious hero who, by means of a hyperbolic embrace of the abnormal identity assigned to her, manages to upset the regime that dispenses such assignments." Jeff Nunokawa's *Tame Passions of Wilde: The Styles of Manageable Desire* (Princeton, NJ: Princeton University Press, 2003), 63.

7. Michael Trask, *Camp Sites: Sex, Politics, and Academic Style in Postwar Culture* (Stanford, CA: Stanford University Press, 2013). Interest in Goffman has increased recently in literary studies, in conjunction with attention to relations between literary form and the organization of social life. See, for example, three books published in 2016: David Alworth, *Site Reading: Fiction, Art, Social Form* (Princeton, NJ: Princeton University Press, 2016); Gage McWeeny, *The Comfort of Strangers: Social Life and Literary Form* (Oxford: Oxford University Press, 2016); and Mark Seltzer, *The Official World* (Durham, NC: Duke University Press, 2016). For a recent reflection on the utility of Goffman's work in the study of literature, see John Plotz, "Having it Both Ways with Erving Goffman," *Victorian Literature and Culture* 47, no. 2 (Summer 2019): 439–48.

8. The phrase "small change of social interaction" appears in Tom Burns, *Erving Goffman* (New York: Routledge, 1999), 22.

9. Michael Delaney, "Goffman at Penn: Star Presence, Teacher-Mentor, Profaning Jester," *Symbolic Interaction* 37, no. 1 (Feb 2014): 87–107, 93.

10. Sedgwick, "Queer and Now," in *Tendencies*, 1–20, 8–9. Sedgwick insisted that, in order to maintain its political salience, "queer" must retain a link to gay and lesbian identity while also addressing other forms of difference. She discusses this tension in relation to "universalizing" and "minoritizing" discourses in *Epistemology of the Closet* ("Introduction: Axiomatic"). In "Queer and Now," just before the passage I have cited about the spinning outward of queer analysis, Sedgwick remarks that attempting to "displace [lesbian and gay] meanings from [queer's] definitional center . . . would be to dematerialize any possibility of queerness itself" (9).

11. Eve Kosofsky Sedgwick, *Epistemology of the Closet* (Berkeley: University of California Press), 22.

12. The phrase appears in the introduction to *Frame Analysis*, 10.

13. Arlie Russell Hochschild refers to Goffman's "black box" psychology in *The Commercialization of Intimate Life: Notes from Home and Work* (Berkeley: University of California Press, 2003), 91. Hochschild, discussing her debt to Goffman, addresses his mixture of attention to oppressed populations and heartlessness. She argues that his works "reflected the poignant vulnerability of the marginal man and woman. But Goffman gave us actors without psyches" (7). Hochschild's concept of affective labor attempts to fill in this gap, addressing the psychological cost of

exclusion. But I would argue that these accounts differ less in substance than in tone and style, since, as I argue elsewhere, Goffman conveys a great deal about the person without recourse to the psyche. For an account that highlights the importance of games to Goffman, see Clifford Geertz, "Blurred Genres: The Refiguration of Social Thought," in *Local Knowledges: Further Essays in Interpretive Anthropology* (New York: Basic Books, 1983).

14. There is critical consensus about Goffman's heartlessness, but not that it was a product of the Cold War. For an argument that suggests the difficulty of framing his research as exemplary of Cold War social science, see Michael Pettit, who writes, "Goffman's career does not fit neatly into a narrative organized around the growth of social scientific knowledge in the service of the American state, especially its military ambitions on the world stage" (Michael Pettit, "The Con Man as Model Organism: The Methodological Roots of Erving Goffman's Dramaturgical Self," *History of the Human Sciences* 24, no. 2 [2011]: 138–54, 139).

15. Foucault, *The History of Sexuality*, vol. 1, *An Introduction*, trans. Robert Hurley (New York: Vintage Books, 1990), 20.

16. George Gonos, "The Class Position of Goffman's Sociology: Social Origins of an American Structuralism," in *The View from Goffman*, ed. Jason Ditton (London: Macmillan, 1980): 134–69, 136. Compare with Joel Whitebrook's claim in relation to Foucault's resistance to psychology that "the notion of the deconstruction of the subject is incompatible with the subject of psychology, for the dissolution of the subject deprives psychology of its object of investigation." Whitebrook, "Against Interiority: Foucault's Struggle with Psychoanalysis," in *The Cambridge Companion to Foucault*, ed. Gary Gutting (Cambridge: Cambridge University Press, 2005): 312–47, 340n14.

17. Goffman, *Relations in Public: Microstudies of the Public Order* (New York: Basic Books, 1971), 260n19.

18. Goffman defined the interaction order in his presidential address to the American Sociological Society, later published as "The Interaction Order," *American Sociological Review* 48 (1983): 1–17. Also see *Erving Goffman: Exploring the Interaction Order*, ed. Paul Drew and Anthony Wootton (Cambridge: Polity Press, 1988), 270.

19. Gary Alan Fine, *A Second Chicago School? The Development of Postwar American Sociology* (Chicago: University of Chicago, 1995). Fine, Philip Manning, and Gregory W. H. Smith strike a similar note in their joint introduction to the four-volume Sage edition of Goffman's criticism, noting that Goffman puts "observational flesh on Simmel's microscopic-molecular theory" (*Erving Goffman*, ed. Gary Alan Fine and Gregory W. H. Smith, 4 vols., Sage Masters of Modern Thought [London: Sage, 2000], ix–xliv, xxxvi).

20. For an exemplary reading of Goffman as a poststructuralist, see Patricia Clough, *The End(s) of Ethnography: From Realism to Social Criticism* (New York: Palgrave, 1992).

21. Erving Goffman, *Frame Analysis: An Essay on the Organization of Experience* (Boston: Northeastern University Press, 1974), 8.

22. Goffman writes: "The term 'strip' will be used to refer to any arbitrary slice or cut from the stream of ongoing activity, including here sequences of happenings, real

or fictive, as seen from the perspective of those subjectively involved in sustaining an interest in them. A strip is not meant to reflect a natural division made by the subjects of inquiry or an analytical division made by students who inquire: it will be used only to refer to any raw batch of occurrences (of whatever status in reality) that one wants to draw attention to as a starting point for analysis" (10). Few critical humanists will find Goffman's use of the term *raw* congenial here. Yet his use of *strip* to describe these sets of occurrence is suggestive. It positions Goffman at once as a student of social reality and as a close reader of film or comic strips.

23. Pierre Bourdieu, "Erving Goffman: Discoverer of the Infinitely Small," in *Le Monde*, trans. Richard Nice, reprinted in Fine and Smith, *Erving Goffman*, vol. 1, xlvii.

24. Louis Menand, "Some Frames for Goffman," *Social Psychology Quarterly* 72, no. 4 (December 2009): 296–99, 296.

25. The literature on national and international surveillance and its links to the history of computing during the Cold War is extensive. See, for instance, James R. Beniger, *The Control Revolution: Technological and Economic Origins of the Information Society* (Cambridge, MA: Harvard University Press, 1986); Paul N. Edwards, *The Closed World: Computers and the Politics of Disclosure in Cold War America* (Cambridge, MA: MIT Press, 1997); *Cold War Legacies: Systems, Theory, Aesthetics,* ed. John Beck (University of Edinburgh Press, 2016); and Matthew Potolsky, *The National Security Sublime: On the Aesthetics of Government Secrecy* (New York: Routledge, 2019).

26. For a discussion of 'sousveillance,' or surveillance from below, as well as its limits, see Simone Browne, *Dark Matters: On the Surveillance of Blackness* (Durham, NC: Duke University Press, 2015).

27. On observational cinema, see Anna Grimshaw and Amanda Ravetz, *Observational Cinema: Anthropology, Film, and the Exploration of Social Life* (Bloomington: Indiana University Press, 2009); Lúcia Nagib, *World Cinema and the Ethics of Realism* (New York: Continuum International Publishing Group, 2011); and Ivone Margulies, *Nothing Happens: Chantal Akerman's Hyperrealist Everyday* (Durham, NC: Duke University Press, 1996). On Mass Observation, see Nick Hubble, *Mass Observation and Everyday Life: Culture, History, Theory* (New York: Palgrave Macmillan, 2010); and James Hinton, *The Mass Observers: A History, 1937–1949* (Oxford: Oxford University Press, 2013). For a broader look at the documentary impulse, see Erika Balsom and Hila Peleg, eds., *Documentary across Disciplines* (Cambridge, MA: MIT Press, 2016).

28. Menand argues that Goffman's work can be understood in terms of a broader obsession with signs of class and status in the 1950s, and in particular with the debunking, deflating intelligence of situation comedy and documentary. Menand identifies a quality of anxious monitoring and self-monitoring across media in the period, with unpredictable ideological effects. Harold Garfinkel's breaching experiments, by which he sought to expose his students to the anarchic consequences of minor situational improprieties, clearly belong to this same moment, and constitute another important frame for Goffman. Louis Menand, "Some Frames for Goffman," *Social Psychology Quarterly* 72, no. 4 (December 2009): 296–99. On breaching experiments, see Harold Garfinkel, "Studies of the Rou-

tine Grounds of Everyday Activities," in *Studies in Ethnomethodology* (Cambridge: Polity, 1984 [1967]), 35–75.

29. Goffman, "Fun in Games," in *Encounters: Two Studies in the Sociology of Interaction* (Indianapolis, IN: Bobbs-Merrill Company, 1961), 15–81, 81.

30. I make an argument for the political value of small-scale analysis in relation to the contemporary discourse of microaggressions via a reading of Claudia Rankine's 2014 *Citizen: An American Lyric* in Love, "Small Change: Realism, Immanence, and the Politics of the Micro," *Modern Language Quarterly* 77, no. 3 (September 2016): 419–45.

31. Butler writes, "cultural configurations of sex and gender might then proliferate or, rather, their present proliferation might then become articulable with the discourses that establish intelligible cultural life, confounding the very binarism of sex and exposing its fundamental unnaturalness" (*Gender Trouble*, 190).

32. Erving Goffman, *Stigma: On the Management of Spoiled Identity* (New York: Simon & Schuster, 1963), 2.

33. Phil Manning, "Resemblances" in Fine and Smith, *Erving Goffman*, vol. 2, 62–63.

34. Alan Bennett, "Cold Sweat," from *Writing Home*, excerpted in Fine and Smith, *Erving Goffman*, vol. 1, 351.

35. Goffman, *Stigma*, 111n15. The previously cited sources in this footnote are Jean-Paul Sartre, *Anti-Semite and Jew* (New York: Grove Press, 1960); Anatole Broyard, "Portrait of the Inauthentic Negro," *Commentary* 10 (1950); M. Seeman, "The Intellectual and the Language of Minorities," *American Journal of Sociology* 64 (1958).

36. In an anecdote reported by a colleague at Penn, Dell Hymes, it appears that the habit of comparison went deep, and that Goffman reflected on his own experience growing up Jewish in provincial Canada in relation to the experience of other stigmatized groups. Hymes remarks that Goffman once said to him, "You forget that I grew up (with Yiddish) in a town where to speak another language was to be suspect of being homosexual." Dell Hymes, "On Erving Goffman," in Fine and Smith, *Erving Goffman*, 48–60, 56.

37. Linda Alcoff, *Visible Identities: Race, Gender, and the Self* (New York: Oxford University Press, 2005), 9.

38. Goffman, "The Interaction Order," 9.

39. Giddens, "Goffman as a Systematic Social Theorist," in Drew and Wootton, 270.

40. Philip Toynbee, *Underdogs: Anguish and Anxiety* (the book was published one year later in the US as *Underdogs, Anguish and Anxiety: Eighteen Men and Women Write Their Own Case Histories* [New York: Horizon Press, 1962]).

41. Toynbee, 9.

42. The right's appropriation of the rhetoric of victimhood in the context of embattled white masculinity or arguments against affirmative action is only one example of how the figure of the underdog can be used to support existing regimes of inequality.

43. Douglas Crimp, "Mario Montez, for Shame," in *Regarding Sedgwick: Essays on Queer Culture and Critical Theory*, ed. Stephen M. Barber and David L. Clark (New York: Routledge, 2002), 66. On the centrality of stigma and shame in queer studies, see Didier Eribon, *Insult and the Making of the Gay Self*, trans. Michael Lucey (Durham, NC: Duke University Press, 2004 [1999]); José Esteban Muñoz, *Disidentifications:*

Queers of Color and the Performance of Politics (Minneapolis: University of Minnesota Press, 1999); David M. Halperin and Valerie Traub, eds., *Gay Shame* (Chicago: University of Chicago Press, 2010); Sally R. Munt, *Queer Attachments: The Cultural Politics of Shame* (London: Ashgate, 2008).

44. Sara Ahmed considers the problem of assuming that "stigma provides a common affective horizon" for the injuries of race and sexuality in "Sensitivity to Stigma: Eve Sedgwick and Queer-of-Color Critique," http://feministkilljoys.com/2013/10/20/sensitivity-to-stigma/; accessed June 19, 2020. Ahmed addresses persistent critiques of Sedgwick for her reliance on a mostly white archive, and suggests the limits of her distinction between voluntary and involuntary stigma. While Ahmed is critical of the universalizing impulse in queer studies, she is moved by Sedgwick's comments on vicariousness and proximity, and accepts queer's ability to do "a kind of justice to the fractal intricacies of language, skin, migration, state." For a briefer exploration of these questions of stigma and political engagement, see Ahmed, *Willful Subjects* (Durham, NC: Duke University Press, 2014), 161-62. Other critics have been less convinced by the queer attempt to make shame or stigma the basis for broader collectivity (although it is true some of these attempts were pursued under the sign "gay" rather than "queer" as in *Gay Shame*). For responses that specifically address the Gay Shame conference that took place at the University of Michigan in 2003, see Larry LaFountain-Stokes, "Gay Shame, Latina- and Latino-Style: A Critique of White Queer Performativity," in *Gay Latino Studies: A Critical Reader*, ed. Michael Hames-García and Ernesto Javier Martínez (Durham, NC: Duke University Press, 2011), 55-80, and Hiram Pérez, "You Can Have My Brown Body and Eat it Too!," in *A Taste for Brown Bodies: Gay Modernity and Cosmopolitan Desire* (New York: New York University Press, 2015), 97-124. For an article that uses shame as a key framework for reading the work of the queer Asian artist Justin Chin, but also criticizes the use of shame in white queer studies, see Chris A. Eng, "Apprehending the 'Angry Ethnic Fag': The Queer (Non)Sense of Shame in Justin Chin's 'Currency' and 'Lick My Butt,'" *GLQ* 26, no. 1 (January 2020): 103-28. Eng writes, "Queer studies scholars who challenge the sentiment of pride by insisting on a focus on shame and recentering sexual practices often reproduce . . . a nostalgic mode that romanticizes the past and inhibits analyses into the entanglements among gender, sexuality, and class" (105).

45. Most significantly, Candace West and Don H. Zimmerman, "Doing Gender," *Gender and Society* 1, no. 2 (June 1987): 125-51. But see also Harold Garfinkel, "Passing and the Managed Achievement of Sex Status in an 'Intersexed' Person," in *Studies in Ethnomethodology* (Englewood Cliffs, NJ: Prentice Hall, 1967): 116-85. This article, now also known by the name of the subject at its center ("Agnes"), has become an important document in transgender history. It makes clear the hard work of performing gender, and especially of maintaining, or managing, cross gender identity in a context saturated by medical and psychological expertise.

46. As Michael Trask argues, the fact that Butler does not cite Goffman constitutes a suppression of a major influence both on the theory of gender performativity and more broadly on the constructionist study of sexuality. Trask argues that, in spite of her antifoundationalism, Butler's reliance on political agency entails a commitment to authentic selfhood. For Trask, fifties sociologists understood social actors as "already attuned to the fictive or rehearsed quality of their identities" (589) and

did not see possibilities for social subversion in the exposure of that fact. Ultimately, he concludes, "Butler appears less committed to repudiating authenticity
or identity than to making these categories as inclusive as possible" (590). Michael
Trask, "Patricia Highsmith's Method," *American Literary History* 22, no. 3 (2010):
584-614. For other accounts of the relation between Goffman and Butler, see Gra-
hame F. Thompson, "Approaches to 'Performance': An Analysis of Terms," *Screen*
(1985): 78-90; Nicky Gregson and Gillian Rose, "Taking Butler Elsewhere: Per-
formativities, Spatialities, and Subjectivities," *Environment and Planning D: Society
and Space* 18 (2000): 433-52; and Philip Auslander, "Introduction," in *Performance:
Critical Concepts in Literary and Cultural Studies*, ed. Auslander (London: Routledge, 2003).

47. Erving Goffman, *Interaction Ritual: Essays on Face-to-Face Behavior* (New York:
Pantheon Books, 1967), 2-3.

48. Consider, for instance, the ending of *The Presentation of Self in Everyday Life*, the
text that grounds widespread claims about Goffman's dramaturgical understanding of the self and social action. In the final pages, referring to his employment of
the "language of the stage," he admits that to "press a mere analogy so far was . . .
a rhetoric and a maneuver." After suggesting that this kind of metaphor should
not "be taken too seriously," he writes, "And so here the language and mask of the
stage will be dropped. Scaffolds, after all, are meant to build other things with, and
should be erected with an eye to taking them down." Erving Goffman, *The Presentation of Self in Everyday Life* (New York: Anchor Books, 1959), 254.

49. Goffman, "The Arrangement between the Sexes," *Theory and Society* 4 (1977):
301-31, 319.

50. The rhetoric of temporal inversion, so important to Butler's account, recurs
throughout the essay, as in the following passage: "It is common to conceive of the
differences between the sexes as showing up against the demands and constraints
of the environment, the environment itself being taken as a harsh given, present
before the matter of sex differences arose. Or, differently put, that sex differences
are a biological given, an external constraint upon any form of social organization
that humans might devise. There is another way of viewing the question, however.
Speculatively one can reverse the equation and ask what could be sought out from
the environment or put into it so that such innate differences between the sexes as
there are could count—in fact or in appearance—for something" (313).

51. Goffman, *Gender Advertisements* (Cambridge, MA: Harvard University Press,
1979), 7.

52. Goffman, "On Cooling the Mark Out: Some Aspects of Adaptation to Failure," in
The Goffman Reader, eds. Charles Lemert and Ann Branaman (Malden, MA: Blackwell Publishing, 1997), 5.

53. Goffman, "Symbols of Class Status," *British Journal of Sociology* 2, no. 4 (Dec. 1951):
294-304, 295. In accounting for the "pressures that play upon behavior," Goffman
had in mind not only the ordinary curiosity of friends, coworkers, and strangers
but also the professional scrutiny of social scientists like himself.

54. Norman K. Denzin, "Much Ado about Goffman," *American Sociologist* 33, no. 2
(Summer 2002): 105-17, 107.

55. In "Much Ado about Goffman," Denzin comments that Goffman offered "a time-
less naturalistic, taxonomic sociology; a sociology that seemed to turn human

beings into Kafka-esque insects to be studied under a glass. He was the objective observer of human folly" (106–7).

56. At the end of "The Interaction Order," Goffman writes, "If one must have warrant addressed to social needs, let it be for unsponsored analyses of the social arrangements enjoyed by those with the institutional authority—priests, psychiatrists, school teachers, police, generals, government leaders, parents, males, whites, nationals, media operators, and all the other well-placed persons who are in a position to give official imprint to versions of reality." Goffman, "The Interaction Order," *American Sociological Review* 48 (1983): 1–17, 17. For an argument about the differential distribution of resources or the capacity to affect others' behavior, see Mary F. Rogers, "Goffman on Power, Hierarchy, and Status." Rogers shifts the focus from power as domination to power as a matter of conformity in everyday life, as do several critics who address the relation between Goffman and Foucault. Mary F. Rogers, "Goffman on Power, Hierarchy, and Status," in *The View from Goffman*, 100–133; Richard Jenkins, "Erving Goffman: A Major Theorist of Power?," *Journal of Power* 1, no. 2 (August 2008): 157–68; Ian Hacking, "Between Michel Foucault and Erving Goffman: Between Discourse in the Abstract and Face-to-Face Interaction," 277–302.

57. George Gonos, "The Class Position of Goffman's Sociology," 136.

58. Gonos does not make this argument on a biographical basis, though he might have. Goffman's desire for privacy (he refused to be filmed, photographed, or taped, and requested that his archive be closed after his death) makes discussion of his biography complex. Yet in spite (or perhaps because) of this resistance, an informal archive continues to grow. A site hosted by the Center for Democratic Culture at the University of Nevada at Las Vegas and edited by Dmitri N. Shalin has collected many documents, interviews, and anecdotes about Goffman by colleagues, students, friends, and relatives. This material attests to Goffman's upbringing in the precarious lower reaches of the middle class, describing the fortunes of Goffman's father's dry goods business in small-town Manitoba. *Bios Sociologicus: The Erving Goffman Archives*, ed. Dmitri N. Shalin (UNLV, CDC Publications, 2007–17), http://cdclv.unlv.edu/ega/; accessed May 7, 2020.

59. C. Wright Mills, *White Collar: The American Middle Classes* (Oxford: Oxford University Press, 1951), 28.

60. Drawing on Luc Boltanski's empirical analysis of the professions and locations represented in Goffman's work, Gonos notes the absence of the traditional working class: instead, the lower ranks of society are populated by domestic servants and petty service workers. See sections 1 and 2 in the appendix to Luc Boltanski's article "Erving Goffman et le Temps du Soupçon," in Fine and Smith, *Erving Goffman*, 290–311, 302–4.

61. Other scholars also attribute this point of view to Goffman, but offer a more negative assessment: In "The Underworld-View of Erving Goffman," Alan Dawe suggests that there is value in Goffman's ability to "convey the terror rampant in the world." But, he argues, Goffman's view of social life, "deformed as it is by the Hobbesian distortion . . . is still sociologically and morally shallow." Dawe continues, "In the end, he is utterly incapable of seeing beyond the mean human possibilities embodied in his sadly limited view of the world."

62. Howard Becker, "Whose Side Are We On?," *Social Problems* 14 (1967): 239–47.

63. Liazos takes Becker and deviance studies in general to task for the tendency to critique midlevel custodians rather than elites. He writes, "The really powerful, the upper classes and the power elite, those Gouldner calls the 'top dogs,' are left essentially unexamined by these sociologists of deviance." Liazos, "The Poverty of the Sociology of Deviance," 105.

64. Goffman, *Asylums: Essays on the Social Situation of Mental Patients and Other Inmates* (New Brunswick, NJ: AldineTransaction, 1961), xviii.

65. Bennet M. Berger, "A Fan Letter on Erving Goffman," in *Dissent*, reprinted in Fine and Smith, *Erving Goffman*, vol. 1, 288.

66. Goffman, "The Insanity of Place" (1969), in *Relations in Public: Microstudies of the Public Order* (New York: Harper Colophon, 1971): 335–90, 390.

67. Gary T. Marx, "Role Models and Role Distance: A Remembrance of Erving Goffman," in *Theory and Society*, reprinted in Fine and Smith, *Erving Goffman*, vol. 1, 67.

68. Bennett M. Berger, foreword to *Frame Analysis*, by Erving Goffman (1974) (Boston: Northeastern University Press, 1986), xi–xviii.

69. Goffman, "On Fieldwork," *Journal of Contemporary Ethnography* 18, no. 2 (July 1989): 123–32, 125–26.

CHAPTER TWO

1. Nikolaas Tinbergen to S. J. and Corinne Hutt, April 11, 1970, Box 1: MS. Eng.c.3144, Folder D1, Niko Tinbergen Papers, Bodleian Library, Oxford University.

2. I am indebted to Richard Burkhardt's landmark study of European ethology for my account of Tinbergen's method and his place in intellectual history. In the following reading, I am specifically indebted to Burkhardt's discussion of Tinbergen's presentation at the Macy conferences and the dispute over the meaning of "ethos" that erupted there. Richard W. Burkhardt, *Patterns of Behavior: Konrad Lorenz, Niko Tinbergen, and the Founding of Ethology* (Chicago: University of Chicago Press, 2005), 399–400. My thanks to Mara Mills for introducing me to *Patterns of Behavior* at an early moment in this project.

3. Niko Tinbergen, "Psychology and Ethology as Supplementary Parts of a Science of Behavior," in *Group Processes: Transactions of the First Conference*, ed. Bertram Schaffner (New York: Josiah Macy, Jr. Foundation, 1955), 75–167, 76.

4. Frank Fremont-Smith, "The Josiah Macy, Jr. Foundation Conference Program," in Schaffner, *Group Processes*, 7–8, 7. On postwar interdisciplinary research, see Jamie Cohen-Cole, *The Open Mind: Cold War Politics and the Sciences of Human Nature*; on Cold War social science and its links to military and government, see David H. Price, *Cold War Anthropology: The CIA, the Pentagon, and the Growth of Dual-Use Anthropology* (Durham, NC: Duke University Press, 2016); for revisionist accounts of this relationship, see Peter Mandler, *Return from the Natives: How Margaret Mead Won the Second World War and Lost the Cold War* (New Haven, CT: Yale University Press, 2013), and Andrew Pickering, *The Cybernetic Brain: Sketches of Another Future* (Chicago: University of Chicago Press, 2011).

5. Thanks to Mara Mills for her help in illuminating the stakes and context of the sociobiology debate. Burkhardt is particularly helpful in parsing the ways that Tinbergen's collaboration with Lorenz situated him both in proximity to and in conflict with sociobiological principles (as I discuss in greater detail below).

6. The field of animal sociology has its origins in the early part of the twentieth century, when it focused on questions of animal psychology. The writing of George Herbert Mead on animal minds shifted the emphasis toward the question of social interaction. See George Herbert Mead, *Mind, Self, and Society from the Standpoint of a Social Behaviorist* (Chicago: University of Chicago Press, 1934). For Tinbergen's contribution to this field, see N. Tinbergen, *Social Behavior in Animals* (London: Chapman and Hall, 1953).

7. Martha Davis, "Film Projectors as Microscopes: Ray L. Birdwhistell and Microanalysis of Interaction (1955–1975)," *Visual Anthropology Review* 17, no. 2 (Fall–Winter 2001-2): 39–49, 46.

8. On ἦθος and ἔθος, see the entry on "Morals/Ethics" in Barbara Cassin, ed., *The Dictionary of Untranslatables: A Philosophical Lexicon*, trans. Steven Rendall, Christian Hubert, Jeffrey Mehlman, Nathanael Stein, and Michael Syrotinski, trans. ed. Emily Apter, Jacques Lezra, and Michael Wood (Princeton, NJ: Princeton University Press, 2014), 691–92. William R. Uttal, *The War between Mentalism and Behaviorism: On the Accessibility of Mental Processes* (New York: Psychology Press, 1999).

9. Burkhardt also comments on the title of Tinbergen's presentation, noting that he named the session "diplomatically" (399). Tinbergen's opening has the character of a charm offensive: "in spite of the differences between American psychology and ethology, the affinity between the two are so close that, if it were not for historical reasons, the two fields would not have different names" (76). The disagreements that break out moments later belie Tinbergen's claim.

10. Burkhardt parses the difference between European ethology and US behaviorism at length in *Patterns of Behavior*. His discussion turns on the distinctions between the lab and the field and between observation and experiment.

11. Sharon Marcus, *Between Women: Friendship, Desire, and Marriage in Victorian England* (Princeton, NJ: Princeton University Press, 2007), 3.

12. See, for instance, Peter Winch's influential argument about the limits of behavioral research in the social sciences in *The Idea of a Social Science and Its Relation to Philosophy*. In the chapters "The Nature of Meaningful Behavior" and "The Social Studies as Science," he argues that human action must be studied as symbolic and self-reflexive rather than mechanical. Yet Winch acknowledges that behavioral analysis can have its uses. He suggests that adopting an "external point of view" may "serve the purpose of drawing the reader's attention to aspects of the situation which are so obvious and familiar that he would otherwise miss them." Winch compares these uses of observational methods to Wittgenstein's use of "outlandish examples" and to Bertolt Brecht's *Verfremdungseffekt*, but he could just as easily have cited Goffman's disconcertingly alien accounts of everyday life. Peter Winch, *The Idea of a Social Science and Its Relation to Philosophy* (London: Routledge, 1958), 110.

13. Skinner writes, "A science of behavior must consider the place of private stimuli as physical things, and in doing so it provides an alternative account of mental life. The question, then, is this: What is inside the skin, and how do we know about it? The answer is, I believe, the heart of radical behaviorism." B. F. Skinner, *About Behaviorism* (New York: Knopf, 1974), 211–12.

14. Annamarie Jagose, "Behaviorism's Queer Trace: Sexuality and Orgasmic Reconditioning," *Orgasmology* (Durham, NC: Duke University Press, 2012), 106–34.

15. On self-divestiture and queer tactics of refusal, see Foucault, *The History of Sexuality*, vol. 1; Leo Bersani and Adam Phillips, *Intimacies* (Chicago: University of Chicago Press, 2008); Nicholas de Villiers, *Opacity and the Closet: Queer Tactics in Foucault, Barthes, and Warhol* (Minneapolis: University of Minnesota Press, 2012); Love, "Forced Exile: Walter Pater's Backward Modernism," in *Feeling Backward* (Cambridge, MA: Harvard University Press, 2007), 53–71; Octavio R. Gonzalez, "Ascetic Self-Divestiture and Queer Relationality in *A Single Man*," *Modern Fiction Studies* 59, no. 4 (Winter 2013): 758–83; and Scott L. Morgensen, "Encountering Indeterminacy: Colonial Contexts and Queer Imagining," *Cultural Anthropology* 31, no. 4 (2016): 607–16. See also Édouard Glissant on "the right to opacity" in Glissant, *Poetics of Relation*, trans. Betsy Wing (Ann Arbor: University of Michigan Press, 1990).

16. For an argument about how asymmetry structures even the most intimate and reflexive work in the field, see Judith Stacey, "Can There Be a Feminist Ethnography?," *Women's Studies International Forum* 11, no. 1 (1988): 21–27.

17. I discuss questions of intention and meaning at length in an article that takes up the relationship between thick and thin description in anthropology and literary studies. See Love, "Close Reading and Thin Description," *Public Culture* 25, no. 3 (2013): 401–34.

18. Tinbergen, "Ethology and Stress Diseases," *Science* 185, no. 4145 (July 5, 1974): 20–27.

19. Hans Kruuk, *Niko's Nature: The Life of Niko Tinbergen and His Science of Animal Behaviour* (Oxford: Oxford University Press, 2003), 257.

20. Kruuk discusses Tinbergen's wartime experience at length in *Niko's Nature*. During the war, Lorenz was a member of the Nazi party, a fact that caused a significant rift between him and Tinbergen both during and after the war.

21. Sula Wolff, "The History of Autism," *European Child Adolescent Psychiatry* 13 (2004): 201–8, 202.

22. Leo Kanner, "Autistic Disturbances of Affective Contact," *Nervous Child* 2 (1943): 217–50.

23. On anthropomorphism in animal research, see Eileen Crist, *Images of Animals: Anthropomorphism and Animal Mind* (Philadelphia: Temple University Press, 1999).

24. See Temple Grandin, *Thinking in Pictures: My Life with Autism* (New York: Vintage, 2006 [1995]), and *Animals Make Us Human: Creating the Best Life for Animals* (New York: Harcourt, 2009). For more connections between autism and nonhuman animals in a disability studies frame, see Dawn Prince-Hughes, *Songs of the Gorilla Nation: My Journey through Autism* (New York: Broadway Books, 2005); Cary Wolfe, "Learning from Temple Grandin: Animal Studies, Disability Studies, and Who Comes after the Subject," in Wolfe, *What Is Posthumanism?* (Minneapolis: University of Minnesota Press, 2010), 127–42; and Sunaura Taylor, *Beasts of Burden: Animal and Disability Liberation* (New York: New Press, 2017). Thanks for Mara Mills for alerting me to Prince-Hughes's work and for conversations regarding autism and animal behavior research.

25. The turn toward the animal in critical theory is associated with the work of Jacques Derrida, Georgio Agamben, Donna Haraway, Timothy Morton, and Cary Wolfe.

But ethology is implicated in other critical traditions, for instance, the work of Gilles Deleuze and Félix Guattari. Janell Watson offers a helpful account of their thinking in this vein, also discussing Lacan's turn away from an early interest in ethology (important to his account of the mirror scene) to develop a linguistic model of subjectivity. Janell Watson, *Guattari's Diagrammatic Thought: Writing between Lacan and Deleuze* (London: Continuum, 2009), esp. chap. 2 ("Capitalism's Triangular Traps"), 55–96.

26. Tinbergen, "Watching and Wondering," in *Studying Animal Behavior: Autobiographies of the Founders*, ed. Donald A. Dewsbury (Chicago: University of Chicago Press, 1985), 431–64. Emphasis in original.

27. Cited in Burkhardt, *Patterns of Behavior*, 399.

28. For a discussion of Lorenz's relation to National Socialism and racialist thought, see Burkhardt, chap. 5.

29. Letter from Niko Tinbergen to Richard Burkhardt, June 19, 1982, Box MS. Eng.c.3156, Folder E2, Niko Tinbergen Papers, Bodleian Library, Oxford University. In an article reflecting on their correspondence, Burkhardt describes this letter as a "subdued" version of a letter written on June 16, 1982, but never sent. In both letters, Tinbergen addressed what he saw as Burkhardt's failure to properly attribute the contributions of Lorenz and Tinbergen. See Richard W. Burkhardt Jr., "Niko Tinbergen: A Message in the Archives," *Journal of the History of Biology* 49 (2016): 685–703, 690.

30. For an account of the move from the field to the lab in twentieth-century biology, see Robert E. Kohler, *Landscapes and Labscapes: Exploring the Lab-Field Border in Biology* (Chicago: University of Chicago Press, 2002).

31. Charles Elton, *Animal Ecology* (New York: MacMillan, 1927). Later in the book, Elton describes how the "grunt work" falls to the "systematist" or taxonomist/collector. "Now, the systematist is not usually a trained field naturalist, or, if he is, he lacks the knowledge of plant and animal associations which is required in order to define accurately the habitat of the specimens he is collecting. The ideal procedure would seem, therefore, to be that as full data as possible should be entered upon labels and handed over to the systematist with the specimens, and that a more detailed account of the environment, and in particular of the animal environment, should be published by the ecologist himself" (167).

32. Harry W. Greene, "Organisms in Nature as a Central Focus for Biology," *Trends in Ecology and Evolution* 20, no. 1 (January 2005): 23–27, 24, 25.

33. Anna Lowenhaupt Tsing, Heather Anne Swanson, Elaine Gan, and Nils Bubandt, eds., *Arts of Living on a Damaged Planet: Ghosts and Monsters of the Anthropocene* (Minneapolis: University of Minnesota Press, 2017).

34. Anna Lowenhaupt Tsing, *The Mushroom at the End of the World: On the Possibility of Life in Capitalist Ruins* (Princeton, NJ: Princeton University Press, 2015), 21. Thanks to the participants in my seminar at the School for Criticism and Theory in Summer 2018 ("Reading the Social World: Observation, Description, Interpretation") for their superb discussion of this book, which has influenced my thinking about it. Special thanks to Josh Kopin and Marco Motta.

35. On the origins of naturalistic research, with a focus on the contributions of Robert Park and Herbert Blumer, see Lonnie Athens, "Naturalistic Inquiry in Theory

and Practice," *Journal of Contemporary Ethnography* 39, no. 1 (2010): 87–125. See also Robert A. Hinde, *Individuals, Relationships and Culture: Links between Ethology and the Social Sciences* (Cambridge: Cambridge University Press, 1987). For a fascinating example of naturalistic research and collaboration between natural and social scientists (and others), see *The Natural History of an Interview*. Wendy Leeds-Hurwitz offers a detailed, thoughtful account of the project in "The Social History of *The Natural History of an Interview*: A Multidisciplinary Investigation of Social Communication," in "Multichannel Communication Codes," pt. 1, edited by Stuart J. Sigman, special issue, *Research on Language and Social Interaction* 20, nos. 1–4 (1987): 1–51.

36. Tinbergen, *Curious Naturalists* (Amherst: University of Massachusetts Press, 1958), 12.

37. Tinbergen and Elizabeth A Tinbergen, *Early Childhood Autism: An Ethological Approach* (Berlin: Parey, 1972). Lorenz shared this view, articulated in his 1973 essay "The Fashionable Fallacy of Dispensing with Description." While Tinbergen's target in his autism research was the interview, Lorenz's was the reliance of quantification in psychological research. Lorenz, "The Fashionable Fallacy of Dispensing with Description," *Die Naturwissenschaften* 60 (1973): 1–9. Thanks to Pearl Brilmyer for drawing my attention to this article.

38. Chloe Silverman, "Birdwatching and Baby-Watching," *History of Psychiatry* 21, no. 2 (2010): 176–89. Silverman also mentions Tinbergen's correspondence with John Bowlby, the psychoanalyst who trained with Melanie Klein and later developed an ethological version of attachment theory. More recently, scholars have returned to this connection, noting Tinbergen's consultation with Bowlby on his depression. See Frank C. P. van der Horst, "John Bowlby's Treatment of Nikolaas 'Niko' Tinbergen's Depressions," *History of Psychology* 13, no. 2 (2010): 206–8.

39. S. J. Hutt and Corinne Hutt, *Direct Observation and Measurement of Behavior* (Springfield, IL: Charles C. Thomas Publisher, 1970), 3.

40. Though it seemed to come out of nowhere at his Nobel address, Tinbergen's interest in childhood autism was long-standing and passionate. This interest occupied him for the last two decades of his life—unlike his interest in the Alexander technique, which faded more quickly.

41. Letter from N. Tinbergen to Philippa Elmhirst, November 24, 1982, Box MS. Eng.c.3146, Folder D34, Niko Tinbergen Papers, Bodleian Library, Oxford University.

42. What the Tinbergens saw as ordinary good parenting was deeply shaped by class, national, and gender norms, as well as by the worship of nature. Although they tended to see autism as the product of the pathologies of the modern world as a whole, their instructions for care (i.e., mothering) were also characterized by classic double binds. In *Early Childhood Autism*, they write, "Mothers should be given precise but tactful advice . . . about the dangers of both under-involvement with their children and over-intrusive behavior . . . We believe that one can learn a great deal from observing female mammals in the process of rearing their young. Their procedure could be characterized as 'watching all the time, but acting only when the baby demands it, either by giving signs of distress or by being reckless.' In this respect it seems that working-class and peasant mothers are, intuitively or of ne-

cessity, better mothers than many intellectuals and over-affluent mothers with few children" (37).

43. Welch to Tinbergen, November 21, 1982, Box MS. Eng.c.3146, Folder D45, Niko Tinbergen Papers, Bodleian Library, Oxford University.

44. Tinbergen to Welch, December 17, 1982, Box MS. Eng.c.3146, Folder D45, Niko Tinbergen Papers, Bodleian Library, Oxford University.

45. One of the key critiques of human ethology, by Daniel Lehrman, which Tinbergen refers to repeatedly in his writing on the topic, was aimed primarily at Lorenz. Daniel Lehrman, "A Critique of Konrad Lorenz's Theory of Instinctive Behavior," *Quarterly Review of Biology* 28 (1953): 337–63.

46. Tinbergen, "On Aims and Methods of Ethology," *Zeitschrift für Tierpsychologie* 20 (1963): 410–33.

47. Desmond Morris, *The Naked Ape: A Zoologist's Study of the Human Animal, Fiftieth Anniversary Edition* (New York: Random House, 2010), 5.

48. Morris, *Manwatching: A Field Guide to Human Behavior* (New York: Vintage, 1977). The method of visual analysis used in *Manwatching* is remarkably similar to Goffman's approach in *Gender Advertisements*, i.e., lateral comparison between gestures using visual media.

49. For a discussion of research ethics in *Tearoom Trade*, see the essays collected at the end of the enlarged edition (1975) by Nicholas von Hoffman, Irving Louis Horowitz, Lee Rainwater, Donald P. Warwick, Myron Glazer, and Humphreys himself. The fullest treatment of Humphreys's work can be found in John F. Galliher, Wayne H. Brekhus, and David P. Keys, *Laud Humphreys: Prophet of Homosexuality and Sociology* (Madison: University of Wisconsin Press, 2004). Galliher, Brekhus, and Keys address the ethical controversies around Humphreys's work, but also make a case for its lasting sociological value.

50. "Unusual difficulties call for unusual strategies," Humphreys writes. Laud Humphreys, *Tearoom Trade: Impersonal Sex in Public Places* (New Brunswick, NJ: Aldine Transaction, 1970), 21. On "oddball measures," Humphreys cites Eugene J. Webb et al., *Oddball Measures: Nonreactive Research in the Social Sciences* (Chicago: Rand McNally, 1966). Compare Humphreys's adoption of the watchqueen persona in the tearoom to Michael Pettit's account of Goffman's similarly unobtrusive (or deceptive) self-presentation in his practice of ethnography and his identification with the figure of the confidence man. Pettit, "The Con Man as Model Organism," *History of the Human Sciences* 24, no. 2 (2011): 138–54.

51. Wayne H. Brekhus, John F. Galliher, and Jaber F. Gubrium, "The Need for Thin Description," *Qualitative Inquiry* 11, no. 6 (2005): 861–79, 876.

52. Helen Macdonald, "Covert Naturalists," http://fretmarks.blogspot.com/2009 /11/covert-naturalists.html (accessed August 8, 2020).

53. Nava shared this anecdote with me, as well as many other insights into ethology and field naturalism, during "Desert Life: Field Studies of Art + Nature in the Southwest," a course run by the Art + Bio Collaborative in summer 2017. My thanks to Saúl Nava and to Stephanie Dowdy-Nava for allowing me to participate in the program and for their guidance and friendship. Thanks also to my fellow students for sharing their expertise with me. More info about the Art + Bio Collaborative can be found at https://www.artbiocollaborative.com (accessed August 8, 2020).

54. Robert Root-Bernstein recounts this story in a brief article on Tinbergen's forays into the visual arts. Describing Tinbergen's drawing, photography, and filmed
documentary, Root-Bernstein also emphasizes the aesthetic pleasure Tinbergen took in natural observation itself. Robert Root-Bernstein, "Niko Tinbergen's
Visual Arts," *Leonardo* 40, no. 1 (February 2007): 68–69. In addition to *Kleew*, Tinbergen also published *The Tale of John Stickle*, which follows a boy engaged in the
basic activities of natural history observation. Tinbergen, *Kleew: The Story of a Gull*
(New York: Oxford University Press, 1947) and *The Tale of John Stickle* (London:
Methuen, 1954).

55. The distinction is not always so clear, however. On the connection between bird-
watching and plane-spotting during WWII in Britain, see Helen Macdonald,
"'What Makes You a Scientist Is the Way You Look at Things': Ornithology and the
Observer, 1930–1955," *Studies in History and Philosophy of Biological and Biomedical
Sciences* 33 (2002): 53–77.

CHAPTER THREE

1. Susan Sontag, "Notes on 'Camp,'" *Partisan Review* 31, no. 4 (Fall 1963): 515–30, 515.
2. David Halperin meditates on a similar ambivalence in the representation and
analysis of gay subjectivity in "Homosexuality's Closet." Via a reading of Foucault
on the question of psychological desire versus bodily pleasure, Halperin writes,
"What gay people need, on this view, is not to be told in more detail, on the basis
of a more thoroughgoing investigation of gay desire and gay subjectivity, who they
really are as subjects; rather, what they need is to escape from models of subjectivity that invite such normalizing scrutiny in the first place . . . The goal of queer
theory, according to this Foucauldian model, ought not to be self-analysis but de-
subjection." David Halperin, "Homosexuality's Closet," *Michigan Quarterly Review*
41, no. 1 (Winter 2002): 21–54, 36–37.
3. William E. Jones, *Tearoom* (1963/2007), 56 mins. For a discussion of the ethics of
"transforming traumatic evidence into visual art" (which nonetheless reproduces
many color stills from the film), see Katherine Biber and Derek Dalton, "Making
Art from Evidence: Secret Sex and Police Surveillance in the Tearoom," *Crime,
Media, Culture: An International Journal* 5, no. 3 (2009): 243–67. Jim Supanick offers
a more positive reading of *Tearoom*, noting how effectively it "reverses the function" of the original film. Supanick, "Last Year at Mansfield: William E. Jones's
'Tearoom,'" *Film International* 7, no. 1 (2009): 12–15.
4. See, for instance, Blas's projects "Face Cages" (2013–16), http://www.zachblas
.info/works/face-cages/, and the Facial Weaponization Suite (2012), http://www
.zachblas.info/works/facial-weaponization-suite/. Also see Blas's essay "'A Cage
of Information,' or What Is a Biometric Diagram?," in *Documentary across Disciplines*, ed. Erika Balsom and Hila Peleg (Cambridge: MIT Press and Haus der Kul-
turen Welt, 2016).
5. The mention of "real existences" forms part of Foucault's preface to the collection of prison records that he edited, "The Lives of Infamous Men." Discussing his
decision not to include literary or fictional accounts, he writes, "None of the dark
heroes [of imaginative fiction] appeared as intense to me as these cobblers, these

army deserters, these garment-sellers, these scriveners, these vagabond monks, all of them rabid, scandalous, or pitiful. And this was owing, no doubt, to the mere fact that they are known to have lived." Foucault, "The Lives of Infamous Men," in *Essential Works of Foucault 1954–1984*, vol. 3, *Power*, ed. James D. Faubion (New York: New Press, 2000), 160. The mention of the sacrifice of the subject of knowledge appears in Foucault, "Nietzsche, Genealogy, History," in *Essential Works of Foucault, 1954–1984*, vol. 2, *Aesthetics, Method, and Epistemology*, ed. James D. Faubion (New York: New Press, 1998), 388.

6. On Warhol's opacity, see Nicholas de Villiers, *Opacity and the Closet*, especially chap. 3. Jonathan Flatley addresses Warhol's opacity and his documentary impulse in *Like Andy Warhol* (Chicago: University of Chicago Press, 2017).

7. Shane Vogel writes, "'Looking for Langston' does less to unearth a gay black past hidden from history than to meditate on the ways in which history—like desire—is dynamic and unfixed." Vogel, "Closing Time: Langston Hughes and the Queer Poetics of Harlem Nightlife," *Criticism* 28, no. 3 (Summer 2006): 397–425.

8. On Bechdel's aesthetics of "documentary witness," see Ann Cvetkovich, "Drawing the Archive in Alison Bechdel's *Fun Home*," *Women's Studies Quarterly* 36, nos. 1/2 (Spring-Summer 2008): 111–28. On Bechdel's process, see Cvetkovich; Anne Rüggemeier, "'Posing for All the Characters in the Book': The Multimodal Processes of Production in Alison Bechdel's Relational Autobiography *Are You My Mother?*," *Journal of Graphic Novel and Comics* 7, no. 3 (2016): 254–67; and "Hillary Chute Interviews Alison Bechdel," http://dykestowatchoutfor.com/my-everlasting -process.

9. Lisa Duggan, "The Discipline Problem: Queer Theory Meets Lesbian and Gay History," *GLQ* 2, no. 3 (1995): 179–91, 181. While this quote makes it sound like Duggan's critique is only directed at queer theory, she also indicts empirical researchers in sexuality studies for their resistance to the theoretical and interpretive insights of scholars in the humanities.

10. Gayle Rubin, "Thinking Sex: Notes for a Radical Theory of the Politics of Sexuality," in *Pleasure and Danger: Exploring Female Sexuality*, ed. Carole S. Vance (Boston: Routledge & Kegan Paul, 1984): 267–319, 284.

11. The thesis of the empty archive of gay and lesbian history appears throughout the scholarship, but perhaps nowhere as memorably as in Martin B. Duberman, Martha Vicinus, and George Chauncey, eds., *Hidden from History: Reclaiming the Gay and Lesbian Past* (New York: New American Library, 1989).

12. Joan W. Scott, "The Evidence of Experience," *Critical Inquiry* 17, no. 4 (Summer, 1991): 773–97, 780.

13. Because of the retrospective narration of the scene, Delany's position in "The Evidence of Experience" is ambiguous: Is he the young naïf witnessing a group orgy for the first time or the mature writer narrating the story of that encounter? Is he the chronicler of this underground world (aligned in that case with social historians) or a member of it (aligned with the subjects of historical study)?

14. Delany, *The Motion of Light in Water: Sex and Science Fiction Writing in the East Village* (Minneapolis: University of Minnesota Press, 2004 [1988]), 173.

15. On the double valence of empiricism, see Jonathan Crary, *Techniques of the Observer: One Vision and Modernity in the Nineteenth Century* (Boston: MIT Press,

1990), and Lorraine J. Daston and Peter Galison, *Objectivity* (Boston: MIT Press, 2010). On the potential within empiricism to destroy foundations, see Jonathan Loesberg's discussion of Walter Pater's appeal to the senses in *Aestheticism and Deconstruction: Pater, Derrida, and de Man* (Princeton, NJ: Princeton University Press, 1991). For a discussion of empiricism in relation to the tradition of novelistic realism, see George Levine, *The Realistic Imagination*: "Literary realism is a self-contradictory program in part because empiricism is self-contradictory, leading to questioning the very experience that is supposed to be the source of our knowledge." Levine, *The Realistic Imagination* (Chicago: University of Chicago Press, 1981), 276. For further thoughts from Levine on the "contradictory implications of objectivity that get exposed when it is lived rather than merely thought," see his essay "The Narrative of Scientific Epistemology," *Narrative* 5, no. 3 (October 1997): 227–51, 228.

16. In perhaps the strongest version of this claim, Scott goes on to argue that the discipline of history is limited by the fact that it has "typically constructed itself in opposition to literature" (793).

17. The linguistic turn refers to nonsynchronous developments in philosophy, history, and the social sciences. The key account of this development in the history of philosophy is Richard Rorty's *The Linguistic Turn* (Richard M. Rorty, ed., *The Linguistic Turn: Essays in Philosophical Method* [Chicago: University of Chicago Press, 1967]). In history and the social sciences, the linguistic turn is associated with the publication of key texts including Clifford Geertz's *The Interpretation of Cultures: Selected Essays* (New York: Basic Books, 1973), Hayden White's *Metahistory: The Historical Imagination in Nineteenth-Century Europe* (Baltimore: Johns Hopkins University Press, 1973), Michel Foucault's *Discipline and Punish: The Birth of The Prison* (New York: Pantheon Books, 1977 [1975]), and James Clifford and George Marcus, eds., *Writing Culture: The Poetics and Politics of Ethnography* (Berkeley: University of California Press, 1985).

18. Cf. Timothy J. Bagwell, "Science Fiction and the Semiotics of Realism," in *Intersections: Fantasy and Science Fiction*, ed. George E. Slusser and Eric S. Rabkin (Carbondale: Southern Illinois University Press, 1987); Fredric Jameson, *Archaeologies of the Future: The Desire Called Utopia and Other Science Fictions* (London: Verso, 2005); and Jeff Menne, "'I Live in This World, Too': Octavia Butler and the State of Realism," *MFS: Modern Fiction Studies* 57, no. 4 (Winter 2011): 715–37. On realism as an "antiliterary" genre, see Levine, *The Realistic Imagination*, 57.

19. Delany, "The Semiology of Silence: The *Science Fiction Studies* Interview," in *Silent Interviews: Race, Sex, Science Fiction, and Some Comics* (Middletown, CT: Wesleyan University Press, 1995), 21–58, 31–32.

20. Delany, "The Second *Science Fiction Studies* Interview: *Trouble on Triton* and Other Matters," in *Shorter Views: Queer Thoughts and The Politics of the Paraliterary* (Middletown, CT: Wesleyan University Press, 1999), 315–50, 317.

21. Kane Race, *Pleasure Consuming Medicine: The Queer Politics of Drugs* (Durham, NC: Duke University Press, 2009), 22. Race credits Scott's analysis with linking material practice to the production of meaning; I am suggesting that Scott, in her polemical turn to a selective account of the literary, emphasizes representation in such a way that material practice is neglected. Scott's parallax view of Delany's text allows space for both readings.

22. Delany, "Aversion/Perversion/Diversion," in *Negotiating Lesbian and Gay Subjects*, eds. Monica Dorenkamp and Richard Henke (New York: Routledge, 1994), 7–33, 9.

23. José Esteban Muñoz, *Cruising Utopia: The Then and There of Queer Futurity* (New York: New York University Press, 2009), 52. While some queer critics have taken issue with Scott's essay, their criticisms tend to suggest that Scott did not recognize how fully Delany anticipates the poststructuralist framing of his work. Lisa Duggan offered an important rebuttal to Scott in her essay "The Discipline Problem": she acknowledges the force of Scott's about-face in the middle of the essay but chastises her for not extending the same reading practices to the work of lesbian and gay historians—whom Duggan argues have not attempted to stabilize identity any more than Delany. Muñoz's reading of Delany constitutes something of an exception, since he considers Delany's work in the context of an argument about institutions of public sex and of queer worlds. But Muñoz also emphasizes this moment in the baths as a "deviation from the text's dominant mode of narration" (52)—as a "glimpse of utopia" that is by definition antirealist.

24. Ricardo Montez has noted the continuity between Delany and social scientific forays into deviant worlds, underlining his relative economic advantage and freedom of movement in relation to the people he encounters. In his essay "'Trade' Marks," Montez considers Delany's sexual and communicative exchanges in the context of commercial sex in gay culture and in a longer history of ethnography as a practice structured by inequality. Ricardo Montez, "'Trade' Marks: LA2, Keith Haring, and a Queer Economy of Collaboration," *GLQ* 12, no. 3 (2006): 425–40.

25. In *American Homo* (chap. 3, n30), Jeffrey Escoffier notes the significance of this date: "In 1963, two of the most influential symbolic interactionist books on 'deviant identities' appeared: Becker's *Outsiders* and Goffman's *Stigma*."

26. Delaney, *Silent Interviews*, 267.

27. Delany delivered "Aversion/Perversion/Diversion" in 1991 at the Fifth Annual Lesbian and Gay Conference on Gay Studies at Rutgers University.

28. Guy Davidson, "Utopia and Apocalypse in Samuel Delany's *The Mad Man*," *Journal of Modern Literature* 32, no. 1 (Fall 2008): 13–32, 24.

29. GerShun Avilez, "Cartographies of Desire," *Callaloo* 34, no. 1 (Winter 2011): 126–42. In his review of *Times Square Red*, Eric Rofes also emphasizes this aspect of Delany's project: "By working across genres (geography, social history, urban folklore, political science, cultural studies), he has created a work of intellectual scope that broadens our understanding of urban renewal far more than a study confined to a single discipline might do. One emerges from a reading of this book with insights from economics, architecture, and social policy as well as from sexology, public health, and urban studies." Eric Rofes, "Imperial New York: Destruction and Disneyfication under Emperor Giuliani," *GLQ* 7, no. 1 (2001): 101–9, 108.

30. Madhu Dubey, *Signs and Cities: Black Literary Postmodernism* (Chicago: University of Chicago Press, 2003), 11. In her larger argument, Dubey describes the difficulty she faced when she "had to reluctantly relinquish [her] assumptions—engrained through long disciplinary training—about literature as the most agile handle on social reality" (13).

31. Delany, "Aversion/Perversion/Diversion," 18.

32. Delany, *Times Square Red, Times Square Blue* (New York: New York University Press, 1999), xviii.

33. Although one can't help wondering about the quality of these friendships, or what getting what one wants might mean in this context, Delany's quantification of the content of these movies recalls not only the methods of discourse analysis but also what has come to be known as the Bechdel test for movies, after the work of lesbian cartoonist Alison Bechdel (http://bechdeltest.com/).

34. A representative moment from John Rechy's *Numbers*: "Again, he tries to remember all the numbers so far. Beginning again: Number one—the one in the movie balcony, the one I stood before, who—. . . Number two . . . number three . . . number four . . . number five . . . number six . . . number seven . . . But now the numbers are scattered." John Rechy, *Numbers* (New York: Grove Press, 1967), 216. For a discussion of counting in the stud file, see Justin Spring, *Secret Historian: The Life and Times of Samuel Steward* (New York: Farrar, Straus and Giroux, 2011).

35. Stefan Bargheer, "Taxonomic Morality: Alfred C. Kinsey and the Natural History of Survey Research," unpublished manuscript provided by the author.

36. On the link between eroticism and sociological knowledge in the novel, see David Kurnick, "An Erotics of Detachment: *Middlemarch* and Novel-Reading as Critical Practice," *ELH* 74, no. 3 (Fall 2007): 583–608.

37. In a relevant discussion of Goffman, Michael Pettit argues that the sociologist's obsession with the confidence man was the trace of his reliance on the technique of participant observation, with its necessary deceptions. Pettit writes, "Goffman celebrated the vantage point of the insincere performer rather than the perspective of a distant and impartial recording device" (145).

38. John Guillory discusses the naturalization of this link in his essay "The Sokal Affair and the History of Criticism," *Critical Inquiry* 28, no. 2 (Winter 2002): 470–508.

39. In his response to "The Evidence of Experience," Thomas C. Holt points out that the essay should not be read as an antirealist polemic: "A careless reading of this essay might convey the impression that discourse is all" (390). At the same time, Holt worries about the evisceration of the category of experience, which he argues can serve as a source of resistance (for instance, in slave societies). Thomas C. Holt, "Experience and the Politics of Intellectual Inquiry," *Critical Inquiry* 17 (Summer 1991): 388–96.

40. Guillory, "The Sokal Affair and the History of Criticism," 482. Guillory suggests that, in the late twentieth century, "the division of the disciplines into sciences and humanities has been triumphantly reconceived as the distinction between knowledge and the critique of knowledge" (505).

41. Theodor Adorno, *Minima Moralia: Reflections from Damaged Life*, trans. E. F. N. Jephcott (London: Verso, 1974 [1951]), 247.

42. José Esteban Muñoz, *Cruising Utopia: The Then and There of Queer Futurity* (Durham, NC: Duke University Press, 2009).

CHAPTER FOUR

1. Samuel Steward, Journal Entry, cited in Justin Spring, *Secret Historian*, 206. As Spring reports, once Steward opened his tattoo shop in the 1950s, he regularly attracted underworld characters: "The tattoo shop was of course a magnet for the very young boot sailors stationed at nearby Great Lakes Naval Training Station,

but it also drew into it the youth gangs of Chicago, the juvenile delinquents, the sexually confused and rootless (sometimes illiterate) young men—the rebels without causes" (212).

2. Edward Sagarin, *The Other Minorites: Nonethnic Collectivities Conceptualized as Minority Groups* (Waltham, MA: Ginn, 1971).

3. Edwin M. Schur, *The Politics of Deviance: Stigma Contests and the Uses of Power* (Englewood Cliffs, NJ: Prentice-Hall, 1980), 11.

4. Eve Kosofsky Sedgwick, "Queer and Now," in *Tendencies*, 9.

5. Judith Butler, "Critically Queer," *GLQ* 1, no. 1 (1993): 17–32, 19.

6. Michael Warner, "Introduction," in *Fear of a Queer Planet: Queer Politics and Social Theory*, ed. Michael Warner (Minneapolis: University of Minnesota Press, 1993), vii–xxxi, xxvi.

7. John H. Gagnon and William Simon, "Deviant Behavior and Sexual Deviance," in *Sexual Deviance*, ed. Gagnon and Simon (New York: Harper and Row, 1967), 2, 12.

8. Although Kinsey's methods were very different from scholars in sociology, his use of a scale of sexual behavior makes clear the continuity he saw between deviant and conforming acts.

9. Editorial headnote, Evelyn Hooker, "The Homosexual Community," in *Sexual Deviance*, 168.

10. Willard Waller, "Social Problems and the Mores," *American Sociological Review* 1, no. 6 (December 1936): 922–33. Schur, *The Politics of Deviance*, discusses this passage on 140–41.

11. For a discussion of debates about sympathy with underdogs in the postwar period, particularly in American letters, see Carla Cappetti, "Footnote Fellows: Cold Wars of American Letters," in *Writing Chicago: Modernism, Ethnography, and the Novel* (New York: Columbia University Press, 1993), 144–55.

12. See John I. Kitsuse, "Coming Out All Over: Deviants and the Politics of Social Problems," *Social Problems* 28, no. 1 (October 1980): 1–13.

13. Sedgwick, *Epistemology of the Closet*, 14.

14. Lauren Berlant and Michael Warner, "What Does Queer Theory Teach Us about X?," *PMLA* 110, no. 3 (May 1995): 343–49, 348.

15. Pierre Bourdieu, *Language and Symbolic Power*, ed. John B. Thompson, trans. Gino Raymond and Matthew Adamson (New York: Polity, 1991), 243.

16. Irving Louis Horowitz and Martin Liebowitz, "Social Deviance and Political Marginality: Toward a Redefinition of the Relation between Sociology and Politics," *Social Problems* 15 (1967–68): 280–96, 284.

17. Herbert Marcuse, *Eros and Civilization: A Philosophical Inquiry into Freud* (New York: Beacon, 1966), 165.

18. Fred Moten and Stefano Harney, "The University and the Undercommons: Seven Theses," *Social Text* 22, no. 2 (Summer 2004): 101–15, 103.

19. Kath Browne and Catherine J. Nash, eds., *Queer Methods and Methodologies: Intersecting Queer Theories and Social Science Research* (New York: Routledge, 2010), 1. I would also point to Lauren Berlant's special double issue of *Critical Inquiry*, "On the Case," as inaugurating an early moment of reflection on method in queer studies. See especially Berlant's introduction to the first volume, in which she explicitly compares standards of evidence and modes of argumentation in the

humanities and the social sciences. Lauren Berlant, "On the Case," *Critical Inquiry* 33, no. 4 (2007): 663–72.

20. Margot Weiss, "The Epistemology of Ethnography: Method in Queer Anthropology," *GLQ* 17, no. 4 (2011): 649–64, 650, 662.

21. For information about this conference, including a list of those involved in planning and organizing and conference participants, see https://gsws.sas.upenn.edu /events/2013/11/01/queer-method-conference.

22. D'Lane Compton, Tey Meadow, Kristen Schilt, eds., *Other, Please Specify: Queer Methods in Sociology* (Berkeley: University of California Press, 2018); Amin Ghaziani and Matt Brim, eds., *Imagining Queer Methods* (New York: New York University Press, 2019). I also understand recent work that aims to historicize the field and to situate it in broader disciplinary histories as contributing to making up the method gap. See, for instance, Robyn Wiegman, "Telling Time: When Feminism and Queer Theory Diverge" and "The Vertigo of Critique" in *Object Lessons* (Durham, NC: Duke University Press, 2012), and Kadji Amin, *Disturbing Attachments*. For an analysis of the way social class and pedagogical practice have shaped the field, see Matt Brim, *Poor Queer Studies* (Durham, NC: Duke University Press, 2020).

23. Jane Ward, "Dyke Methods: A Meditation on Queer Studies and the Gay Men Who Hate It," in *Imagining Queer Methods*, 259–76, 262.

24. Valerie Traub is responding to a set of short essays about her book *Thinking Sex with the Early Moderns* published in the "Queer Methods" special issue of *WSQ*. Traub, "A Response: Difficulty, Opacity, Disposition, Method," *WSQ* 44, nos. 3–4 (Fall/Winter 2016): 336–42, 337.

25. Biddy Martin, "Extraordinary Homosexuals and the Fear of Being Ordinary," *Femininity Played Straight: The Significance of Being Lesbian* (New York: Routledge, 1996), 45–70, 70.

26. Keja L. Valens, *Desire between Women in Caribbean Literature* (New York: Palgrave Macmillan, 2013), 90.

27. Robyn Wiegman and Elizabeth A. Wilson, eds., "Queer Theory without Antinormativity," special issue, *differences: A Journal of Feminist Cultural Studies* 26, no. 1 (May 2015).

28. The allusion is to Michael Warner's foundational definition of queer as arrayed "against the regimes of the normal" in his introduction to *Fear of a Queer Planet*. Michael Warner, "Introduction," *Fear of a Queer Planet: Queer Politics and Social Theory* (Minneapolis: University of Minnesota Press, 1993), xxvi. I have written about the tension between the ordinary and queer exceptionalism in "Wedding Crashers," *GLQ* 13, no. 1 (Winter 2007): 125–39.

29. Susan Fraiman's 2017 *Extreme Domesticity: A View from the Margins* engages in depth with these questions. Fraiman makes a persuasive argument that "contempt for domesticity is in part an effect of bias against spaces and practices strongly associated with women" (3). Fraiman looks to examples of nonconforming domesticity, including several queer and transgender examples, in order to argue that practices of care and homemaking can be separated out from conservative and sentimental ideologies of domesticity. While I agree with her desire to develop less punitive accounts of domestic life, and her interest in the longings of vulner-

able subjects for "continuity and security" (11), I am more hesitant to distinguish between conforming and nonconforming practices of domesticity. Is it possible to distinguish in all cases between normative and nonnormative desires for safety and stability? As I argue, in the era of gay marriage and what has been called the violence of inclusion, it becomes increasingly difficult to judge which point of view is from the margins and which is not. Susan Fraiman, *Extreme Domesticity: A View from the Margins* (New York: Columbia University Press, 2017). For an influential account of queer domesticity and its discontents, see Maggie Nelson, *The Argonauts* (Minneapolis: Graywolf Press, 2015). Nelson's book is influenced by queer theory but also takes exception to it, critiquing the association of normativity with women and children. For more critical accounts of the rise of normativity in queer life, see Jin Haritaworn, Adi Kunstman, and Silvia Posocco, eds., "Murderous Inclusions," special issue, *International Feminist Journal of Politics* 15, no. 4 (2013); Chandan Reddy, *Freedom with Violence: Race, Sexuality, and the US State* (Durham, NC: Duke University Press, 2011); Dean Spade, *Normal Life: Administrative Violence, Critical Trans Politics, and the Limits of Law* (Durham, NC: Duke University Press, 2015); Christina B. Hanhardt, *Safe Space: Gay Neighborhood History and the Politics of Violence* (Durham, NC: Duke University Press, 2013); and Jasbir K. Puar, *Terrorist Assemblages: Homonationalism in Queer Times* (Durham, NC: Duke University Press, 2007).

30. Harvey Sacks, "Doing 'Being Ordinary,'" in *Lectures on Conversation*, vol. 2, ed. G. Jefferson (Oxford: Blackwell, 1992): 215-21, 216, emphasis in original.

AFTERWORD

1. Michel Foucault, "Two Lectures," in *Power/Knowledge: Selected Interviews and Other Writings, 1972-1977*, ed. Colin Gordon (New York: Pantheon, 1980), 80.

2. Walter Benjamin, "Theses on the Philosophy of History," *Illuminations*, trans. by Harry Zohn, ed. Hanna Arendt (New York: Schocken Books, 1968).

3. Goffman, "The Insanity of Place," *Psychiatry* 32, no. 4 (November 1969): 357-88, 387.

4. For one example of a call to shift the object of sexuality studies, see the introduction to David L. Eng, Judith Halberstam, and José Esteban Muñoz, eds., "What's Queer about Queer Studies Now?," *Social Text* 84-85 (2005).

5. Rubin, "Thinking Sex: Notes for a Radical Theory of the Politics of Sexuality," in *Pleasure and Danger: Exploring Female Sexuality*, ed. Carole S. Vance (Boston: Routledge and Kegan Paul, 1984), 267-319, 293.

6. Hiram Pérez, *A Taste for Brown Bodies: Gay Modernity and Cosmopolitan Desire* (New York: New York University Press, 2015), 1.

7. Sedgwick, "Preface to the 2008 Edition," *Epistemology of the Closet* (Berkeley: University of California Press, 2008), xiii-xviii.

Index

Page numbers in italics refer to figures.